NEW YORK TIMES Bestseller

Bettyville

A MEMOIR

GEORGE HODGMAN

"A remarkable, laugh-out-loud book." —The New York Times

PRAISE FOR

Bettyville

"A humorous, bittersweet account of Hodgman's caring for his aging, irascible mother."
—Vanity Fair

"A gorgeously constructed memoir . . . Hodgman creates an unforgettable portrait of his mother, Betty. . . . He evokes her with wit and tenderness."
—The New York Times Book Review

"Intimate, heartfelt . . . *Bettyville* explores the difficult terrain of long-held roles within a family, the changing landscape of a small Southern town with a long memory, and the strain of growing up gay under the disapproving eye of otherwise loving parents. Hodgman's sharp wit carries the book ever forward."
—Minneapolis Star Tribune

"A superb memoir . . . Hodgman is by turns wry, laugh-out-loud funny, self-deprecating, insecure to the point of near suicide, and an attentive caregiver despite occasional, understandable resentments. . . . I have read several hundred American memoirs; I would place *Bettyville* in the top five."
—The Kansas City Star

"By turns hilarious and poignant, Hodgman reflects on matters such as coming of age in the 'Show Me' state, negotiating the world of New York publishing and—most of all—seeking common ground with his strong-willed mother. . . . What holds the book together is Hodgman's confident and engaging narrative voice—somewhere between the folksy humor of Garrison Keillor and the acid wit of Oscar Wilde."
—St. Louis Post-Dispatch

PENGUIN BOOKS

BETTYVILLE

George Hodgman is a veteran magazine and book editor who has worked at Simon & Schuster, Henry Holt, Houghton Mifflin Harcourt, *Vanity Fair*, and *Talk* magazine. His writing has appeared in *Entertainment Weekly*, *Interview*, *W*, and *Harper's Bazaar*, among other publications. He lives in New York City and Paris, Missouri.

* * *

Praise for *Bettyville*

"Rarely has the subject of elder care produced such droll human comedy, or a heroine quite on the mettlesome order of Betty Baker Hodgman. For as much as the book works on several levels (as a meditation on belonging, as a story of growing up gay and the psychic cost of silence, as metaphor for recovery), it is the strong-willed Betty who shines through." —*The New York Times*

"Kindness. The word is scribbled throughout the margins of my copy of George Hodgman's new memoir. If you think of that word as a sentimental squish, if you believe memoirs are best built for retribution and self-promotion, let Hodgman change your mind. . . . His memories help him sort through the inventions of shame. His desire to empathize, his focus on goodness, his search for hope allow him to find the beauty in the hour of now. If I could prescribe a cure for the seeming hopelessness of both growing older and taking care, I would prescribe *Bettyville*. When I want to be reminded of the genius of decency, I will return to George Hodgman's words." —*Chicago Tribune*

"Hodgman writes with humor and self-mockery that bring levity to the painful, central subject of *Bettyville*: caring for a parent on the threshold of death. . . . He captures a generation of widows who came of age at a time when it was taboo to air vulnerabilities and emotions. Hodgman is gay and cosmopolitan, but he only talks about his sexuality once with Betty, who confesses his father had never discussed it with her, even privately. . . . A moving book about what remains unsaid and undone."

—*The Economist*

"In the course of this brave, tender story of finding and forgetting, the author becomes whole again through his mother's losses. . . . Through caring for her, he develops the courage to be honest with himself and with Betty, and she, in turn, acknowledges her son for who he really is. In the end, we can thank Hodgman for reminding us that human kindness can survive almost anything. Among the wide audience that his memoir deserves, I find myself hoping that it reaches those kids still in hiding who, after reading it, may find their own Bettyvilles much easier to bear."

—*The Atlanta Journal-Constitution*

"In this achingly honest memoir, you feel for Betty, for George, for their misunderstandings, grievances, neuroses. You cheer their wit, their playfulness, all the good love between them. A warm, intense delight."

—*The Charlotte Observer*

"A witty and poignant portrait of a son and his mother reconciling their differences and learning, among other things, how to cook, come to grips with caretaking, understand unspoken sexuality, and treat each other with patience, love, and self-respect. Surely we all have a beautifully complex and hilarious (if not semi-dysfunctional) relationship with our mothers, but none of us are likely to commemorate it with the skill and humor of Hodgman."

—*Los Angeles Magazine*

"Hodgman transforms the caregiving experience into a story that is both funny and affecting. Fans of Roz Chast's *Can't We Talk About Something More Pleasant?* should take a look."

—*Newsday*

"Affectionate, humorous, and sometimes bittersweet . . . A love letter to fading little towns, to that resolute generation of Americans who lived their lives with grace and a stubborn zeal. After you have finished reading *Bettyville* you'll admire this gentle memoirist. And you will love Betty." —*Dayton Daily News*"Without a doubt, you'd be forgiven for reaching for a tissue while you're reading this book. Heck, you might want a whole box of them—but there's a lot more to *Bettyville* than heartstring-tugging. I found joy inside this story, in between its inevitable sadness. Hodgman keenly remembers his small-town childhood from all sides: churchgoers and alcoholics, kindness and bullying, adolescent crushes, baffling foes, and off-limits subjects that no small-townie discusses. . . . Be prepared to laugh a little, but be prepared to cry, too, as you're reading this fine memoir." —*Myrtle Beach Sun News*

"*Bettyville* is a superior memoir, written in a witty and episodic style, yet at times it's heartbreaking. . . . Filled with a lifetime's worth of reflection and story after fascinating story." —*Library Journal* (starred review)

"Hodgman writes with wit and empathy about all the loss he's confronted with. Betty's poor health is mirrored by the failure of towns like Paris, whose farms and lumberyards are now Walmarts and meth labs. Coming out in the age of AIDS, he lost the people he was close to when he had nowhere else to turn. . . . When things are left unsaid between parents and children, it leaves a hurt that can never be completely repaired, but love and dedication can make those scarred places into works of art. *Bettyville* is one such masterpiece." —*BookPage*

"An exquisitely written memoir about the complicated but deeply genuine love a son feels for his courageous, headstrong, vulnerable mother in the twilight of her life. George Hodgman is stunningly clear-eyed and yet so darned big-hearted. *Bettyville* is just wonderful."

—Jeannette Walls, author of *The Glass Castle*

"A beautifully crafted memoir, rich with humor and wisdom. George Hodgman has created an unforgettable book about mothers and sons, and about the challenges that come with growing older and growing up."

—Will Schwalbe, author of *The End of Your Life Book Club*

"I was completely engaged, not just because of George Hodgman's great ear and his sense of timing, but because he delivers Betty to us in such a manner that she steps off the page. Beyond the humor and the pathos, the quotidian and the bizarre, there remain profound lessons about life and love that I will carry away."

—Abraham Verghese, author of *Cutting for Stone*

"This bejeweled pillbox is rich and funny and heartwrenching and might just cure you of your ills; if those ills include loneliness or feeling like you don't belong—you are not alone."

—Nick Flynn, author of *Another Bullshit Night in Suck City*

"One of the great benefits of reading memoir is that it offers the reader more people to love. I love Betty, and I love George Hodgman, whose beautiful book this is. Read *Bettyville*. Laugh, weep, and be grateful."

—Abigail Thomas, author of *A Three Dog Life*

"This story of a sensitive Midwestern boy coming to terms with his homosexuality, his drug addiction, his clueless parents, his all-out war with shame, is nothing short of epic. It is, in every sense, a tale about the power of love." —Marie Arana, author of *American Chica*

"With great tenderness, honesty, and a searing, sardonic humor, George Hodgman has written a love letter to his mother, at once a penance and a tribute. In doing so, he has given us Betty, a character for the ages. This is a beautiful, illuminating book." —Dani Shapiro, author of *Devotion*

Bettyville

A Memoir

George Hodgman

Penguin Books

PENGUIN BOOKS
An imprint of Penguin Random House LLC
375 Hudson Street
New York, New York 10014
penguin.com

First published in the United States of America by Viking Penguin,
a member of Penguin Group (USA) LLC, 2015
Published in Penguin Books 2016

THE LIBRARY OF CONGRESS HAS CATALOGED THE HARDCOVER EDITION AS FOLLOWS:
Hodgman, George.
Bettyville : a memoir / George Hodgman.
pages cm
ISBN 978-0-525-42720-9 (hc.)
ISBN 978-0-14-310788-0 (pbk.)
1. Hodgman, George. 2. Adult children of aging parents—United States—Biography. 3. Caregivers—United States—Biography. 4. Aging parents—Care—United States. 5. Mothers and sons—United States. 6. Sons—Family relationships—United States. 7. Gay men—Family relationships—United States. I. Title.
HQ1063.6.H63 2015
306.874—dc23
2014038536

Printed in the United States of America
7 9 10 8

This book is dedicated, first and foremost, to my best friends, my parents:
George A. and Betty Baker Hodgman.
Every word about them is written with love.

It is also for my grandmothers,
Margaret Callison Baker and Virginia Rachel Hodgman;
my great-aunt Bess Baker; my aunt June Baker;
and Alice Mayhew, always loyal, ever generous.
Finally, it is for Madison and Paris,
where so many I care about have walked.
I will always remember you, good people.

If only one knew what to remember or pretend to remember. Make a decision and what you want from the lost things will present itself. You can take it down like a can from a shelf.

—Elizabeth Hardwick, *Sleepless Nights*

1

Missouri is a state of stolen names, bestowed to bring the world a little closer: Versailles, Rome, Cairo, New London, Athens, Carthage, Alexandria, Lebanon, Cuba, Japan, Santa Fe, Cleveland, Canton, California, Caledonia, New Caledonia, Mexico, Louisiana. Paris, our home.

Then there are the funny-named places. Licking is a favorite, along with Fair Play, Strain, Elmo, Peculiar, Shook, Lone Jack, Butts, Lupus, Moody, Clover, Polo, Shake Rag, and the T towns that always end my list—Turtle, Tightwad, Tulip, and Tea.

When I cannot sleep, I try to see how many I can still name, an old game played with my parents when I was a kid looking out the car window at the rolling brown waters of the Mississippi.

Something has awakened me, though inside there is only the sound of the air conditioner and outside it is pitch black and quiet, but for the trains. The clock says 2:30, give or take. I won't go back to sleep. Where am I? Not in my apartment; there are no sirens, horns, or streaks of neon shining through the blinds. This is not Manhattan, not Chelsea, not West Twenty-third Street. I am home, in Paris, Missouri, population 1,246 and falling. Living here, I say to myself, for just a few more days or weeks. For now. Until Carol, the good-hearted farm woman who helps watch out for Betty, recovers from surgery on her rotator cuff. Or until my mother can be admitted to an assisted living facility. Until there is rain, or Betty's spirits mend, or I get a regular job again. Until something happens here on Sherwood Road, and my mother is gone, and I must close up shop.

I hear Betty's voice from the hall: "Who turned up the air-conditioning so high? He's trying to freeze me out."

And here she is, all ninety years of her, curlers in disarray, chuckling a bit to herself for no reason, peeking into our guest room where I have been mostly not sleeping. It is the last place in America with shag carpet. In it, I have discovered what I believe to be a toenail from high school.

On the spare bed, there is a quilt with stars and crescent moons, figures of girls and boys joining hands along the borders, and the embroidered signatures of long-gone farm women, including my great-aunt Mabel's. I am installed here, along with the Christmas wrappings, the desk of Betty's uncle Oscar, and the bed I slept in with my grandmother as a boy, listening to Mammy's snores and the sound of the furnace startled into service. My grandmother's home in the village of Madison, ten or so miles west of us, where my mother grew up, was nicknamed the House of Many Chimneys. In the garden by the back door there were pink roses, which my grandmother, half blind and old, fretted over constantly, nicking her fingers on the thorns.

The hallway light is on. Betty has been in the kitchen, cadging a snack as she does in the middle of the night after being awakened by the need for the bathroom or dreams that make her cry out. Something—her dreams, her thoughts, her memories—hounds my mother at night. A light sleeper, she toddles around in her thick white socks, clearing her throat loudly, veering slightly from side to side, turning on the coffee, which will be cold by morning, checking to see if everything is in her own odd idea of order. After she has gone to bed, I try to light the path she takes to the kitchen in the dark, leaving on the lamp in my father's office, along with one in the foyer, to provide a trail to guide her through the hall.

"Are you awake?" my mother asks.

"I am now," I say.

Betty, whom I recently discovered sorting through the contents of my suitcase, turns on the overhead light in my room, wrinkles her brow, and peers in like a camp counselor on an inspection tour, as if she suspects I might be entertaining someone who has paddled in from across the lake. She must keep an eye out. I am a schemer. There are things going on behind her back, plans afoot, she fears. She has no intention of cooperating with any of them. When the phone rings, she listens to every word, not sure if she can trust me with her independence. I don't blame her. I am an unlikely guardian. A month ago I thought the Medicare doughnut hole was a breakfast special for seniors. I am a care inflictor.

She's not easy to corral. Her will remains at blast-force strength. "It's a hot day, but I'm going to that sale," she murmured last week in her sleep as outside the temperature soared past a hundred and, in her dream, she jabbed her finger up to place a bid. She is testier with me than anyone, sometimes slapping the air if I come too close. There are days I cannot please her. Carol, who has worked in nursing homes, says that old people who are failing get the angriest with those they are most attached to, the people who make them realize they are no longer themselves. But Betty's crankiness is an act, I think, a way to conceal her embarrassment at having to ask anything of anyone. When I do something for her, she looks away. Accustomed to fending for herself, she hates all this.

"I was worried," Betty says. "You said last night you couldn't sleep. I was worried you wouldn't sleep tonight." She stares at me.

"No, I'm sleeping. I'm asleep. Right now I'm talking in my sleep."

"You're in bed in your clothes again."

"I dozed off reading."

(Actually, I go to bed in clothes because I am waiting to be called into action, anticipating a fall, or stroke, or shout out. She seems so frail when I tuck her in. I keep the ambulance number, along with the one for the emergency room, on my bedside table.)

"It isn't a good thing for people to go to bed in their clothes . . . The *Appeal* didn't come today," she complains.

Our little town's newspaper, which reports civic events, charitable campaigns, and church news—including the "Movement of the Spirit" at the Full Gospel Church—has appeared erratically recently, possibly because of the increasingly short-staffed post office. This is the kind of lag that can throw my mother into crisis mode. She wants what she wants when she wants it.

"Did someone call today? From the church? I can't find my other shoe, the Mephisto."

I say we will look in the morning, and my mother, somewhat satisfied, almost smiles. For a second, there is the old Betty, who does not often appear now, my old friend.

In St. Louis, when we turn off Skinker onto Delmar, not far from the University City gates, Betty always points out the place where, as a young woman, working as a secretary at Union Electric, she waited for the streetcar. She seldom mentions the past, but loves to return to that old streetcar stop. Back in the 1940s, after the war, she was a pretty girl with wavy light brown hair, fresh from the "Miss Legs" contest at the university. Listening to her memories, I see her in a cast-off coat, not long after the war, looking down the tracks toward Webster Groves where she stayed with her aunt, called Nona. There is innocence in her expression, excitement at her new city life as she stands by other women in expensive dresses, the sort that Mammy never allowed her to buy. Sometimes I wonder whether she wishes she had gotten on that streetcar and ridden it to some other life.

By the time my mother realized that she was smart or saw she had the kind of looks that open doors, she had already closed too many to go back. "I just wanted a house with a few nice things," she told me once. "That was my little dream."

Betty—actually Elizabeth, or, on her best stationery, Elizabeth Baker Hodgman—doesn't see well at all. Certain corners of the world are blurred. Her hearing sometimes fails her, but it is often difficult to determine whether she is missing something or simply choosing not to respond. Also, she is suffering from dementia or maybe worse.

Some days she is just about fine, barking orders at Earleen, our cleaning lady, sharp enough to play bridge with her longtime partners. Other times, though, she is a lost girl with sad eyes. I am scared I am going to break her. I am new at all this.

We have hunts for liquid tears, or checks, or hearing aids, or the blouse Earleen was supposed to have ironed for church. The mind of my mother has often drifted away from peripheral matters. She has always been busy on the inside, a little far away.

Now more than ever, she is in and out, more likely to drift off into her own world for a minute or two. Or sit staring for long spells with a vacant look. Or forget the name of someone she knew, back then, before she had to worry about not remembering. In the afternoons, her whimpers and moans, her little chats with herself are all I hear in the house. The nights, especially just before bed, are the worst. She knows something is happening to her, but would never say so. We circle around her sadness, but she will not let me share it. Acknowledging anything would make it real. These, I fear, are her last days as herself.

My mother always drove fast, never stayed home. In the old days, we sped across the plains in our blue Impala, radio blaring DJ Johnny Rabbitt's all-American voice on KXOK St. Louis. She took me to the county line where I waited for the bus to kindergarten. My mother—"too damn high strung," my father said—stayed in the bathroom fussing with her hair and smoking Kent cigarettes until the very last minute. "I look like something the cat drug in," she told herself, frowning into the mirror.

When she finally came out, I'd be sitting on the hood of the car, my Batman lunch box already empty except for wads of foil and a few hastily scraped carrots.

"I'm a nervous wreck," I'd cry out. I was an only child, raised mostly among adults. I repeated what I heard and didn't get half of what I was saying.

"Why are you just sitting there?" she'd yell as if I were the one delaying things.

Those mornings, heading to school, I learned to love pop music, a lifelong fixation. My mother and I sang along to "This Diamond Ring" by Gary Lewis and the Playboys, "You've Lost That Lovin' Feeling" by the Righteous Brothers, and Petula Clark's "Downtown." Betty took her shoe off the foot she used for the gas pedal and almost floored it.

I like fast things, and the highway between Madison and Moberly will always be one of the places where I will see my mother, hair wrapped in rollers under a scarf, wearing a pair of sunglasses, taking me off into the big wide world.

"What are you looking at, little demon?" she would ask.

"Don't bug me," I'd say. "Mind your own business."

"You are my business."

"Betty," my father often said, "no one would mistake that kid for anyone's but yours."

I was Betty's boy.

This year, Betty had to give up her driver's license after backing into a ditch. Now she must sit home, awaiting invitations. "They won't even let me go to the grocery store," she says. Her eyes are wistful and her fingers, with their chipped pink polish, are itchy for the feel of the car keys.

Suddenly, Betty yells out. "Oh God," I think as I run to her, trip on a hair curler and barely escape ankle injury. "What is it?" I ask as I approach her door. "What is it?"

"Say," she begins, "you didn't get toilet paper."

We go through enough toilet paper for an army. I think she is involved in some sort of art project. A kind of Christo thing.

"I'll get some tomorrow," I say.

"That suits me," she answers, pausing before asking, "Did you make me a hair appointment?"

"I told them it was an emergency."

It is 3 a.m. I steal a cigarette from my mother's old, hidden cache and sit out on the step in front of our house in the dark. The mailbox made by my father is falling apart now. I would fix it, but am not handy. Nor do I assemble. A trip to Ikea is enough to unhinge me. I would prefer a spinal tap to putting together a coffee table.

I am running out of meals I know how to prepare. Tonight, feeling nostalgic, I rolled out tuna casserole made with Campbell's Mushroom Soup and crushed potato chips.

"I didn't know anyone still made this," she said.

"I was trying to think outside the box . . . Mushrooms are vegetables. Or are they a fungus?"

"Be still."

Mushrooms, I realized, *are* a fungus. I had served my mother a fungus casserole. With barbecue potato chips.

"There is no such thing as a perfect parent." Betty always said that. But to me she was perfect. Especially when she thought she was not. In grade school, on holidays, the mothers brought refreshments. Popcorn balls—crunchy white confections with the popped kernels held together with sorghum—were my favorites. When it was her turn to bring treats, Betty asked what I wanted. I said, "Popcorn balls." She said, "Oh brother," and lit a cigarette.

The kitchen was not her natural habitat. Her tendency to never turn things off led to exploding percolators and smoky puffs from toasters. A few days after my popcorn-ball request, I found Betty in front of the oven in her hair rollers, which were held in place with pink picks that tended to turn up all around the house. The kitchen, never a page from *Good Housekeeping,* was strewn with bowls and baking sheets. Sticky lumps of popcorn and fallen curlers were everywhere. On a tray there was a strange grouping of misshapen popcorn balls.

When I said they were supposed to be all the same size, Betty appeared exasperated, harassed, so forlorn and disappointed. She had failed. Nothing was right. She thought she had to be some kind of model mother.

I reached for a ball and took a bite. "I think these are the best I've had," I told her as I stuck some of the picks from her curlers into the balls so they would look a little snazzy.

"Why are you doing that?" she said. "Go outside and throw something."

My mother should not live alone now, but vetoes all conventional alternatives. I try to pretend I am in control. It is my time to play the grown-up and I don't want the part. "Don't put me in a place with a lot of old people," she says.

"Fine," I say to myself. "I'll go."

In my apartment in New York there are tumbling piles of books and, in the refrigerator, cartons of take-out food I forgot to throw out. By now it must have sprouted new life forms. I imagine squatters with grimy faces, warming their hands over fires crackling from large rusty barrels. Chickens are running everywhere, clucking and bursting madly into flight. I am probably going to have to stay here in Missouri and become a horse whisperer.

I have three pairs of pants and about five summer shirts, food-stained from my culinary efforts. This visit, for my mother's birthday, was supposed to last two weeks. It is getting on two months. I lost my job; I have the time. I am not a martyr. I am just available, an unemployed editor relegated to working freelance.

I think about leaving, but cannot seem to make it to the plane. My fingers will not dial the American Airlines number and I realize that my place in New York would feel very empty if I returned. I miss the company of people from work. I'd miss Betty too. Turns out I am a person who needs people. I hate that.

"Don't leave me," Betty says, if I go to bed before she is ready also. "Are you going to leave me?" If I start to move my work to my father's desk in the back of the house, forsaking the card table near the couch that is her center of command, she begs me to stay. She sits beside me all day, always wants me near, a real change from the woman who was always shooing me away, off to camp or college, or the next phase, off to be independent. If I allow someone else to take her to the doctor—the foot doctor, say, not an emergency situation—she is angry for a day or two. This is how it is now.

My mother is scared. I cannot believe it. But she will not speak of her fears. She is locked up tight. She keeps her secrets. I keep mine. That is our way. We have always struggled with words.

I am never certain quite what I will wake up to. Recently, as she was preparing for our daily walk, I discovered her trying to put her sock on over her shoe. This interlude, I know, cannot last. My life, such as it is, is on hold. I am worried by how we are living now, scared of drifting, losing footing on my own ground. Soon she will need more than I can provide, but she is not ready to give up. Despite her vision, her fading hearing, her stomach problems, and the rest, she tries to hold on in this place that is so familiar, her home.

It is the smallest things that trouble my mother most—the glass broken, the roast she cannot bake right, the can opener she cannot command to do its work, the TV remote control she cannot operate. Tell her the house is on fire and she will go on with the newspaper. Tell her you cannot find her address book and she will almost fold. Yet she has always been a determined woman, a force. She has been my rock and I am convinced that, at some level, she has survived to give me—a gay man whose life she has never understood—a place to call home.

In her wake now, a path of open cabinets, dirty Kleenexes and crumbs, cantaloupe seeds on the couch and the floor, bills she intends to pay, food left out to spoil. I polish the silver, fix her meals, buy her new bracelets, leave Peppermint Patties under her pillow, drive her to her battalion of doctors. I buy mountains of fresh fruit, still—like ice cream—a luxury for a woman raised in the country during the Depression. Even after decades of relative prosperity, a bowl of fresh strawberries remains a thing of beauty to her, a wonderful surprise. She spies them with the delight of an excited girl.

I try to imagine anything that will make her a little happier. If only, just once in a while, she could look a little happier. I know that her days are numbered in this house, built by my father, where deer run in the backyard and Sara Dawson down the street watches for Betty's light in the mornings, in the kitchen window where so many times I have seen my mother's face watching out for me as I turned into the driveway. For both of us, finally, I know, these are our final days of home. I am a loner, but I hate to lose people. I can only imagine how scary it is to know that the person one is losing is oneself.

2

In Missouri in springtime, the rivers rise and the rolling fields stretching acres and acres, miles and miles, gradually go green as the farmers fret over the wet ground, wondering when it will be dry enough to disc and get the crops out. In the mornings, old women wander through wet grass, bending with dirty hands over jonquils or bursts of peonies, rising to inspect children walking to school or hang summer clothes to air in the breeze.

In April and May, torrents of rain come, lightning chars the tree trunks, and the branches fall, and the thunderclaps crash. Creeks and rivers flood the river bottoms and roads. Betty hit the gas and drove through the water, never acknowledging anything unusual.

More twisters touch down here than ever now. A few years back, the town of Joplin, a few hundred miles away, was nearly destroyed by a funnel cloud that gathered force as it made its way across the plains. Many people died. The world took note.

Betty had little to report. These things happen. That is life. One year, near Paris, a farmer was taken up in the winds. Betty did not register the event, just marched on. She is from determined stock.

According to a family story, my mother's grandmother Anna Callison began a journey one spring morning at the age of eighty-five, departing from Union Station in St. Louis. She traveled alone by train halfway across the country, to Virginia, where as a girl during the Civil War she fetched a drink of water for Traveller, the horse of General Robert E.

Lee. She headed back to catch a glimpse of Traveller's bones, which had been recently excavated, to remember the morning when she saw the general, the war, the days when she was a girl. No one could stop her. Not Mammy, or Nona, or Uncle Oscar.

"That old woman was crazy," Betty says.

Spring is long gone now; it is August and the heat has been record breaking. No rain since June. Even the river bottom looks like desert and the corn in the fields is burning on the stalks.

On the television news at 6 p.m., I learn that members of the Missouri legislature, some of whom carry guns into sessions, are considering a bill to ban the imposition of sharia law. There is a controversy over a resolution forbidding teenagers access to tanning beds without parental permission. Betty scrutinizes the television.

"They are going to start arresting teenagers for illegal tanning," I tell her.

"You're not as funny as you think you are," she replies. My humor makes her look as pained as she did at parties when my father, a tenor, and never bashful, belted out barroom ditties as the other husbands strained to mutter a word. I am irony. She is no nonsense. Our lives have been lived on different planes.

I like staying up all night, hunched over a manuscript, playing with the words and sentences. I like setting out for somewhere early in the morning when no one is stirring. When I scan my existence, I can recognize no recognizable pattern. At home in New York, I listen to music, read books, fish old photographs from trash cans on the street. I like the unconventional, the city and its stories, castoffs and characters of dubious reputation. My mother has sometimes lived her life for the neighbors. I have never been able to remember the neighbors' names.

"Who *is* that?" Betty demands to know as a kid roars by in his pickup as we back out of our driveway into the early evening. "Now where is *he* going?" On the corner, where the city is excavating and there is a pile of dirt, she demands, "What are they doing? It looks like they've dug a big hole. You better watch out."

She is wearing the jeans she will never take off and a blouse with wrinkles she cannot see. For many days this pairing has been her choice. I have given up trying to control her clothes. God grant me the serenity to accept the clothes I cannot change.

We are thirty minutes late for a dinner so I hit the gas, and in moments we are turning onto 24, heading out of town. We pass a church, not so well kept up, where the sign that usually displays Bible verses beckons with a request: PRAY FOR RAIN. Prayers are frequent around here, especially this summer. Angels are hoped for. A woman nearly killed in a car crash on I-70 claims to have seen an angel crossing the road before her car veered out of control.

We pass the place where, some years back, Major's Drive-In Theater blew down in a bad spring storm. We pass shiny black cows. Mammy always talked about how pretty she thought black cows looked against green grass. But the grass is not green this summer and Mammy is a long time gone.

Betty sighs as she surveys the fields. "It's a good thing we don't have to try to sell lumber to the farmers this year," she said. "Lotsa luck." She hugs her purse, a bag of flowered cloth I purchased for her birthday and she declared too youthful. "I thought you didn't like that purse," I commented. "It's bought and paid for," she says. "I'm not going to turn my nose up at it."

This is the real country, not a place for rich weekenders. Tractors putt along highways where vapor rises and tar melts. We go by one of the lumberyards our family used to own, closed decades now, where a meth lab was discovered in an outbuilding. Betty turns her head rather than see the place. Some man keeps a collection of boa constrictors on the premises now. Recently one escaped to slither down Rock Road toward the home of my high school typing teacher, an excitable woman, unprepared for a morning of snake wrestling. To my way of thinking, the only proper place for a boa is around Cher's neck at the Golden Globes.

Dinner is at the home of Jane Blades, my old friend. We are late because Betty has demanded her gin and tonic, her five o'clock ritual. When Betty asks whom Jane is married to, I say, "No one you know." She says she hopes Jane does not have to support him. "Whoever he is." Betty never thinks anyone has married the right person. Some speak of love and romance. This is not my mother. A ring on the finger is not, in her opinion, a ticket to high heaven, but she is usually curious about the quality of the diamond.

"I shouldn't even be going," Betty says. "I'm an ugly old woman. I'm an old battle-ax."

"How do you think I feel?" I ask her. "I don't have a pair of decent pants I can button over my stomach."

"You could take off a few pounds."

"Did you fix your hair that way intentionally?"

"Just be quiet. Don't say a word."

"I'm probably headed for a gastric bypass."

"Stop," she says. "Don't talk. . . . Al Roker had one."

"What?"

"A gastric bypass. He had it on *The Today Show*."

"During the weather report?"

"Everyone could see it. I thought Earleen would never shut up about it."

Betty peers at the huge metal barbecue on Jane's patio. "What is *that*?" she asks. "I don't know," I say. "A school bus?"

When Jane comes out, we hug, but Betty draws back. Her family, the Bakers, did not hug socially, and she is not a woman who cares much for such. Nor is she often sentimental. Inside a silver locket she has worn for years, a gift from my father, are the stock photographs of strangers it came with. When she speaks of dying, I tell her how sad I will be. She waves my words away. "The world goes on," she says.

Jane's house is nice, but a little bare compared to ours, cluttered with antiques laden with hat-pin holders, candy dishes, decanters, ashtrays, and figurines. Many of our things are dusty, but Betty can't see well enough to recognize this. One could safely say that she considers the absence of bric-a-brac a social problem roughly comparable to malnutrition.

My father, the unofficial architect of the lumberyards once owned by my mother's family, supervised the remodeling of Jane's house decades ago. He gave my friend his greatest compliment. She did not, as he always put it, dillydally over everything. When I bring this up, Jane says my dad made her laugh, Betty says nothing. She never mentions my father, dead since 1997. She is always silent about loss.

"Oh God, what a character," Jane says of Big George.

My mother stares at me.

Inside is Evie Cullers, a colorful soul whose light blue sweatshirt says COUNTRY KWWR, MISSOURI'S SUPERSTATION; it looks clean enough for a baby. A former floral designer, now in her sixties, Evie sometimes bemoans the poor quality of current funerals and warns of the pitfalls of cremation. "They burn everybody on the same tray and there is a potential for getting one person's ashes mixed up with another's.

"If I'm gonna be livin' in a urn," she declared, "I'm not crazy about the idea of having a roommate."

I love Evie because she is a character; Betty is sympathetic to her as both have vision problems. "I was over to Wal-Mart," Evie tells me. "I was searching for something in the drug section and asked some kid for help, said I was visually impaired. He said he'd get someone. Five minutes later, I hear over the loudspeaker, 'Blind woman needs help in drugs.' I mean, what else do they say on the loudspeaker at Wal-Mart? 'We got a bitch in toys'?"

Betty's eye difficulties, not quite as serious as Evie's now—thanks to a legion of doctors and treatments—began when I was in grade school when her retina detached during a surgery for a condition called latticed retinas that Mammy had as well. There have been eight or ten surgeries since then, culminating in transplanted corneas. It has been decades since she has seen clearly, but no complaints have been uttered. She has played the hand she was dealt, bluffing her way at night or on cloudy days. Just like Evie.

We stand around the kitchen island. Betty accepts a glass of wine, but I decline because I have to. I'm nervous, but can't drink; I can't take anything that isn't prescribed. I have a history. Twenty years ago, I was snorting lines of speed before I went to work. When I crashed I never told Betty what had happened. I knew she would try to help, but I knew what she would think of me.

I listen as everyone talks about their children. Betty, not one to fuss over wee ones or beg to hold a baby, pays little attention to the pictures being passed. She is quiet, as she is in public these days. She seems to have declared herself beyond participation. Sometimes she seems to fade away. By the time she goes to bed, when things get bad, she will have fewer pieces left in place.

Camilla, Jane's sister, who has worked construction all over the world, including in Iraq, talks about Baghdad. The city, she says, barely exists now.

"Just like here," remarks Evie. "Stoutsville is just gone. We had banks, stores, a restaurant, even a movie theater. And the trains. Every time I heard the whistle, I'd run down to the tracks to wave at the engineer. In summer, the gypsies would come and steal everything. They wore bright colors and drove old cars. Mama would tell us to get under the bed when they were around. People said they liked to run off with children.

"There's not a kid here anybody'd take now."

"In ten years," says Camilla, "we could be sitting around this table and there could be no Paris at all."

. . .

Places like Paris are vanishing. Main Streets in all the towns around are boarded up. Gone are Lillibelle's Dress Shop, Mrs. Bailey's department store, Nevin's Florist, the barbershop where old farmers emerged after a cut and card game to take a pinch of chewing tobacco from the pockets of their overalls. We are decades past the last picture show. Wal-Mart, staffed by those known as Wal-martians, has taken its toll. There is a bail bondsman, and on television, a place called Family Pawn advertises relentlessly. "I've never pawned anything," Betty has confessed to me. "Have you?"

I read histories of the place I am from—the Civil War battles, the characters, the traveling Chautauquas, the old houses that lined the shady streets when Paris was the heart of "Little Dixie," a bastion of Southern sympathy. Long ago, there was an opera house; a grand hotel; a woolen mill that produced yarns, flannel, and blankets. There was a pottery works; a flour mill; plow, wagon, and shoe factories; tobacco warehouses; a feed store; a livery stable; a factory where cigars (Queen of Paris) were made and a wooden Indian stood out front. At Murphy and Bodine's Clothing Store, a huge stuffed bear in the window displayed men's coats and hats.

Things are different now. A book I read said three things changed rural America: the breakup of the family farm; Wal-Mart; meth.

After dinner, Jamie Callis, who graduated a year before me, arrives. The immediate center of attention, she is bawdier than I remembered and I am miffed; I want the spotlight. In the kitchen, Jane whispers that this is Jamie's first time out since her husband, a veteran, committed suicide. A few days ago when Earleen told Betty all about this, my mother interrupted: "Stop, stop. I can't hear that. I can't hear it."

Betty shyly edges her hand toward Jamie's; she wants to offer something, but cannot reach her without calling attention to herself, and when she sees that I am looking, she withdraws.

. . .

Driving home, we pass Jamie's big old house, which was her parents', and Betty notices a flower bed at the edge of her driveway. "I hope her flowers make it," Betty says. "Hers more than anyone's. Look at that woman. A lot of people would fold. She's carrying on. I like her."

Later, Betty and I are watching the news. She looks up, unhappy. "I'm ignorant, aren't I?" she asks. "Jane's sister's gone everywhere. I've never been anywhere much. I never went far."

Ignorance has always been one of my mother's greatest fears—for herself and for me. Growing up, she emphasized that I would be going to college. She planned for me to become a lawyer, like my father's father, in St. Louis. I didn't see it.

When I was a kid, I had no notion of what could happen to me. I knew that, somehow, I did not fit exactly; but this was my home. I loved my home.

I still hear the sound of the clothes falling in the dryer on the other side of my bedroom wall in our old house. On hot nights I lay with my head at the end of my bed to catch the breeze from the humming fan. Out my window, I could see the field, planted with soybeans. All summer long, Bobby Buck and I ran between the rows of beans all afternoon; at night after supper; and then after dark, when it felt dangerous to go barefoot, as we always were. A curled-up snake might be waiting underfoot. Some animal might spring up. I closed my eyes and took off.

Across the street lived the Masons—J.C. and Maggie and their kids, Kevin and Missy. J.C., who drove a big gravel truck, or Maggie took us all to grade school in their sea-green Chrysler, its ashtrays overflowing with cigarette butts. "Your love," the radio played, "is like a itchin' in my heart," or "Come on, come on boy, see about me." Early morning in Missouri: fog billowing around the grain elevators, streets slick with ice, blue windows, big women in aprons behind the diner counter beating the hell out of egg yolks.

"Tell me a joke," Missy cried, her small face streaked with a bit of breakfast, swimming in the hood of a parka circled with dirty fluff. "Say a joke. Say a joke. Say a joke." I was always trying to be funny. I remember Missy, maybe four years old, in winter, with skinned knees in a torn pair of shorts and a pair of her mother's battered high heels, making her way across the highway, hair full of flakes of snow.

Most kids lived on farms. Some of the country kids brought the same lunches every day: one strip of bologna on a slice of bread folded around with a dot of mustard. One girl had skin so dry from walking in the cold to feed that no one would touch her when we played games.

I read books and worried. Sometimes when company came I hid in the front closet, among the coats, with their just dry-cleaned smell and blue plastic wrappings. In summer I hung around the house, filling the captain's decanters with Dr. Pepper, which I drank from my parents' wineglasses. I watched TV, mostly soap operas: *As the World Turns, Love Is a Many Splendored Thing,* and *The Edge of Night*. When something remarkable happened, I called my aunt June, long-distance, to discuss these events. June—married to my mother's younger brother, Bill—was a former beauty operator whose home was decorated with furniture from her parents' funeral parlor in Kansas. She always thought she knew who had done the murders. "I can tell," she said, as if gifted with special insight into homicide, a special benefit, she implied, of being raised in the funeral home business.

In the afternoons I peeped into the tavern to see who was drunk or rode my bike to Mammy's where a handful of old ladies—Winnie Baker, Betty's aunt; her sister Maude Eubank; Ruth Holder; and Bess Swartz—often played canasta. Mammy kept score with a pencil she sharpened with a kitchen knife and stuck in her pinned-up braids. She reminded the women, when they excused themselves, not to put paper in the toilet, which was temperamental. I sat on the front porch, listening and reading *Ladies' Home Journal,* particularly absorbed by the monthly column "Can This Marriage Be Saved?" though I somehow knew I would never be kissing the bride.

I sometimes walked with Mammy to Mildred's Beauty Shop, where

I read *Photoplay* and *Modern Screen* as the blue-haired ladies lined up, waiting for the dryers in their bibs and wave clips, their new hair colors dripping in rivulets down the sides of their heads. Mammy didn't go to Mildred's that often. When it was possible, she washed her hair in rainwater, collected in a flat tin pan, kept on the top of the well, amid the pink roses covered in coffee grounds and eggshells, their branches held together with nylon stockings.

Before bed, I check Facebook where Jamie Callis has written, "Why can't we go back in time? Joyful family and love." I hear my mother talking to herself as she does when it gets late and she seems particularly anxious and confused. "What's wrong with you?" she asks herself over and over. "What's wrong with you?" For a minute, I think she is talking to me. But she would only be so ferocious with herself.

"Are you okay, Betty?" I ask. "Are you okay?" Standing in the doorway of her room, I see her wagging her finger at someone who is not there. "I'm fine," she says. She is yelling at me all of a sudden. "I'm fine."

She is so frustrated, ashamed of herself. I want to go to her, give her a hug, but she would just draw back.

"You're my buddy," I tell her.

"Am I?" she asks. "You know I wouldn't want just another damn sweet old lady," I say.

Later when I look in, she is dozing with the covers kicked off and her purse in bed beside her, making the odd, sweet noises old people make when they sleep. When she opens her eyes, I put an old soft towel in the dryer to warm up and then spread it around her feet, which she complains get cold at night.

3

Here in Paris, too anxious to linger after the alarm, I get up early to edit in the quiet. A freelance book editor I am struggling to balance Betty, manuscripts with snarled sentences—and my checkbook. Last night, I was up late on the phone with one of my clients, a loon from Los Angeles who believes he has dug up an unprosecuted Nazi still stomping around Germany. Instead of actually acting on my edits, he has e-mailed hundreds of documents to be summarized for entry into the text. I have had very little sleep. My sympathies are veering toward the Reich.

Mornings in New York, I could be found editing books through the night, at the Malibu Diner on West Twenty-third Street. I sipped my coffee, watched the street and the people, scrutinizing the cops mingling with ancient ladies with drop earrings, streaks of red on their faces, and blaring lipstick—old showgirl types, their often-tinted hair in dry curlicues, who come out early to order rye toast and soft-boiled eggs.

I have always lived alone. My life as an editor of books and magazines has been spent lingering in the white spaces between lines of copy, trying to get the work perfect. I was raised to get it right. I was raised to work. These were some of the things my mother taught me by example.

Betty started playing the piano when she was a girl. She has a way with the instrument, but it was my father's voice that people really noticed. Big George was known for singing. The possessor of a voice that could boost celebrants and move even casual mourners, he performed at weddings and special occasions in Madison and Paris. Betty accompanied him. One night, I remember her practicing the "The Lord's Prayer" over and over so many times I got a headache.

"Stop playing 'The Lord's Prayer,'" I screamed out from my bedroom.

"Don't bug me," Betty yelled back. "I'm in a mood."

When my father came home, later than usual, I threw my arms around him as my mother asked where he had been. She said they had to practice for a funeral the next day. We hadn't had much dinner. Betty never really ate, just pushed her food around on her plate. She wanted to stay thin.

"Thy kingdom come," my father sang, *"thy will be done."* His voice filled the house. They went through the song over and over as I slept on the couch. The warmth of my father's hand on my back brought me back. When I got up, he stood me in front of him with his hands on my shoulders and my feet on his work boots. He walked me all the way to my room like this as Betty kept on at the piano.

Betty kept practicing just to make sure she got it right, got it perfect. I had listened to my mother so many nights, playing the church songs over and over; I could sleep through it. But my father, a man with a temper, never could. Big George got up, furious.

"Dammit, Betty. Dammit," he said, his voice loud and angry, "leave that alone and come to bed. I am worn the hell out."

"No one," my mother yelled back, "wants to hear the pianist hit a clunker when they're about to go into the ground."

All through school, I worked as hard as I could, tried to win approval. From anyone. I was so hungry for something. My quest to be perfect never really stopped. I tried at work, on every project, at all the jobs I held. For a long time, as I moved from job to job, I was always praised and got promoted, over and over. But I never got it quite right.

I am not sure my mother believes she ever got it right either. I don't think she believes that either one of us have ever really hit the mark. I struggle with my moods. They come in big waves, erratic and intense, though I hide them. I have had to fight at times to stay upright. But here my mother keeps me going. I just get up. I crack the eggs, pick the pieces of shell out of the bowl, and flick them across the room with my fingertips.

This morning, as usual, there was coffee, ready and waiting. Every night Betty changes the filter and puts the water, some of which she always manages to spill, into our old, huffy-puffy machine. During her night missions she turns it on for when I come in. She is very conscientious about this; it almost is the last task, aside from the laundry, that she is able to complete successfully. Although she can still play the piano occasionally for church, she cannot cook, or clean, or do anything that requires organizational ability or thinking ahead. She makes the coffee too weak, but if I try to intercede before she gets to it, she looks hurt. It is her job. And she thinks I use too much Folgers. "Coffee's high," she says. "Coffee's high priced."

Procrastinating, trying to avoid the Nazi hunter's last crazed draft, I snag this and that from the kitchen. A day that begins with four coffees, two cinnamon rolls, and several trips to the refrigerator for caramel praline ice cream is likely to lead a person into risky emotional territory. If that doorbell rings it had better not be a Jehovah's Witness.

"What is that stuff you drink at Christmas?" Betty asks when she gets up. "What is the name of that stuff you drink at Christmas? I lay awake half last night trying to remember the name of it."

"Eggnog," I say.

We are to drive to Columbia to the hairdresser later. If we don't leave by noon, we'll be late and Bliss, Betty's hairdresser at Waikiki Coiffures, will throw a fit or, as she has threatened, cancel my mother's appointment. I hate Bliss. She stares at my mother's clothes on the bad days when we don't get things quite right. Betty pretends not to notice, but I see how it hurts her feelings. There is a lot she pretends not to notice these days. She doesn't even seem to take in the weather.

This is the third month of the drought. There may be hope for beans, but not for the corn; the farmers are cutting it down for silage. I have never known exactly what silage is, but I wonder if it would enhance a dinner salad.

Our flowers, miraculously, have survived, mostly. I am trying my best to keep them alive. In the mornings my mother stands at the window in the dining room, where the silver is tarnished now, in front of a wicker stand where she once kept geraniums, gazing out at the roses for as long as she can bear to stand up. Her face in the pane is like streaks of a watercolor. Even though she is old, I think she is more beautiful than ever, softer. You would never guess her age until she speaks. I do my best to make sure that when she looks in the mirror, there is someone who is familiar though sometimes nothing else is. When dealing with older women, a trip to a hairdresser and two Bloody Marys goes further than any prescription drug.

The pink rosebushes came from my grandmother's garden in Madison. My uncle Bill, adept at an astonishing range of skills, moved them here for Betty after my grandmother gave up her house. "I am grateful to Bill for that," she says. As if there is not much else she gives him credit for. "It was a hard job. He worked and worked. He worked hard."

When I lie awake worrying about what will come next, I wonder if my mother is contemplating, as she stands at that window, what will become of her mother's roses—transplanted by her brother's old rough hands, pruned by my father, watered and tended by the family through decades of harsh summer sun—after she is gone. Caring for things—flowers or people—has never been my strong point. I worry about doing right by my mother. She deserves someone who can help her better, someone who can change a flat or stuff a turkey. My life has been unconventional. I have walked the streets of New York City, lived in studio apartments, eaten tons of takeout. I have made only desultory attempts at personal arrangements. In fact, I have no personal arrangements.

Maybe it is impossible to come home again and not to wonder how it is that things turned out quite this way, why I am here, how it came to this, how it is that I cannot quite find the appropriate term for my "life-style," why it is that my mother simply shakes her head when I share details of my existence, why she cannot bring herself to speak of my life.

My mother has never tried to be anyone but herself. "At least I'm out and out with my meanness," she says. "I'm not a sneak. I hate a sneak." When I was growing up, we tussled a lot, but never really fought. Yes, Betty had her blowups, her bad days, her little tempests, but there was also the sly way she winked when I came home in the midst of one of her bridge games; the way she rolled her eyes at Mrs. Corn in church just for me to see. I was her conspirator and she made me laugh or want to reach out, sometimes, to protect the part of her that rarely showed, her secret soft spot. At the country club, where she could turn a game of golf into a disaster movie, her face took on a wistful look as she watched her ball plunk down a few feet from the tee. Once on Ladies' Day, Doris Rixsey took the golf club from her hand and said, "Honey, let's just go have a highball."

If Betty turned against you, she would take you on, but if she loved someone, they would never stand alone. She has a force, a strength that make her gentle moments especially tender. During my first year of school, my friend Alan Million's mother died in childbirth. I was home, pretending to be sick. When Betty broke the news, she pulled me to her knee. I was an only child; the deaths of parents terrified me; I lived in fear that mine would be taken from me. Betty knew how upset all this would make me.

When I got up in the dark that night to get in bed with my father, Betty was missing and I was scared, but I found her sitting on the couch in the living room. She looked bereft, and when she saw me, held out her arms. "Who will take care of Alan?" I asked. "His father," she said, "and everyone in town will keep an eye out for him. People will help him. He won't be lonely."

I lay on the couch with my head in her lap for the rest of the night; she did not shoo me or run me away. After my father got up, Betty made cinnamon rolls, the kind she always managed to tear apart trying to get out of the container, the kind that came with icing that made her scream out when it squirted suddenly from the tube.

Lunch today is clam chowder from a can. Betty sticks the dirty spoon in the pocket of her robe. Something is clearly worrying my mother, and therefore I am worried too. Our moods fold into each other's more and more as the days pass. "What is that stuff you drink at Christmas?" she asks once more. "What is that stuff called?"

"Eggnog," I say. "Eggnog."

She gets obsessed.

Betty is cross, moored to the couch. She frets, but will not move or get ready to leave for the hairdresser's. She fumbles her way to the refrigerator, refuses to put on her clothes, and remains in her nightgown and robe. "I'll get dressed in a minute," she promises, as usual. "I will in a minute."

I ask again, "Please, go get your clothes on, please, please, please." She looks away, does not respond, shifts into a position that suggests even greater fixedness. As I leave to take my shower, she picks up her book, oblivious to my concerns, to the demands of the world. Something in her has just let go of all that.

When I was eleven or so, my parents were going out and I was trying to get my mother moving, for my father, who was waiting in the car, as always. Betty was standing at the mirror in her bathroom, struggling with makeup from tubes and jars, nervous, fitful, irritated. Her hands shook as she struggled to apply mascara, not a task at which she excelled. The other mothers were jealous of Betty's appearance. But my mother wasn't sure enough, inside, to believe what everyone else saw.

"Go," I wanted to scream. "Go." I knew what it was like to always be kept waiting. I always had to wait for Betty too. At school, everywhere, our Chevy was always last to round the corner.

Mammy was putting something into the oven. I was sitting on the bed in the midst of a pile of dresses, selected and rejected, tossed off. On Betty's dresser, her cigarette had burned down to the very end. I took a puff before stubbing it out; it was glamorous, but a fire hazard. Mammy, who was to stay with me that night, was always there, never said she couldn't come. Whatever she was doing she put it aside for Betty and me. She knew my mother needed to get out, that she got blue and just went to bed when she didn't.

In the garage, my father gunned the engine of the Impala. I heard him yell, "What the hell is the matter, Betty? Quit your dillydallying." My mother turned from the mirror, muttering, "Ugh . . . ugh, ugh, ugh," then stuck her tongue out at me and grabbed her purse. Finally.

"Your father," she said, "thinks I'm hard to put up with." She loved to give him a little trouble.

It wasn't a rare thing for my father to get angry; once, the bookkeeper at the yard and I watched as, red-faced, he slammed his fist down on his desk, changing my notion of what a person might be capable of on a day of hard trials. But he rarely exploded at me. Suspicions of some reserve of rage lurking inside my father's powerful frame would probably be unfounded. He carried what was probably the normal amount of anger. Stored up, though, it was released in sudden storms that left him red-faced and almost tearful.

Determined to get my mother out the door, I am back in the family room, showered and shaved with still-wet hair. Betty brings her book closer to her eyes, hides her face. I lose it. When my mother refuses to act like herself, I get angry, because it scares me.

"Mother, get ready, *now,*" I demand. "We should have left at twelve." With every word, my voice grows firmer.

"Why didn't you tell me?"

"I told you again and again." Then I lose patience completely and raise my voice. You might say I almost yell. You might say I almost give up.

Shocked and hurt, she seems disbelieving. Slowly, she manages to lift herself off the couch, but falls back. She tries again and again. Her face is red, ashamed. When I go to her room to check on her, I find her lying on her back in bed, legs lifted as high as she can manage, trying to get her pants on as best she can.

When Betty is finally dressed, I take her hand and lead her toward the car where she rebels against her seat belt. When she demands water for the trip, I stop at Abel's convenience store, where early in the mornings whiskery men in old boots gather in groups to smoke and cuss out Obama. "He should just head back to the asshole factory where he came from."

"How's your mama?" asks Destiny, who rings up my gas. Everywhere I go, people inquire after Betty. They want to stop in, bring food, help. They miss seeing her.

"Came in here one day and said she could get fresher produce at an antique store," said the man at the IGA.

I can't take her place. When I pull up to the bank window, the cashiers look askance, knowing my habit of getting my card stuck in the cash machine. At the grocery store, the checkout girls grow anxious upon my arrival, well aware of my tendency to trip and topple displays.

As I come out of the store, I see Betty's face through the windshield, the very image of stubbornness. I wish I were on drugs. Yesterday at the meat counter when they asked what I needed, I whispered to myself, "Xanax. And a little crack on a bagel."

My friends worry that I am falling into a hole here, that this time away is really giving up, running away. Since I lost my job, I don't know quite who it is I am now. Suddenly I feel older. In New York, my closet is full of clothes that still smell a little like youth. I cannot bring myself to get rid of them. Betty and I are both crossing bridges we would rather avoid. Luckily to distract us there is *Wheel of Fortune,* a show we despise so avidly we cannot ever miss it.

I have always been my work. And now here I am, suddenly, after all these years, home. I am not exactly the black sheep of my family, but it is not like I am grazing in pastels.

Getting back into the car, I hit my head on the door frame and yell out. Betty asks, "Are you all right?"

"I'm fine," I say. "It's just something that will kill me later."

All the way to Columbia, Betty complains about my driving; she is less daring these days where speed is concerned. As we are passing through Hallsville, she asks the question again.

"What is that stuff you drink at Christmas?"

"Eggnog."

Finally, we make it to Waikiki Coiffures, where I always expect to find the operators in leis: *"Aloha, Missy Betty. Welcome to our island kingdom!"*

We are a bit late, but they take her, though I get dirty looks. "Betty, you need some new shoes," Bliss says, glancing at my mother's feet and then at me as if to say, "How can you let her out of the house in these?"

I get a coffee at Lakota and stroll past Jock's Nitch. Columbia is the home of the University of Missouri, my alma mater, and the store sells T-shirts and jackets with the Tigers' logo. I buy Betty a fleece-lined jacket for fall and a long-sleeved T-shirt in gold, one of the team's colors. Both are emblazoned with large tiger heads, ferocious and ready to spring off the fabric. Betty went to school at the university, but couldn't afford to join a sorority. At football games with my dad, she never glanced at the field, only at the Tri-Delts and their outfits.

After her appointment, Betty lowers the visor over the dash to inspect her hair in the mirror. Not one of Waikiki's most successful endeavors, it is a lacquered bubble, blown back in a way that suggests shock.

"This is the worst yet," Betty says, downcast. My mother has not had what she considers a successful hair appointment since around 1945.

I present her with her new clothes, and she wears her Tiger jacket all the way home, despite the temperature hovering just under a hundred degrees. "Do you think it's too warm for the heated seats?" she asks. They are her favorite of our car's features.

I say I think so, but she flicks hers on anyway. I wait for smoke to rise from her rear end. She is quiet for a while, then asks, "That girl from dinner. Her husband killed himself . . . She drives the school bus."

"Jamie, you mean."

"She must feel low. I have some things I want to give to someone. Would that insult her?"

"I don't know, Mama."

"She's working herself ragged and her husband served this country."

As we drive, Betty remarks on the sky, light blue with a few thin lines of color. Before the sun starts to fall, the light illuminates the flat land that extends on and on, miles and miles and miles, with nothing to obstruct our view until, finally, it merges with the horizon. The clouds go back and back in rows, each hanging slightly lower than the one before it, one visible after the next and trailing tatters of white.

The sky is our sea here, our object of contemplation in all its moods and shades. My father taught me to observe it. As I watched him gaze at it as a kid, or a bored teenager, or on early-morning trips back to the university, or later, on the way to the airport in St. Louis, I began to see what he did. I watched for my favorite effect—the way the clouds, in morning and at sunset, jutted out into the blues and pinks like islands in a huge bay of light, gradually thinning as they stretched out into what seemed like the waters of the ocean.

Often he would pull over, take his camera from the glove compartment, and snap some shots while I wondered if we would ever reach our destination. My father loved to watch, in autumn, the long scarves of lonely birds, flying, finally together, toward home.

"It's all going to be okay, Betty," I say later, back in Paris, when she gets her nighttime worried look and starts to make her sounds: "Hmmm, hmmm, hmmm." And for one long moment, I let myself slip into denial and believe it.

Betty asks again about the eggnog, as I write a note to my friend Stephen, an artist, who has lung cancer and is probably dying. "What's up, Florence Nightingale? Are you ready with my enema?" he asked me a few weeks ago on the phone.

For a while, Stephen and I met at the Starbucks on Greenwich and Bank at 7 a.m. daily for lattes and old-fashioned doughnuts. His mother still lives in Texas, and whenever there is a storm warning, she wakes him at odd hours of the night to proclaim, "The storm is coming. It's heading this way. It's heading this way."

He imitated her expertly, and we laughed, and about once a week I asked him to retell me my favorite story, a tale he excelled at repeating: There was a time in his life when Stephen kept very late hours, and one night, in the Village, at a twenty-four-hour convenience store not far from the river, he encountered a fine black sister of the self-created feminine persuasion whose deportment suggested that her business might possibly involve certain amorous transactions.

She had a bit of glitter on her face, a pile of errant hair, and a derriere of some considerable dimension tucked into some snug-fitting denim shorts. On top, she had on some kind of loose-fitting garment. Her eyes—large and saucerlike—gave the impression that she had recently ingested some mood-enhancing chemicals. When Stephen encountered her, she was in the back of the store, trying to stuff a large canned ham under her top. Then, proudly, she marched through the checkout, protecting herself with a purchase of maybe a Butterfinger or something.

But perhaps because of her state, she suddenly lost it and did a kind of swoon thing or whatever and the ham dropped out from underneath her top with a large thud. The cashier looked at her. She looked at the cashier, then at the ham, and announced, "I can't be coming to this store no more. People be throwing hams at me."

I love the citizens of the city night. For many years, I was one of them. I had adventures. My life has been an odd hotel with strangers drifting through and friends sometimes growing concerned. At times I was known to show up at work seven days a week, logging in at odd hours and setting off complicated alarm systems. For years, always feeling a little resentful, I walked past town houses where lamps revealed marble fireplaces and beautifully organized bookshelves. Like the assortment of strange relics in our basement, I have some cracks, broken chips, missing pieces. I have spent my life trailed by voices in my head saying, "You're no good. This isn't right. You're not right." My skin is sometimes the most uncomfortable garment of all. I have wandering eyes that do not easily meet the glances of others. When shaking hands with new acquaintances, I still wonder if my grip is right. Is it manly enough? I tell too many jokes. In a city of arrogant wristwatches, I have rarely been able to keep a Timex running right.

As a child, I kept broken things from around the house or taken from the trash in the bottom drawer of the bureau in my room. When I was finally grown, when it seemed that life would be inhospitable here, I fled—to Washington, Boston, New York. I will never forget my father's face—his sad, lonesome look—when I left the house to go east.

I give last-minute gifts, haphazardly wrapped, travel on fantasies and imagined furloughs, late-night planes, booked too tardily for discount rates. I have no condo, summer home, or good investments, or family of my own. I have no husband, or domestic partner, or even beloved pet. Betty would never guess quite how things have been. If pressed to do so, she could not really imagine how I have lived. I never wanted a house with a few nice things. Or did I?

I am exhausted. Before I go to bed, I look in on her, as always. There is a pungent smell coming from her room.

"I'm here to check on you and your hair," I say.

"I sprayed it," she says. "I don't know if it will work."

"You're a mean old woman, you're not a bit good," I tell her.

"I can't believe you're not in the penitentiary."

In the middle of the night, I hear her in the utility room, washing, banging down the lid of the washer, whispering to herself, turning on the dryer. Although she always seems to turn up in clothes with stains, she washes the same stuff over and over and over, usually at odd hours. Night after night, she washes and washes and I listen as she talks out loud, cries out. It is Friday and I do not know what Saturday will decide to do with us here on Sherwood Road and I cannot let myself jump ahead to imagine next week, or next month, or next year.

Before sleep, I go outside to check the stars, so much more visible here than in New York. They calm me after seeing Betty under siege. I turn on the coach light by the driveway; I leave it burning all night every night. We are expecting no guests but it says that we are still alive, not ready yet to disappear into the dark.

4

A few days later: When I get home from town, the garage door is up and Betty stands at the door to the empty space, wearing no shoes. After fifty years, I can read her; at this moment, anyone could. She conceals her deepest affections, but registers dissatisfaction without hesitation. Her emotions are heightened; this is part of her condition. Her face is angry; her body is angry. When I get to her, she is nearly frantic.

"Where have you been? Where were you? I have to get to the church. You have to take me to the church. How could you forget me? You knew this was the day. You knew this was the day. You were there when they called this morning. You heard. You heard them say there was a meeting."

In fact, I have not remembered that I was supposed to drive her to the Memorial Committee meeting at four. I try to apologize, but no. Her anger has been building since who knows quite when. Although she is mostly dressed—this time, of course, she has made a real effort to be on time—she is trembling. But there is something behind her panic, besides the fact that I have forgotten her. She cannot find her shoes.

"What," she asks me, in desperation, "have you done with my shoes? Why do you treat me like this? Where have you put my shoes?" I tense up and run toward her, afraid that she will trip on the rug in front of the door.

This morning began with the long stretch of sky hinting at pink. In the baked backyard, I spotted a young deer straining its neck to feed from the low-hanging branch of one of the trees my father planted years ago. Staring, the deer tilted his head to the side and assessed me quizzically. At Abel's Quick Store, the girl behind the counter, wearing a badge saying TRAINEE, stared at me in much the same way. I have become an object of puzzlement to all species. I have no rear or hips and a fat tummy. It's like what used to be my ass has somehow shifted to the front of my body. There is no pair of pants made on the planet that does not fall down when I wear them.

At home, Betty ignored me, something brewing. Soon the phone began to ring, a rarity, one call after another. First came the tidings of one of my mother's old friends. Her daughter has had a baby. She feared it has an oddly shaped head. Next, someone from the bridge club: She has a bladder infection. So prevalent are references to bladders in my mother's circle that I have come to think of them fondly, like a quirky, hard-to-control family who might soon be arriving for dinner.

Next it was the church about the meeting later, then a recorded message announcing Betty's upcoming appointment with her GP. Refusing to answer the telephone herself, my mother balked at even being called to the receiver. On the line, she oozed the frustration of a mob boss dissatisfied with the morning tallies from Vegas. By the third or fourth summons, she was greeting her callers with, "Speak!"

Then came Waikiki Coiffures. When I started to put Betty on, the shop's owner stopped me, asked, "Are you her son?"

"Maybe," I said. "Is there a problem?" Apparently Betty almost fell on her last visit; the owner cannot risk a lawsuit if Betty tumbles down next week. I say we are not litigious types; we are peaceful folk, despite occasional fits of rage after a comb-out. I beg her understanding. But no: From here on, my mother will have to be accompanied by someone who will wait while she gets her hair done.

I watched Betty, who eyed me gravely, her sixth sense for trouble in high gear. Yes, she is sometimes shaky on her feet, I told the caller. But the biggest problem, I argued, is her shoes. The woman agreed. She said the soles on Betty's sandals are worn down enough to make her trip.

After hanging up, I explained the situation to Betty, who slammed her book down on the couch. "I'm ninety years old and everybody in town is telling me what to do!" When she clicked the TV remote control device, I swore she was pointing it at me. "Be still," she yelled. "Just be still."

Betty complains constantly about her feet. New shoes, she claims, cause her agony. (She has always taken pride in the fact that she wears a narrow size. Now she insists on the same size, though her feet have swollen.) During fittings, she cries out. Fellow shoppers stare at me, fearful she is being attacked. I point at the clerks, mouth, "Shoe people," in a shocked stage whisper.

In my mother's mind, no pair is right; nothing feels good. Her feet are tender, and when I attempt to guide them carefully into her Mephistos, she behaves as if she is being tortured. She can no longer bear even the slightest discomfort of any variety. For several years, despite our efforts at malls across the region, we have found no footwear that does not cause her pain. At Saks in St. Louis, a clerk pulled out a pair of flats by Jimmy Choo. "Listen," I begged her. "We are not talking *Sex in the City* here." She glanced at me as if I had blasphemed. I bowed my head, chastened.

A pile of rejects grows higher by the couch. Betty refuses to put them on or try to break them in, relying instead—even in winter—on the beat-up sandals and her ancient Mephisto "runners." This morning, after the call from Waikiki, she brought the newspaper up over her face and stuck her feet under the coffee table when I reached for a pair of the new shoes. As I withdrew, I caught her peeping out from behind the paper quite satisfied with her obstruction. I wondered if my 12-step group might pass some sort of humanitarian injunction allowing me to ingest one tiny Xanax on an emergency basis.

· · ·

This was the beginning of the War of Shoes. Since man first staggered across the earth, wars have been waged over God, land, money, freedom. This will be a battle for control over one small territory that remains my mother's own: her feet, a dry landscape below the region of swollen ankles, a terrain coursed by rivers of fragrant lotion, of calloused patches, broken veins, errant toes. On this field of battle I have vowed to lay my body down. Withdrawing to my bed, I planned future maneuvers. My hostages, I decided, would be stowed in the crowded confines of my bedroom closet.

If I were starting a Betty Museum, I would make an exhibit out of the sandals with their worn, thin straps and soles indented with my mother's dark footprints. These shoes are relics; they sum up our last years here on this planet. I treat them kindly; they have served us well, through weather in all forms and days of challenges, through so many moods and ups and downs. In my bedroom, I tucked them into the closet on a high shelf. There would be repercussions. But this was war.

At the city office, located in the old elementary school, where I had gone to pay a bill, I made a quick detour into the historical society, located in this same building, to reread a few of my favorite items, including the tale of Ella Ewing, an eight-foot-four-and-a-half-inch "giantess," who traveled with P. T. Barnum, sharing the bill with a twenty-three-inch-tall Russian dwarf called Peter the Small. Her shoes are displayed at the state capitol. Bending the rules a bit, the woman behind the desk allowed me to borrow a clipping about Ella's life.

My family, our friends, all our days reside on these shelves. For several months now, I have tried to piece together my mother's life, the past she will never mention.

According to my grandfather's obituary, Joseph William Baker, whom I never knew and who was rarely discussed by his children, disposed of his first business, a hardware store, in order to enter World War I. The fighting ended before he could report for duty and he started over from scratch, opening the lumberyard in Madison and working hours that extended from before sunup to long beyond the fading of daylight. He took a wife, Margaret, often called Marge or, later, Mammy. Photographs reveal a young woman with a wistful face and thick, pinned-up braids who taught at country schools to which she rode on horseback, even in the rain, through the trees and bean fields.

The first child of Margaret and J.W., a son named Harry Clay, was born in Madison in 1921. On August 4, 1922, my mother—Betty Baker—arrived. A few years later, there was another son, my uncle Bill.

Accounts of my mother's first year on earth describe the most extreme temperatures ever recorded, all around the globe. In Missouri, so oppressive was the heat that citizens in St. Louis slept in Forest Park under the stars, cooling themselves in breezes drifting in from the Mississippi. I envision Mammy, up with the babies through the hot nights, walking through fireflies to pick white grapes from the arbor or sitting on the back step, under the walnut tree, brushing her hair out in the dark, as she did before sleeping. She would soothe the little ones with washcloths moistened with well water as her husband—a light sleeper with shadows about his eyes—lay awake, worried over the day to come and the state of his business.

During 1922, 144 biscuits were served each morning at the Poor Farm in Monroe County, where residents included the insolvent, imbeciles, and the insane. According to one account, some of those confined "uttered nary a word for days on end while others chattered to themselves of imaginary trips to destinations as far flung as Mississippi and Alabama." For suppers, the matron of the institution, Mrs. J. P. McGee, served 207 chickens in 1922, all raised by herself with the help of an inmate known as Stick Horse John. Between 1924 and 1928, 187 property owners in Monroe County were forced to sell their homes or properties at trustees' or sheriff's sales.

Children died often and early of the influenza virus. In an old diary of my mother's there are only two kinds of entries: the noting of piano recitals and the names of classmates lost to flu. Most of the pages, though, are blank. Today Betty remains closemouthed about what was.

In Paris now, there is almost no one she knows. Gone are the abattoir, the jeweler; the fountain at the courthouse goes without its goldfish. Gone are the fine old families who lived in the big houses on Locust and Cooper streets and wintered in Biloxi. Gone are the women who served weak coffee, labeled "troubled water" by my grandmother, in demitasse cups. No more are the old friends who arrived unexpectedly with embroidered baby clothes, canned peaches, or jars of pale green gooseberry jelly. My mother's family name brings little recognition. Once more, the weather is the most frequent topic of conversation. The lakes are down, their beds cracked and dry like parched mouths. From the stately houses in the river towns—Boonville, Louisiana—one sees banks, vulnerable to fire, above the currents of the waters that eddy in slow, languid circles.

Betty asks for food made from her mother's recipes: pimento cheese, lemon pies, burned sugar cakes, oysters, peppered fiercely and baked with crumbled saltines. She craves fresh peaches, sorts through old baby announcements and birthday cards, worrying slyly over whom she will likely offend as she changes her mind, over and over, about which of my cousins will inherit her gravy boats, gold bracelets, and silver salvers. Like most who live now in the place where she is from, she does not care to contemplate the past or to consider the future. Here and now is trouble enough.

The clock says it is after four. Betty says she will never make the meeting, beats her hand on the table. They will think she is too old. They will say she shouldn't even be on the committee, that she can no longer keep track of the expenditures. "They will say I forget," she keeps repeating. Her hand beats the table again and again and again. "Why did you leave? Where did you go? Why today? Why don't you ever pay attention?"

My mother yells for her shoes. Only the sandals will do. I give up immediately, all vows rescinded. The war has been brief, but filled with shock and awe. I get the worn sandals from the closet, and when she sees them, when it is confirmed beyond denial that I have hidden them, a new wave of hurt and anger emerges as she sits down at the kitchen table and tries, unsuccessfully, to put them on her feet, a task that she cannot manage because she is so enraged at me, at her feet, at the people at the church, at herself, the way she is.

"Calm down," I say, taking her hand, which she pulls away, slapping me away. "Please, Mama," I beg her. "Please, please, Mama. It is all right. It is okay. You're all right. You're okay."

"Am I?" she asks. "Am I? I don't think so. I don't think so."

For the meeting, she has put on her good black pants that we found at J. Jill. Mean tattletales, they keep record of every day's spills, every crumb or bit of lint, everything she has brushed against, every speck. Tight at her bulging waist, baggy over her narrow legs, they hang down over her feet. Sometimes, because of her vision, she cannot make out how much of her life has accumulated on her outfits and just doesn't realize how badly they need to be cleaned. How unforgiving the eyes of the world can be, even over small things: She knows that now. A trip to bridge has sometimes become a lesson in humility.

Bending down , face-to-face with the sandals, I salute my victorious adversaries and brush off the legs of Betty's trousers with my hands. Her fingers, resting tentatively on my shoulder for one fleeting second, when it seems that she has almost lost her balance, are trembling. Her shoes, her good old shoes: She thought I had just walked off and left her.

From the sink, I bring a damp cloth to erase a dusty streak on the trousers. Her gaze meets mine, but quickly she looks away from whatever my eyes show.

She is under siege, from scary thoughts, from new shoes, from a son who does not understand, from a world that cannot comprehend the confusion and pain of the secret battle she does not acknowledge to anyone, maybe not even herself—the struggle to stay, to hold on, to maintain. She stares up at me, her elbow on the kitchen table, her hand gripping her forehead as if it is too heavy to hold up. Her eyes, where clouds have settled in, which seem to grow larger, more liquid every day, are full of fear, her expression anguished. How hard she is trying here. No one knows. Age is taking everything away. Now I, the one who she counted to be on her side, have taken her shoes, the only ones that still soothe her tired, sore feet that carry her load. She is so hurt.

This is what I see in her face: the wandering one, the one who is letting go, and the anguished one, the one who remains, but who knows she is losing, barely holding on. They coexist, alternating, the one gradually ceding to the other. As the surrender progresses, she becomes more and more anxious, sometimes even terrified.

"Betty's okay," I whisper. "Betty's fine. Betty's home. Betty's okay. Betty's fine. Betty's home." When I finally get her in the car, she looks at me as if she has lost the only person in the world she trusts. I get her to church, hold open the car door, help her in and down the basement stairs, a flight of concrete steps that terrify her always. Reluctantly, she grabs my arm and holds on tight. In the meeting room, gathered around the table, the other members of the committee are waiting and not everyone looks like they have maintained their patience. As she starts into the room, she rallies; she straightens her shoulders. She heads into the fray, reaching for my arm as I leave to say that she is sorry. When my mother walks into the meeting, I think of all the people quietly doing so many things that are hard.

There was a day once, a few years back, before I realized how bad her eyes had gotten, when I had left her at the church to practice. Detained at the lawyer's office, I was late to pick her up. When I returned, I saw no other cars in the parking lot and glimpsed Betty, walking close by the side of the church, keeping both hands on the wall of the building, moving tentatively toward the side yard to wait by the steps for me. There was no sun; it was a cloudy day. She moved very slowly, as if just ahead there might be something waiting, something that might take an old woman down forever.

My mother speaks of the night when Mammy fell and broke her hip as the moment when her mother stopped being herself. Betty is petrified of falling. It is what she fears above all. Already she has gone down twice, once bruising her tailbone. She will not admit—even to herself—that this ever occurred. Yet in the hall at night, I hear her: "I can't fall. Don't fall. Don't fall. Don't fall."

My parents were at a party the night my grandmother's accident occurred. After they left the house, after I was forced to watch Lawrence Welk, after I was asleep, my grandmother tumbled down some steps and broke her hip. I slept on, not hearing her cries. My parents found her when they returned and I woke to the voices of the ambulance men. For the rest of her life—and she lived to be a very old woman—my grandmother used a cane, and then later a walker, which she called her horse, to get around.

I woke up, very late, to find my mother sitting on the edge of my bed, gently patting my back.

"Ssshhh," she said. "Sssshhhh." Maybe she was crying; I couldn't tell for sure. We hadn't said our prayers together as we always did. It seemed now especially that we should not miss. "Do you want to say our prayers?" I asked.

My mother said nothing, just kept patting my back. I do not know if Betty's sorrow stemmed from her mother's loss of independence or her own. Mammy would need care. There would be another person depending on my mother, a situation to make a woman like her feel more hemmed in. That wouldn't be easy for anyone. Mammy felt terrible for falling.

. . .

After we return from church and Betty calms down, I shower and nervously attempt a shave. I realize my face is bleeding from razor cuts, which I attempt to stop with the application of tiny shreds of toilet paper. They cling to my face. Of course, this would be the moment I decide to go out. I don't think I can bear to sit in the house one more night. After freshening my toilet paper, I clean my glasses—butter sucks on bifocals—then mix pineapple with cottage cheese, bake a piece of salmon, and give Betty an early supper. I hesitate to leave her, but when I say I am going, she nods.

In the Columbia paper, I have read about a program at the synagogue called "Coming to America," featuring elderly Jews telling the stories of where they are from and how they came to this country. I decide, as I have time, to take the route through the country past a little store run by the Amish where I take Betty to buy pies. By the time I reach the area where the Amish reside, the sun is setting. I watch the men and women in their heavy dark clothes, in which they must be baking, gathered on porches or walking in from the fields. By the side of the road, a group of little girls in aprons marches together toward the store, carrying dishes covered in white cloths. One girl lags behind. Her bonnet is untied and the strings hang down her chest. Her cheeks are dirty and her boots appear to be unlaced. She stomps angrily down the path, oblivious to the rest. She looks angry; I sense rebellion. I can almost hear her screaming: "Enough with the churning!" This one may just be heading off the reservation. I imagine Betty as a girl like this, inclined toward irritable moments and headstrong, determined to go her own way. I like a girl like that.

5

Always open—late nights and early mornings—Rexall Drugs was run by Lennos Bryant, a pharmacist and longtime mayor of Madison known for his annual ascension of the water tower to put up Christmas lights visible for miles. Also in attendance at the store was his wife, Nadine, a registered nurse with an eye for fashion. From her closet came turbans, stoles, aged fur pieces with heads and wandering eyes, sarongs, dresses draped with huge cloth flowers or glittering jewel-like objects. She attracted praise for her attentiveness to the sick for whom she served as doctor, as the town had none. But she specialized as well in unpredictable acts—leaving poison out for dogs that congregated in the business district—that made her less popular. On certain Sundays, her Chevrolet could be seen on the highway, swerving back and forth across the lanes as she supervised the driving instruction of her four-year-old grandson.

The Rexall was adorned with a black cat clock whose swinging tail marked the hours. My father parked us at the counter as Nadine—her wet hair shaded slightly blue—gave herself shampoos in the soda fountain. My father loved her, egged her on to further feats of eccentricity. On this particular day, however, he finished his cherry Coke before I did and looked shocked when Nadine picked up his drained glass and began crunching on the ice.

"Nadine!" exclaimed Lennos.

"He doesn't have any germs," replied Nadine. "Look at him."

My father laughed until he remembered why we were there. Then he looked at me gravely and said, "I gotta tell you. Your mother has a plan."

. . .

Every few years, when the rains come right, it is impossible not to notice that the place where we live is blessed with picture-book beauty. Maybe it was the pastoral greenery or the glory of nature that led Betty—a woman petrified of the water and not inclined to feast on its products—to wake one morning and imagine her husband and son standing at the edge of a sludgy current, fishing poles in hand, joined in appreciation of each other and the wonder of it all.

It was 1969 or so, and not long after my father sat me down at Rexall, the two of us found ourselves preparing to go. Fishing.

"Good lord," said Big George, "I guess tomorrow is the day." We were watching the movie on Channel 7, as we did Friday nights. My father was drinking beer. Betty was gone, and as he was inclined to ignore her preferences when the two of us were on our own we had let our dog, Toto, whom Betty detested, into the house. Both of us were sneezing as I powdered our irascible animal.

"Sonuvabitch," my father yelled out as Toto scratched himself lewdly. "We gotta do something about that damn dog." Our breathing became even more difficult.

"Sonuvabitch," I screamed in imitation. I loved a cussword uttered with abandon.

"Don't talk like that," he said.

"I like that word," I answered.

"I know," he agreed. "It is a good one."

Sometimes on nights like this, my father went on about World War II, when he was stationed in Saipan at an oxygen plant. Some people associate war with death and suffering, but Big George spoke of his years in the South Pacific as if they were the most golden days he could remember, which made me feel a little bit hurt. He often told me about the day when his base was bombed and he almost died. The planes flew so close that he was able to spot a Japanese pilot's long yellow scarf blowing in the wind. He never spoke of the thousands of American boys who died on Saipan. My parents never mentioned bad things at all.

Once a year, he went off to St. Louis for a reunion of his army buddies on the Hill, the Italian section of the city on the South Side. He didn't have that many male friends in Madison. I don't think I could have named one. I didn't have that many either. It was fairly difficult to gather a band of boys to stage a re-creation of the Academy Awards with me as the favored nominee for everything.

"Good lord," my father said, anticipating the fishing expedition. "Of all the damn things . . ."

"Of all the damn things . . ." I repeated. "Of all the damn things . . ."

"I guess I'm supposed to get a damn pole," my father said. "I guess we'll have to buy some damn worms."

"Where," I asked, "do you buy the damn worms?" I was no Huck Finn, though I thought the hat was interesting.

"Hell if I know," he said, "but someone will know. I don't think we'll have to put an ad in the paper."

I continued to powder Toto—a loyal but randy terrier who pursued every bitch in Monroe County. Domestic life did not come as second nature to him. Asked to perform even the most rudimentary trick, he yawned and sauntered off to lick his well-used private parts. He seemed to like my father, who had found him on the street and took care of him mostly. Me, he had reservations about. Each day when Big George arrived home, Toto swaggered over to his station wagon, looking aggrieved and obligated to report that the boy-dog bonding thing just wasn't working out.

Until 1972, when I was thirteen and we packed up to head a dozen miles down Highway 24 to Paris, my parents and I lived in Madison, a town of 528 people, where Betty grew up and her father built the family's first lumberyard. Big George ran the place. When we pass through Madison now, I see my father standing in front, crying out something a little shocking at passersby, or raising his hand as my mother and I drove by.

"What is he up to?" Betty would ask. "No good."

Rolling down the car window, she would yell at my dad, "Get to work.

"What am I going to do with him?" my mother always asked.

"Hit the road, Betty," he cried back.

Big George fancied himself a little bohemian. In the late 1960s, when the hippie signs proclaimed FLOWER POWER, he painted the refrigerator in the family room completely black with one big blooming white flower. He could draw anything, and, wishing I could too, I sat watching him for hours as he sketched a caribou from the *World Book Encyclopedia*, the profile of John F. Kennedy, a sleeping dog, my mother's face from a photo taken when she was in college. In the picture she looked shy and innocent; in the sketch, through my father's eyes, even more so. He worked on that portrait night after night, but she didn't like it. It was the same old problem; in person or on paper, she never thought she looked right, even when captured by loving hands.

My father's big hands were rough from work, but gentle too. When laboring in the yard, he touched the leaves and shrubbery with kindness. Standing behind my mother, latching a necklace or strand of pearls, he brushed the hair away with delicacy, always kissing her neck when he finished his task. I came to see my mother through my father's eyes, which took in what few others recognized, her sweetness, vulnerability, and the sadness that sometimes came over her silently.

Betty and I were nervous characters, and when we were on the downswing, the house was still except for the sound of my father making jokes, trying to wash our cares away. When we would return to the world, we would find him, sitting in a chair on the patio with a beer, stroking the ears of Toto, who had grown accustomed to my capricious affections and my mother's tendency to send things into a bit of a whirlspin.

There seemed to be some kind of rule that my father could never have anything he wanted. He lived for us.

. . .

On the morning of the fishing trip, I located a glass jar with a top and dragged the snow shovel out of the garage. Digging tentatively into the earth, I left a fairly shallow impression and collapsed on the ground as Toto eyed me skeptically. Already I found life exhausting, and it seemed to have the same opinion of me, but eventually I did find a couple of worms and managed, with a kitchen fork, to get them into a jar. "Two will be plenty," I said to Toto. "We won't be staying long." I had a plan.

Big George looked woebegone when he arrived home with a pole and more nasty worms in a small box. Work, hard work; this was the Baker family religion, but my father was the good-time sinner man who never quite got the faith. My uncle Harry, who supervised the running of all four of the family's lumberyards, had a way of suggesting, as he peered over his accountant's half-glasses, that no one else could ever do quite right. My father tended to ignore him when it was possible; he was as easygoing and personable as Harry was shrewd and financially adept.

We headed to Moberly, to Rothwell Park where there was a pond or lake or something. Daddy took along a six-pack of Budweiser. I was determined that whatever happened, I would not touch a fish. I left the jar with the worms I had found, dead by this point, on the kitchen table for my mother to find with a sign that said, ENJOY YOUR LUNCH!

My father did what he always did when we traveled together alone. "I want you to have a happy childhood," he told me before asking about school, my life, my friends. Sliding as far as possible toward the car door, I never knew quite what to say to please him. I wanted him to believe that all was well, but could not really make the case.

"I'm not right," I blurted out to him once.

"No one is," he answered. "They just think they are. Too many people think they've got it all figured out. But they don't."

This idea was going to come as quite a shock to many people I knew.

"No one?"

"Look inside a person and everyone has problems. I work in a damn lumberyard. My father was a lawyer. He was number one in his class."

All the way to Moberly, my father sang, as he always did in the car. From his old single man's life as a salesman, he kept, in a rarely opened cabinet in the family room, the records of Benny Goodman, Louis Armstrong, Dizzy Gillespie, Billy Eckstine, Count Basie, Duke Ellington, Paul Whiteman, Tommy Dorsey and his Orchestra, Lionel Hampton, the Mills Brothers, Woody Herman, and Nat King Cole.

"Mona Lisa, men have named you," he sang as he dried off after a shower, always folding his towel carefully and hitting every inch of flesh. I thought the method was something he had picked up in the army.

At Rothwell Park, after my father finally succeeded in assembling the pole and baiting it, he retired to the grassy bank to drink beer. There I stood for fifteen minutes or so, holding the pole, hoping that the fish were elsewhere, preferably in some far-off bay. My father checked the sky for rain with some frequency and chugged on a Bud.

About every five minutes, I shot him a look that said, "Isn't this enough?"

"Fish, dammit," he said. "Fish." In return, I made a face, turned back around, and threw the fishing pole into the lake. Already I was a believer in the power of the grand gesture.

"Damn, George," my father yelled as I plopped down beside him.

"Daddy," I said, "you know and I know that this is just a shit waste of time."

"Don't talk like that," he said. "Your mother is going to blame me for this. I am never going to hear the end of it. Some boys would be damn grateful for a fishing pole like that."

Then he gave me a sip of beer.

After the fishing ordeal, my father and I wound up eating hamburgers at the country club bar where my father's cronies wandered through the bar in their golf shoes. "I guess you wouldn't want to learn golf," my father began. But I was reluctant. I did not care for the shoes.

"Am I a brat?" I asked.

"Borderline," he responded.

Soon, another thought occurred. *Funny Girl* was playing in Columbia. I did not know Barbra Streisand, but anyone who tripped on her pants leg at the Oscars was my kind of woman. I had read the reviews of the movie, knew the songs from the record, and had memorized the number to call for showtimes. My father shrugged, threw down the last of his drink, gave in. We saw the movie. When Barbra declared, "I'm a bagel on a plateful of onion rolls," I wanted to cheer.

When it was over, my father remarked, "That Jewish girl can sing." Afterward, we dined at Rice Bowl Shangrila restaurant, which I considered the height of sophistication. All the way home, I talked about Barbra until my father turned from the wheel and said, "Please, George, hush. You've got to straighten out and fly right."

For days, I spoke in Brooklynese 24/7. I narrowly escaped injury when, standing on a bar stool in my bathrobe, lip-synching to "Don't Rain on My Parade," I fell to the floor after what I considered a particularly devastating climax. Betty came rushing, kneeling down to check for fractures as I rubbed my head, thinking, "Oy!"

A city kid who grew up in St. Louis as the son of a successful attorney, my father—who snoozed over the stacks of sale tickets he brought home nights—was from a family of huggers, eaters, drinkers, people who dragged us, way past my bedtime, to suppers at fancy restaurants with waiters in tuxes, appetizers, tanks of lobsters with snapping claws.

Granny was one of five sisters, all with waves of platinum hair, whose parents, or grandparents, or someone, had come to a town near St. Louis called Pacific from Vienna, for reasons I cannot say. Maybe they thought things worked out for the Gabors.

Granny wore black dresses, strands of pearls, loved to entertain, stuffed bills into the hands of ragged men on the streets. "God love him," she always said when she passed those without. Her sister Sade Sizer was smoky-voiced, with the tendency to scatter burning ash. She turned the air around her blue with curses. When she descended on St. Louis from Chicago with her husband—an ice magnate—my father watched his aunt, face circled by cigarette fumes, holding court like a bawdy empress while Granny trailed her, checking the carpet for anything smoldering. He savored a character, loved things a little wild and crazy.

Sade, though, frightened my mother. Granny's sister was the sort discomfited by a younger woman whose beauty bested the kind she herself acquired at the Marshall Field cosmetics counter.

"Have another drink, kiddo," Sade told Betty. "Don't ya wanna get a little peppy?"

My father's family always gathered by the piano to sing, watched by Betty and me, along with Granny's friend Bertha Cox, whose blond wig (necessitated by sparse, filament-like hair) was purchased in a room at the Chase Hotel "from a traveling salesman," Granny always emphasized, "a Chinaman!"

Like my dad, Granny loved Nat King Cole.

"Rambling rose, rambling rose, why you ramble, no one knows."

Betty watched how Granny served, did everything. She dressed up for them all, wanted never to disgrace herself.

"Relax," Daddy said, pulling her head to his shoulder but never getting it to stay.

When Granny sang, I saw my father's face in hers; I saw him in everything she did, definitely in her eyes, which, when turned on me, revealed what felt like suspicion. I loved her, but sometimes a look from her could poke like a pin. Already I knew that she was an enforcer of what I sometimes violated: the rules for boys and the rules for girls. Once she saw me gesturing along with the Supremes on television and her glance said it all.

My mother believed in the rules. My father had some rebellion in him, but the others could always jerk him back easily into enemy territory. Sometimes, though, we could find a secret space.

Sade told tales of nightclubs, gangsters, and strange phone calls arriving for her maid, who claimed to be Castro's daughter. She often arrived with lavish gifts, once outdoing herself with two shiny silver cranes with long beaks and thin elegant legs. One bent down as if to feed, the other stretched its long neck toward the sky. Granny put them on the dining table and I sat looking at them reflecting the light, these exquisite birds from Sade's enticing world. When I told Granny they were the most beautiful things I had seen, she looked back at me quizzically. Throwing me off guard, though, rescue arrived in a husky voice.

"Toots, we gotta get you to Boca," Sade told me. "I think you're kind of a fish out of water."

She was sitting at the dining table and I went to stand beside her and did not move for the longest time. Maybe this was someone who could be on my side.

Betty was in awe of the city, loved it when Granny treated us to club sandwiches, held together with colored toothpicks, at the tearoom in Stix, a world of women and the tap of high-heeled shoes. Models moved past the tables. I was always the only boy brought along; I loved the models and began to pose for class photos with head thrown back and eyebrows raised in a way I considered suitable for print work.

While Betty and Granny shopped, I bypassed the toys and went upstairs to the furniture floor, to the model rooms, complete in every detail. I sat in them one at a time—living rooms, dens, family rooms, dining rooms, master bedroom suites, rooms for babies, little girls, teenage girls, and boys. When I sat down, tentatively, in the boys' room, complete with bed with wheels meant to resemble a racing car, sports souvenirs, soldiers marching on the walls, baseball bat lamps, I realized I did not feel at home.

It wasn't that I wanted to reside in the girls' rooms, it was simply that no place fit me right. I liked a mock-up of a basement hideaway featuring an armoire with what I considered an ingenious secret—a Murphy bed—and some framed movie posters, including one from *Casablanca*.

After the clerks got tired of my lying on the beds and pretending to wait for room service, I rode the escalator down to the basement snack bar where I waited on a bar stool, watching the hot dogs turn on the rotisserie and listening to the big black girls talk and talk. "You wanna dog, sugar?" they'd ask. "You wanna big hot pretzel? Baby, you hongreee? You look like you like to put down the groceries."

Things My Parents Told Me When I Was Very Young:

1. "Don't stand that way; you're posing."
2. "That book is for girls."
3. "Your hair is too long. It looks effeminate."
4. "Why would you want to wear that?"
5. "You've been hanging around with the girls again. I can hear it in the way you talk."

One year, I purchased a yellow scarf for my dad for Christmas, as a kind of commemoration of what he had seen during the war. I pictured him wearing it with his herringbone "Going to the City" winter coat. There was no doubt in my mind that he would get the connection with the Japanese pilot; I guess I was a kid with strange ideas of what might make a father smile. As Big George opened the box, I prepared for a moment of glory, but he wound up giving the scarf to Preach Burton, the minister of what was then known as the colored church, along with a polka-dotted costume vest he purchased one year for a New Year's Eve barbershop quartet. Daddy said that yellow was an effeminate color, but I didn't think so.

In our backyard there is a bent-over clothesline and the wrought-iron chairs on the patio are rusty, in need of paint. No one has sat upon them for a decade. We never use the backyard, once filled with the trees my father planted and tended—willow, oak, crape myrtle, maple, hawthorn, flowering crab—some now bare with spindly limbs, the victims of this or that. My mother just shakes her head at the lost ones—when she actually lets herself look. When most people die, she says it is a "blessing." But the trees are a different story. Even my mother grieves openly for my father's trees.

Now a hired man, who talks way too much, waters and cares for the yard, which Big George gradually expanded year after year, mowing farther until it stretched almost all the way down to the forest.

"You can always tell me anything." That is what my father often said to me when I was a kid. But I never did.

6

GEORGE: "That casserole I made Saturday is much better today."

BETTY: "Maybe I'll try some more around Friday."

The late-morning sunlight filters through the old carnival glass vases and heavy tinted bowls on the sill of the bay window in the living room. The objects from auctions that adorn this room are, to my mother, worth only their value and represent her shrewdness, her skill at acquisition. When she holds them up to inspect them, she does not imagine, as I do, the others who once picked them up, though she handles anything that belonged to my grandmothers with extreme care. She has some fine and costly things, but it is a pair of small Chinese figurines, two children, boy and girl, meant to sit on a shelf dangling their legs, that are her favorites. "Don't ever break these," she has told me. Only recently have I discovered that my father bought them in Chicago for twenty dollars. It is these little slips that pass so quickly, almost unnoticed, that occasionally show her feelings, that make them seem as fragile as the figurines. Her emotions are her most delicate possessions, rarely taken out, even for company. When a hint of them breaks through, I want to coax them forth, but she is just too reticent.

"I love them too," I said to her yesterday, glancing at the Chinese children.

"Oh, they're nothing," she said, changing her tone of voice and posture. "They're worthless."

I am pleased she never purchased antique dolls. Few things irk me more than an antique doll, publicly displayed. Particularly off-putting are those perched in small rockers in bonnets.

I wager that down the street, Edna Mae Johnson, still uncomfortable in her new teeth, is bent over her embroidery in her crazy, messed-up house, squinting at her tiny stitches as she stands back to admire the small flowers that blossom over the cloth.

Betty will not get out of bed. When I ask if she is thirsty, she just shakes her head. She is agitated, and when she gets this way I can't focus on much else. Her state of mind affects everything in the house, me especially. I take it in and pace around the house. I want to do a good job here; it is important to me. I want to do right by her.

When I set the trash out earlier, a neighbor informed me that the game warden has released bobcats in the forests nearby to help control deer. He saw a bobcat a few nights back in the parking lot of the high school's vocational agriculture center. The building was, until fifteen years or so ago, a garment factory where the women workers on break gathered outside the door, smoke from their cigarettes rising around them.

Where do the women work now, after their divorces, or when their husbands die, or when bad luck strikes, or the harvest is squat? Not here. They drive to Columbia or other towns nearby to work in hospitals or clean the houses of doctors from India and Pakistan. The country roads are full of headlights at night as they often work odd hours.

"Buck Johnson is getting married again," Earleen says. "It's his fourth. You'd think by now he'd a either figured it out or quit." She is ironing in the kitchen. On the nearby couch, I try to close my eyes. She is not the most diligent housekeeper in America. She runs a rag over a counter so fast, it barely has time to collect a crumb. The vacuum control is always shifted to the lightest setting so it won't be hard to push. But she's game for just about anything. At Christmastime, during a somewhat madcap decorating spree, Betty had Earleen and me searching for ornaments that I broke before puberty. Earleen, trying her damnedest, kept pretending to look until finally confiding to me, "George, I don't know where this shit is.

"How do you think your mama is doing?" she asks me now, setting down the iron and coming to stand by the couch as if there is the possibility that I might not hear her.

I wish my mother would appear at the door of the kitchen and say, "Hey, let's head to the Junction for a catfish sandwich."

"I would do anything for your mama," Earleen says, going on and on. "She's the same age mine would be if she had lived, you know.

"Gettin' old is for the birds, but your mama's a doll. I tell you, when you're not here, I'm on the case. I'll spring like a jackrabbit if I need to.

"My mama was a Indian. She was beautiful," Earleen has often remarked. "I look just like her.

"Was you gonna take a nap?" she asks now, returning to the ironing board. "I never can sleep of a day. I got too much on my mind."

She continues; her only enemy is silence. "I've cleaned for Betty since my boys were kids." Her oldest son, Ethan, is a mechanic. Jackie Roy is a nurse at a VA down in the section of the state we call the Boot Heel. A few years back, he cared for a boy back from the army with a hole in his head the size of a quarter. Earleen worried about the soldier as if she had given birth to him.

I wish my mother would appear at the doorway of the kitchen and suggest, "Say, I'm going down to the Dollar Store to buy a birthday card."

Last night my cousin Lucinda, who tries to appeal to my interests, invited Betty and me to a benefit for the *Missouri Review.* Throughout the dinner I fretted, knowing there was a reading to come. Glancing now and then at Betty, I wished for brevity. I hoped that our entertainment would not be a poet. But no: A poet it was. Despite the weather, she was wearing a jacket of a sort of faux zebra, trimmed in leatherette with tassels on the buttons. Her name was Jude Nutter.

"Where," my mother asked, quite loudly, "did that jacket come from?" I cringed, as Betty glared at me with an expression with which I am very familiar. It seems to suggest that I am personally responsible for every particle of bullshit loose in the world.

"What was her name?" my mother asked loudly, after the introduction.

"Nutter," I said. "Jude Nutter."

"What?" my mother, incredulous, asked.

"Jude Nutter," I repeated. "Her name is Jude Nutter."

"Nutter," my mother said again, even more audibly than before. "N-U-T-T-E-R?"

"Yes," I repeated again. "Nutter. N-U-T-T-E-R."

My cousin looked slightly uncomfortable as Jude nodded at our table, sensing some disturbance. Betty smiled back, gave a bit of a wave, as if to acknowledge the attention. I knew things were going to get worse when Jude confided that she had grown up in a house on a lot adjacent to the Bergen-Belsen concentration camp.

She continued, telling us about her special kinship with insects, which she likes to feel on her body. This is sensual and pleasing for her. I waited, but Betty, intent on her brownie, made no remark. I began to breathe more regularly. Then Jude started to recite her first poem, a work that opened with an image of flies on the bloody eye of a dead lamb. Again, Betty shot me the look. It is always me. I am *always* responsible.

"How," Betty pondered loudly, "did we get involved with this?" She threw her half-consumed brownie down on the plate as if it were a horseshoe. Jude Nutter mourned the lamb.

The second poem began. Jude Nutter read to us of finding the dentures of her deceased mother in a small container in the bathroom. Soon, there were Germans. Then there were the teeth. Then the insects. Then the teeth again, the haunting melancholy of the mother's gaping oral cavity. Finally, the poem built to a dramatic conclusion: Jude kissed the teeth and threw them into a river.

"She's going to have a hard time topping that," said Betty.

At times, my mother maintains her capacity to see much and often surprise. Especially in public, with others. But after the reading, she wavered, wandering into confusing territory. It is astounding to me how quickly Betty can fade from her normal self into the disorientation that upsets her, leaves her wringing her hands. If she is engrossed in something—a meal, a book, a poetic experience involving insects—she is okay, but without something to focus on, she gets a little crazy in the hours before bed. Dementia patients suffer from a phenomenon called sundowner's syndrome, which worsens their symptoms at night.

In the car going home from the reading, Betty's defenses fell; the act failed. "Stop, stop, stop," she yelled out at every sign, slamming her right foot down as if hitting the brakes. "Slow down, slow down, slow down," she commanded, though I was well within the speed limit. Her noises—the mutterings and whimpers, the troubled utterances—signaled the approach of high anxiety. "Are you okay?" I asked.

"I'm fine," she said, as if she could will it so. "I'm fine."

At home, panic crossed her face in tiny waves. A dropped pill led her to cry out, as if something sharp had stabbed her. When a toothpaste tube fell into the sink, she seemed to lose all hope but giggled as her face crumbled. Arriving in her room, I found her seated at the edge of her bed in her nightgown with her shoes still on and her good black pants fallen around her ankles. "Let's get the shoes off," I said, taking over and managing to get her ready to sleep. The sight of her bare feet was enough to suggest that life is just too tough, but they are survivors, these old codgers, and beautiful in their human way.

Finally she closed her eyes, but cried out several times as her mind, unwilling to rest, continued to fret. Early in the morning, I woke to go to the bathroom and found her in the family room, going over the bills she stacks and restacks. I lay down, though this made her angry. "I have things to do here," she told me. "Things to do. *Things to do!*" She was mad at me for standing guard. That is what it is; I am the guard to her, the one who has taken over her castle. When I woke up at 5 a.m., she was gone, back in her bed, but not sleeping: There were the sounds, her little cries out.

Today, I am crazed. My head is full of voices: Everyone up there is talking, yelling. No one thinks I am dealing with Betty correctly. I hear the voice of a writer in Washington, D.C., telling me that my relationship with Betty is "codependent." Friends in Manhattan yammer in the corners of my brain about my destroying my career by staying in Missouri. My relatives plead for Betty's entry into assisted living. My father and Mammy join in the fray. In my head, the dead are pushy, opinionated, and easily offended. At Starbucks, they scream into my cerebellum about the price of venti lattes and the calorie content of chocolate graham crackers.

Suddenly, a voice I believe to be my mother's joins the committee of commenters. She draws out every word, articulates seemingly every letter with extreme care. Wait a minute, this is not Betty. The God of Brain Waves has made an error. This is *Meet the Press,* I am almost certain. I am hearing Peggy Noonan. And she is concerned, very concerned. Shut up, Peggy. Shut up, shut up.

I am doing my best here. I will make it back to New York, but frankly, to spend some time in Paris, Missouri, is to come to question the city, where it is normal to work 24/7, tapping away on your BlackBerry for someone who will fire you in an instant, but crazy to pause to help someone you love when they are falling.

If I have a deadline to meet, I stay awake, working all night. Around 2:30 or 3:00, I take a break to get a bit of breeze, hit the twenty-four-hour convenience store for coffee and doughnuts, drive the loop around Paris, which takes me to the top of a hill, near the cemetery. From the four-way stop where I pause—aside from the occasional semi whooshing by, there is little other traffic at this hour—I look out at the town: the courthouse dome, Main Street, the loose scattering of lights, blue and yellow, twinkling around the hills that hold the houses on their shoulders. I like the feeling of being the only one awake for miles and miles.

. . .

"We're the new Mississippi," says Jane Blades, who works in social services. Rural America is going ghetto. Because the high school no longer offers a foreign language, the kids who attend Paris R-II High do not qualify for admission to any of the state universities. In the doctor's office, an old classmate tells me that there are no longer cheerleaders at the school. "Now how can you build spirit without cheerleaders?" she asks me, crestfallen.

"It's the never knowing" goes a song I like that plays on the radio here, *"that keeps us going."* In Paris, religion is the great comfort. The most popular verb here is "pray." People gather together to lift their requests for the survival of sick children, the vanquishing of tumors, the securing of loans. At church recently, I have heard a special prayer for a dying child, offered up by his father, a tenderhearted rodeo clown. WE PRAY WITH OUR BOOTS ON says a sign advertising the Cowboy Church on the side of a pickup. Global Prayer Warriors are called forth on the Internet in times of trouble.

When I look at our town from the top of the hill at night, I think of all the people waking up, facing the day, their problems, imagine their voices, their prayers for themselves, their children, the neighbors and friends they have known for years rising up with hope into the lightening sky.

There is far too much illness in this county, including a large incidence of cancer, blamed on pesticides used during the 1950s and '60s. Illnesses are a constant topic and housewives chat in the aisles of the grocery store about the merits of various chemo procedures. Gossip about the state of the neighbor's marriage has been replaced by intense discussion of his vital organs. A law firm called Tolbert, Beadle, and Musgrave advertises on TV constantly, courting victims of mesothelioma on Channels 8 and 13. Cancers wipe out whole families or parts of them.

A friend of mine who grew up near Middle Grove can list all the people who lived near his family's farm who have battled the disease. His father died of it. His sister died of it. He has fought it himself for almost twenty years. "A good day," his mother told me, "is when everyone is alive."

On streets in towns around here, old houses tumble, drawing meth cookers who start fires at night. Helicopters filled with state police look for dealers who hide in trailer homes and campers in the woods. In Columbia, where the elderly, including Betty, go to the doctor or for tests at the med center, MS-13—a deadly gang that drifted north after Katrina—is being held responsible for a series of "senseless shootings" and is said to be involved in drug trafficking, robbery, murder, prostitution, and arms trafficking. On the streets of this once peaceful university town, it is possible to acquire military-style ammunition that can pierce a policeman's protective vest. There are rumors of young women inducted into white slavery against their will. The husband of my mother's friend Betsy was approached by a youthful prostitute in the parking lot of Red Lobster. "We were there for Crabfest," Betsy said.

"That brings them out," I replied.

There is frequent mention of depression and bipolar conditions. "It used to be hysterectomies and then there was mastectomies," Evie Cullers says. "Now it is always something up in the head."

This is not a locale whose residents are waiting desperately for the latest version of the iPhone. This is a place where the Second Coming would be much preferred to tomorrow's sunrise, the world of the Dollar Store, the Big Cup, the carbohydrate, and the cinnamon roll—a region of old families, now faded, living in trailer homes, divorcing and having illegitimate children. But there is also kindness, such kindness, the casserole on the doorstep from someone who does not expect to be acknowledged, the wet morning flowers in the mailbox.

And then there is my mother, one of the last truly fashionable women in Monroe County, even now. She fusses over the catalogs, always determined to find the perfect blouse. People still remark to me on her outfits, her style. Our friend Linda Lechliter says that when her mother died, she could find no one in Paris who would even take her dresses, which didn't fit Linda herself. You can't get the women here into anything but jeans, Linda claimed. "And these were nice dresses," Linda said, "beautiful dresses. And not a soul in this town to wear them."

At the parking lot of Hickman's IGA, our grocery store, I notice, on one of my late-night rides, the sunburned kid who mows our lawn sitting on the hood of his car, all alone, hugging his knees, waiting in the dark, watching the occasional car go by. I have also seen him sitting around at the car wash or chasing squirrels down the street in the evenings in his dirty clothes. Aside from a few old people and little kids, there are few pedestrians in Paris; everyone drives and practically lives in what they call their "vehicles." I don't know this kid's name, or his family, or if he has one at all. He looks like he might belong to one of the wanderers—sham ministers who found churches and make off with the dough; women on the dole, unmarried or divorced, who drift in, rent old houses for next to nothing, and disappear, leaving a kid or two old enough to kick off the gravy train. You see these young ones, not even out of their teens, walking on the sides of the highway in the early mornings and wonder what they have been up to.

It is always the wandering ones, the underdogs, the eccentrics, the castoffs who tell me their stories. Leslie, whom I met in graduate school, had a distant relationship with truth. From her I learned never to trust anyone who ever lived in Los Angeles. Then there was Esther, an old woman who pushed her stuffed cart along Perry Street. We met at a laundry called the Stinky Sock. Cookie, the black drag queen, wore enormous bejeweled crosses and earrings with healing crystals, small Statues of Liberty, and large glittery crescent moons. Jason was a homeless Puerto Rican street kid I took in. At night he wrapped his head in towels to try to silence the voices he heard when he tried to sleep. In my apartment he left a stocking cap I keep on a vase as a small tribute and a leaky plastic jar with colorful floating fish that he bought at a discount store for my birthday.

. . .

The first of these characters arrived in my life early on; he was a family friend who drifted through our lives. Wray Chowning resided in Madison, in his parents' old house, a place so covered with vines that the brick barely showed. Preach Burton mowed the lawn, which received no other attention. It lay flat and half brown, like an old carpet. In the front hallway stood a huge grandfather clock coveted by Betty and a desk of cherrywood with thin elegant legs that slightly curved. My mother said the desk was of the Queen Anne style and that it wasn't really right for a man's house. Who knew these rules could attach themselves to even a piece of furniture? Though I told no one, I felt united with Wray. I understood, somehow, that we had a bond. I was a kid trapped between feeling something and knowing nothing.

Mammy often asked my mother to drive by to see if Wray's car was in the driveway. It bothered her if it was not. It worried her if it was. I could see that Mammy wanted to reach out to him. She took pies and cakes, but sometimes, even when his car was parked out front, he didn't come to the door when we knocked. "I'll bet he's just sleeping," Mammy always said. "Maybe he's just sleeping." Betty tended just to shake her head. She and Mammy both knew Wray was drinking. Even I had picked up that this was his problem. Mammy, whose brother had also been a drinker, seemed to understand what came of a life trapped inside a bottle of disappointment.

Wray was unmarried and lived alone after the death of his father and the closing of their family's dry goods store downtown. He did not work. Though his clothes suggested some involvement in large concerns, he seemed to have none. For holidays or special dinners, he came to our house or to Mammy's, never sitting in the living room with the men, but always drifting toward the kitchen. His face went red when my father or Harry or Bill laughed in the other room, and he did not join in the talk at the table, just listened, fingers shaking so that Betty's aunt Bess would reach out for the dishes to spear him some meat or ladle out the gravy.

My father said his name in a way that was both too nice and not nice at all. Wray. *Wray.* Daddy added a kind of flourish that somehow diminished his greetings and their recipient and left me anguished. It seemed like my father had sided with the enemy.

Usually when Wray came to our house, he was invited with the ladies, the widows—Mrs. Bloom who ran the silver shop in Moberly; Betty Riley, a doctor's widow who went to Mississippi every winter to ride horses. My father plied him with cocktails. Everyone else tried to get Wray not to drink, but my father always kept asking, again and again, if he needed a refill. On holidays, Big George always got him drunk and my mother's brother Bill Baker would catch my father's glance and roll his eyes or chuckle when Wray stumbled or slurred his words. Big George was nice to everyone, but somehow Wray was okay to laugh at, even when he was present, just sitting there, bothering no one. My father served his cocktails with a twist of contempt that I could taste too when he held out the glass. Maybe it was just for entertainment for my uncles. Maybe it was because it was a relief for my father to have someone farther outside the circle than he was. No one kicks you harder than a pal on the bench who sees his chance to join the team.

The Chownings were among Madison's fine old families, a circle with the Bakers on the periphery that included the Thompsons, who knew Harry Truman and wrote to him if someone in Madison changed their party alliance. There were also the Threlkelds, and the Atterburys, whose son, Newton, dead for years by this point, had been Wray's great friend when they were young. When people spoke of Wray, they always brought up Newton too. Newton had married and left for Jefferson City. Wray, it was implied, was lost without him and began to drink, more and more.

Wray had hair of pure silver; any tarnished part was carefully combed over. He wore cuff links, suits tailored in St. Louis, shirts so fiercely pressed that life dared not intrude. He smoked extralong Salems lit by a shiny gold lighter meant to resemble a fountain pen. He was always the first to leave the gatherings. In the pocket of his vest there was a shiny watch, produced just after meals when he took it out to suggest he had some other pressing engagement. Sitting beside him at the table, you could hear it, ticking out the minutes until he could safely get away.

There was something about him that scared me. Bill called him a "mama's boy." From early on, I had a sense for secrets, for the places where people were hiding things, the spaces where words went unsaid, the moments when someone at the table shifted the subject away from something or someone. Mostly, I shied away from Wray. I didn't like the way they treated him, the way my father said his name. *Wray, Wray, Wray.* I can still hear the way he said it. My father's rendition of the name made too fancy by its extra letter was almost enough to make me cry. This was my father, the one who I believed would always be loyal. Who said I could tell him anything.

My parents were gone for the weekend. Maybe a lumbermen's convention. I was staying with Mammy, who was walking by then on a cane left over from someone. Constantly she asked me to check the thermostat to make sure we weren't using too much power.

One of the most intriguing aspects of a visit to Mammy's was the gun kept under her pillow—a pistol, metal, cold, and surprisingly heavy for its size—given to her by my uncle Bill for protection. Betty said she would like to use it to shoot Bill.

During one of my stays at my grandmother's, Mammy realized that she was supposed to play bridge, and a neighbor named Edith came to the rescue. She tried to get me to sleep in Mammy's bed so she could watch *Love of Life.* This seemed unfair. After Edith left the room, I grabbed the gun. As a joke, I took it into the living room and pointed it at Edith. "Lordamighty!" she screamed, throwing her hands up. "Lordamighty!"

I gave up the gun with no discharge, but this was not the end of it. Edith told Mammy, who told Betty. "Edith will tell this all over town," Betty remarked to my grandmother.

"Well, he didn't shoot her," Mammy said.

I remember checking several times for the gun on the weekend I am recalling, but it was nowhere to be found. On Saturday, Mammy burned an angel food cake. Later, she baked another, as the dessert was for Study Club. She beat the batter up as the radio played. It was Oldies Hour: "Someone's Rocking My Dreamboat."

That night, Mammy popped popcorn, as was her custom on our nights together. She talked to me about life, said what she had wanted most for her kids was for them to see the world.

On Sunday, Bill and June arrived with their two dogs, Tammy and Heidi, to take us to see Mammy's brother, Uncle Oscar, who had not yet left his home in Clarence, not far from the farm where Mammy grew up.

Bill sold tractors in Mexico, although he remained a partner—with Harry, Betty, and Mammy—in the lumberyards. Spitting out the windows and clearing his throat, he traveled the countryside with June and the dogs at all hours in a grimy baseball cap in search of round balers to buy and sell. Before he married, he slept in rooming houses run by old widows but lived on the back roads. Late nights found him at a roadhouse in Moonglow or sipping a Bud in some truck stop, mulling over newspapers. He met June at the Black Orchid Lounge in Joplin. A still youngish "widow woman," she had been a beauty operator before the five farms in Kansas, Missouri, and Oklahoma that she inherited from her first husband made her a rich woman. The owner of a mink stole that I tried on in secret during a Thanksgiving dinner, she always gave me special attention.

June smoked profusely and served her seventeen-year-old toy terrier, Tammy, coffee with cream in the mornings to get her going. "In the mornings," June would say, "Tammy needs her fuel. Just like me!"

It was late fall, November perhaps, not long before the winter set in. The Missouri sky was nearly white with smoky lines of cloud. Back home, in Madison, after the trip, there was a curious event, a car in Mammy's driveway with the windows rolled up and a man behind the steering wheel who would not roll down the windows or speak at all. He just gazed ahead, as if frozen. We had no idea of his purpose here or when he had arrived. It was Wray. He frightened me. I did not want him there.

Bill approached the car, tapped on the window, but Wray remained fixed, oblivious. He did not react. "You all right, Wray?" Bill asked. "You all right?" But Wray did not turn; he ignored Bill completely. For a while, Bill stood by the car. Then June, holding Tammy, went up, knocked gently on the window, and waved the dog's paw. "Tammy wants to see you, Wray," she offered. Mammy finally said, "Just leave him. Let him be. He's not doing anything wrong." Eyeing Tammy, she turned to me and mimicked strangulation.

I could not take my eyes off Wray's face, his hands on the wheel, which he gripped tight. Where was he going? He was always on his own.

Inside, Mammy served the burned angel cake to Bill and me. June would not leave Wray. She sat for a long time on a lawn chair on the front porch, holding Tammy and smoking her Dorals. From the window, I watched the smoke from her cigarette eddying through the cold air. "Sometimes," she said, after finally coming into the kitchen, "if you just sit with a person, you can get 'em to feel a little better." She poured coffee for herself and Tam, prepared a tray with cake and coffee for me to set on the hood of Wray's car.

When I came back in the kitchen, June was still talking. She said that Wray had somehow gotten on "the wrong road." It is easy sometimes, she says, for a person to get on the wrong road. She nearly took such a detour after she lost a baby, Mary Ann, and then her first husband. She said she went through a rough patch. Bill cleared his throat to end the talk. It was getting too personal and he winced, as he had a way of doing if certain kinds of things came up in conversations.

Outside it was getting dark, but Wray still did not move. When Bill and June left, I kept watch at the window. Mammy came over sometimes to stand behind me and try to make out what was going on. Gradually, the car disappeared into the dark. In the morning, Wray was gone.

"It's just a sickness," said Mammy of Wray's affliction, "that's all." But it wasn't. He was more than sick. He was loathed by many, it seemed. He was the kind of man whom our town seemed to hate, though he himself seemed to be the only one he had ever injured. Elsie Van Sickle talked about Wray's "toots," his trips to St. Louis on the train, and his stays at hotels downtown where, her voice implied, nothing good went on.

Mammy called Wray every few days. Once he did not pick up the phone for a whole weekend and Mammy sent me to take him a skillet full of eggs and bacon. "Just open the door if it's unlocked and leave it. Don't go in unless it seems like he needs help. I can't do it. He could be in there naked."

Miss Virginia, Mammy's neighbor, drove me to Wray's in the red Chevrolet that she acquired after she retired. Like Bertha Cox, she wore wigs and kept a row of them on Styrofoam heads on the top of the piano in her living room. Her favorite resembled a thatched roof in an African village. In emergency mode, she did not even put one on, but added a loaf of bread and a can of Vienna sausages to my deliveries. Upon arrival at Wray's, I found myself more and more nervous. I balanced everything as I walked up the sidewalk to Wray's new apartment in the Senior Housing Complex. Tentatively, I opened the aluminum screen door. It was unlocked, as was the main door with the little knocker.

Wray was on the couch in a robe and nothing else, sick and queasy with eyes so glazed over that they could barely be distinguished from his gray face. The robe was untied and I tried not to glance below his pale chest with its swirls of hair. But I did; I could not stop myself. I left the food on a table near the door and picked up Wray's glasses from the floor. As I had worn glasses for so long and was nearly blind without them, I was especially sympathetic. I had inherited the Bakers' weak eyes.

When Wray glanced at me, a flood of blood was set loose under the skin of his face. It spread. His hands were shaking too bad for him to eat.

Back in the car, I told Miss Virginia what had happened as a small tear made its way down her rouged cheek.

. . .

As the years passed, I learned more about Wray, and whenever his name was mentioned, I got worried. The secrets around him were frightening to me. Often, Betty and I traveled to Moberly to visit her uncle Oscar at the Maple Lawn Lodge for elders. To Oscar we had delivered jelly rolls, prune juice, cottage cheese containers filled with ambrosia, and jars of ink in which he soaked his used typewriter ribbons. He kept a typewritten journal of his bowel movements (June 24: COMPLETE EVACUATION), which I pored over when Oscar and Betty left the room.

After we left Oscar, while Betty shopped for groceries, I always went to the library, where it seemed there was something I felt driven to find hidden in the books. There were three floors, thousands of books. On a shelf, in a pile, in a newspaper or magazine: I had to be there somewhere. There had to be someone whose inside felt like mine. "What are you looking for?" a librarian asked me one day. "You always look like you are looking for something. Can I help you?"

"I don't know exactly. I don't know."

Hiding back, far into the shelves, I read the *New York Times* Arts and Leisure section, books about movie stars, and occasionally, when there was nothing else to riffle through, stories about the war, where I hoped to find some mention of Saipan. I loved the name of that place where my father had been stationed, out there somewhere by the ocean: *Saipan, Saipan, Saipan*. Often in one of my scariest dreams I saw the Japanese pilot flying in the plane, his yellow scarf blowing in the wind, my father running on the beach for his life.

In one volume of photographs, there was a shot of a naked soldier working in the tropical heat, taken from the back. I looked it up again and again. When a librarian approached, I slammed the book closed, but the picture was imprinted in my brain.

Something had told me, from the first time I heard the word "homosexual," that it applied to me. Absolutely unknowing about anything concerning the subject, I located a book called *The Gay Mystique* at the

Moberly library that I camouflaged by placing it inside another, larger volume. Turning the pages, I scanned the room, more seriously on guard than ever before. I thought of stealing the book. No one else within hundreds of miles would want to read it; no one would care if it went missing. Finally, in what I considered a show of courage, I ripped out the back pages, the "Resource Guide." Included was the address of a gay newspaper, *The Advocate.*

Because I was truly desperate for *something,* and as it was summer and I could be at home to intercept the mail, I sent five dollars to San Francisco, asking to be mailed as many issues as that might buy. I waited, checking the mailbox every day. When they finally appeared, just as I was about to give up, the papers were a confusing revelation. Taking them in, I was filled with many questions. I read one sex ad with shaking hands, then quickly rolled up the papers in a rubber band and hid them.

Five minutes later, I was dragging them out again to look at another ad. Then I put them back and then I got them out again. Then I put them back again and then I got them out again. A few days later, my mother, who has a homing device for anything below board or off-kilter, discovered them under my mattress.

All during the day she found the newspapers, my mother turned her face away when I approached. She looked stricken. I would try never to inflict this hurt again. In an instant, a thousand choices were made. This was the beginning of many silences to follow, our struggle with words. At the time, I thought the silences, the secrets, did not matter. As it happened, they did. This is what I have learned: To build a life on secrets is to risk falling through the cracks. "Shame is inventive." I read this in a book somewhere awhile back and it has haunted me for years. Shame can make a joke. It can reach for a bottle. It can trip you up when you don't even know it is there. It can seep into everything without your ever knowing.

7

On Saturday morning, I stop for cinnamon rolls at the small farmers' market held in front of the courthouse by bespectacled Amish matrons in bonnets and farm women outfitted in shirts with flowered yokes. This indulgence is needed by neither of us at 701 Sherwood. I envision my future as that of a person who will have to be cut out of a couch.

Already, it is steamy, well into the nineties. Today is the All Town Yard Sale and tables in garages across town are loaded with old clothes, housewares, figurines of Jesus and cartoon characters, scenic landscapes framed without glass, lamps without shades, children's watches and battered toys, pill organizers I am tempted to lick for crumbs. Vans with baby shoes dangling from the rearview mirrors circle yards. On the back gate of a pickup, a hand-lettered sign is taped below a tractor decal: IN MEMORY OF BOBBY T. I keep my eyes peeled for an elderly gentleman whose favored mode of conveyance is a rusty aqua-colored golf cart festooned with American flags. Skinny little black girls in colored barrettes dance around their large, determined-looking mothers in their pastel stretch shorts who search for school outfits and near-fit shoes.

"Thank you for taking care of me." That is what Betty said last night, apropos of nothing, really. I was looking at places in the kitchen where the linoleum is coming up and wondering if I could glue it down without permanently adhering myself. Admitting she had, in her mind, run up a debt clearly troubled her, even though it was just to me. She was grateful, though she never seems to really take in what staying here is costing me—my life, really. Probably because she cannot bear to consider it.

"What kind of man would do that, come home and live with his mother?" There are a lot of things I couldn't care less about people saying, but I don't want to be thought tragic, because I'm not. I may not have a life partner or a bunch of kids. But I have had loves you can't quite put a label on, though now I am reconciled to being on my own. Discussions of gay marriage make me feel spinsterish. Yes, my brothers and sisters should be allowed to wed. In my experience, it is gay dating that should be outlawed.

A long time ago, in New York, a man I wanted to maybe settle down with, an architect not much for sharing confidences—my kind of person—told me that I didn't meet well. "I met you, didn't I?" I asked. He just stared back. I could not make him understand that I cannot summon myself when I most want to, when there is someone I need to please. When I care for someone I find it a difficult thing to admit. I even find it difficult to say that I find it difficult. I have been called emotionally unavailable. I prefer to think of myself as temporarily out of stock.

The architect didn't pan out. "You're high maintenance," he said. He was right. I take a village.

He is currently in Brooklyn somewhere, married to an artist with a multicolored Mohawk. I imagine they are living happily now in a beautifully refurbished loft space or perhaps a teepee. Maybe they have adopted a child from that little country in Africa where Madonna goes.

In our house we keep to a regular schedule. Betty's in the family room by nine, eagerly awaiting her breakfast. Frying up bacon, I assess her mood and condition, pour out her pills—Aricept, Namenda, estradiol, Celexa, and Enablex—and check to see if any need to be refilled. This morning, waiting for her, I hear a few yelps and a dog's low growl, a funny kind of barking that suggests a halfhearted attempt to sound ferocious. Someone has dumped a stray, as they do here in the country. You see them, often past their prime, padding along the shoulders of the highway, looking hot and bedraggled. Outside, I see a reddish-brown creature, medium-sized but barely more than a puppy, bounding out of our garage with a bit of what looks like potting soil sticking to his nose. I am tentative at first, having no interest in emotional entanglement. He looks needy. I am wary. I am needy too, and all I can handle. But before too much time has passed, I reconsider, tentatively.

"Hey you," I say, hunching down. The little dog—a bit of many breeds, it seems—circles me, sneezing. He has yellow half circles above his eyes, like eyebrows. When I ease myself toward him, he lurches, then pulls back. He growls a bit but plops down in front of me, looking curious. I feel slightly offended. He is unsure, which is fine. I am not accustomed to creatures won over easily.

When I get close enough to flick the soil from his nose, the pup bounds up, tail seemingly wagging his entire body, licking me sloppily while he dances. How happy! What do you know? Lost and hungry but hardly down and out. I throw my arms around him, lose my balance and fall back, banging my rear on the concrete as he eyes me and lets out another loud sneeze. When I give him a chaste peck on his ample snout, he pulls back shyly, as if unprepared for such advances.

I bring ice water for the pup, hoping that he will drink and be on his way. Actually, I want him to stay. It strikes me that this is something that could happen. I could have a dog. Why not? Even I could have a dog. Yet I command myself not to encourage him. A drink in this weather is a necessity, the obligation of any humane person, but to go further is not fair and I am no teaser. This is not going to happen. I am not here forever. I cannot take him on. I don't want a commitment. When I head back into the house, he woofs. I start to turn back, but will not let myself.

Today, Betty is not peppy; her tongue is dry and her speech is slightly slurred. "You're just an old sleepyhead," I say. "Did you rest last night? Did you do okay?"

"I did okay," she says, as I pour water and get her one of the bendable straws she favors. "I dreamed your father bought three thousand dollars' worth of cats." Cats are our least favorite animal. In the old days, driving to kindergarten, I always thought my mother sped up if she saw one crossing the road.

As I cook, I tell Betty of the warnings on the news of a "Porkalypse" or "Bacongeddon" because of the drought. "No corn, no pigs," she says. "I'll eat an Eggo when that time comes. Suits me."

After breakfast, Betty hunkers down in her gown on the couch in the midst of a pile of newspapers and books by Nicholas Sparks and Anna Quindlen, anything we can get in large print. When she finds a book she likes, she reads it again and again, but will never admit she has actually enjoyed it. "It was all right," she says. "Better than most of that stuff you get. Better than that Rachel Maddow. She goes on television looking like she is about to play baseball."

Sometimes, out of nowhere, I can see the little girl my mother once was in her eyes. She is funny and sweet, bossy and mischievous. "Tell that woman," she says when Carol leaves the room, "that I don't want Brussels sprouts and that I want strawberries on my ice cream every time." She bangs her fork down on the table. She fusses if she does not want to do something: "Stop bugging me about everything," she commands when I hold out her medicine capsules. "I am too busy," she adds, peeking around her book to see what I am going to do. "Don't boss me, mister," she exclaims, as she pitches *Pride and Prejudice,* which I have recommended, across the couch. "This is like what some old schoolmarm would give out." She does not like television. "I pay for hundreds of channels and it's all trash," she declares. "There is a channel where all they do is sell knives!"

The morning passes—with the occasional growl or yelp from outside. Our moods rise and fall, though at different times. Betty and I are conflicting lines of music, but sometimes come together in a moving or explosive way. I am, if the truth were known, more volatile. Monitored by graph, my emotions would resemble a chart of a frenetic third world economy.

On the phone, a friend, Benjamin, whose novel I am working on, tells me that his mother's name is actually Betty, but at age fifty she changed it to Daphne. My Betty does not seem to get the humor. "Be still," she says and turns away.

Outside, I hear the occasional whining noise: already—tears, emotional manipulation, guilt. I can't take it. I have enough problems. I need a Global Prayer Warrior. When I go out with some leftover breakfast sausage for the dog—a bad move, I know—my friend is tearing around one of the neighbors' yards, that maniacal tail still making its fast, swooshing loops. I whistle and his ears shoot up. He rushes toward me, almost walking on his hind legs before he falls forward. Leaping up on my chest, he devours the sausage with a single chomp, and starts to lick my face as if I am a leftover he cannot quite identify. In seconds he is attempting to drag a bag of antidepressants out of my pocket. My kind of pooch.

He is young and full of life—attributes I am not normally crazy about—but there is a tenderness, a vulnerability, especially when his ears fall back. I find myself once more scooping him up in my arms, feeling his paws on my shoulder, his moist nose on my ear. Love hits me. I don't like it. I don't want it. This flirtation cannot go anywhere. I am a flight risk.

When I tell him to get along on his way, he scrunches down again as if I have hit him. I turn away, head back to the house, but, turning for a parting glance, I see that he is lying on his back, paws nabbing at air. "Get along, little doggy," I say. "Get along." But I whisper it and hope he does not hear me.

After lunch, my mother is silent for a while, then makes her much-repeated pilgrimage to the laundry room. She washes more clothes than Prissy in *Gone With the Wind*. I am convinced she is taking in laundry from other neighborhoods. We are both spillers. During a brief snack time, I can turn a white button-down into a Jackson Pollock. She covertly launders her personal items. If I approach from behind as she tosses a pair of panties into our Speed Queen, she peers over her shoulder as if I have caught her disposing of a murder implement. "Do you have to follow me around all the time?" she demands. "I have some personal business in here."

On the way to the washer, Betty pauses at the mirror in the dining room. "My hair looks awful. How did it ever get to looking like this? That girl who did this ought to be shot." My mother's hair life has always been complex. It isn't just vanity; that hair is everything she can't quite control. In the 1970s, she went to bed for days after getting a bad "frost job." Said my father, "Well, I guess you'll have to shave it off." She screamed back, "You just don't know what it's like!"

My cell buzzes. I anticipate no good news. The Nazi hunter has been raving about a conspiracy against him at the Simon Wiesenthal Center. But no, it is American Express. In recent months, our relationship, never blissful, has entered a period of all but open warfare. They like to be paid promptly. I see the company more as a long-term financial partner. Our conversation makes me feel small in every way except size. If I save my money, I will be able to retire in Penn Station.

Yesterday I spent hours on the phone, sorting through Betty's insurance policies, attempting to assess what would be covered if she entered an assisted living facility. I dialed cities across the plains—Omaha, Wichita, Tulsa. "Slow down," I told them as they rattled off their explanations. "I have special needs." There is more paperwork to sort through. Stuff that I would normally procrastinate about for decades needs doing right now. My to-do list begins with chores already done so I can cross off things right away.

Every day after lunch, Betty and I walk—down Sherwood Road to Hickory, then right on Cleveland, and then another right on McMurry, passing burned lawns and trees whose leaves are turning prematurely brown. Betty never wants to go, but once we've begun, she sets forth the best she can. "Just try to keep going," I tell her. "Well what choice do I have?" she asks. "I'm not just going to lie down out here."

Today, as we head out, I look fondly at a tree in our front yard, a big leafy oak that my father planted when we moved to this house almost forty years ago. It is dying. From its branches hang small brown balls, harbingers of a disease that, according to the yardman, is taking even the oldest, strongest oaks all over Missouri. This tree, I love. I can see my father, with his hair frizzed up, watering it with the hose during its nascent stages before giving it a good dousing with a few tossed-off shakes of Budweiser. I blame its disease on global warming.

I steer Betty out of the driveway. Looking small under the spreading branches, she stares up with a quizzical look as if she knows the tree is sick, but says nothing. Her balance is shakier and shakier, but she tries to forge ahead with no help, emitting the little grunts and groans that have become normal during these expeditions. A wad of Kleenex is stuffed into her hand. Less than halfway home, her nose always begins, inexplicably, to run. "I have to blow my nose," she yells out. We must halt completely. Walking is hard enough without another task to handle simultaneously.

By the time we pass the house of our minister, she wants to turn back and her face has lost all color. "She's on a cruise," she says of the reverend. "Nobody at church can figure out where she gets the money." Her look suggests I am involved in this.

Suddenly the dog reappears, dancing his dance, licking my hand, and moving to Betty to give her a good sniff and slurp. She grimaces, eyes him cautiously.

"Who are you?" she says. "Get out of my way. What are you doing?" Mr. Dog backs off. "Is that dog going to the toilet?" Betty demands to know. "I don't want to see any dog going to the toilet . . . Who was that dog we had?"

"Toto."

"What an animal!"

By the time we are heading back up our driveway, Betty is leaning on my side, tentatively, as if someone might catch her doing it and criticize. Before we reach the door she is gripping me desperately.

A woman named Barbara who is friendly with my mother sells health insurance, and when she arrives at our house to try to interest me in a policy, I get anxious. I don't do policies. I don't do forms. But I like Barbara. We bond over our appreciation of the festive charm that our neighbor's still-lit Christmas snowman brings to the summer nights. Betty, on the couch, coughs. She wants to hear everything we say, but I talk softly, to get her goat, and Barbara follows my lead. Betty frowns.

"I'm not hard-sell," Barbara says. "I just want to help you make some decisions. Important decisions."

I look at her with terrible seriousness. "I don't care what you say," I tell her. "I am keeping my baby."

The line is a risk, but I am desperate for attention and figure we might as well test this relationship. When she laughs, I know that I have found someone and reach down to a shelf under the toaster shelf. "Would you like an Oatmeal Creme?" I ask. They are made by Little Debbie and are, for me, a crack equivalent. "I've been moderate today. I've only eaten about eleven."

"I don't think so," she says. "I'm kinda semi-dieting."

Barbara looks at me in a kind of hopeful way, asks about New York, says she had always wanted to take her stepson for a visit. "He is artistic," she says. "You know, like that." I get the signal. Who wouldn't? But I want no heart-to-hearts today. I want to have fun. Laugh. It's so nice to have someone here.

When she begins to talk about the policies, I can tell she is as bored as I am. She is originally from Minneapolis and misses sushi: yellowtail, spider rolls. I say I like tekka maki, but am disgusted by roe.

"Why did you come to Paris?" I whisper to Barbara. She says she married someone here, someone I knew in high school. Then she blurts out that her stepson is gay.

The boy, a year out of high school, lives in Jeff City, where he waits tables and acts in some kind of theater troupe. He never comes home. "I was the one who had to tell him that I knew," she says. "He didn't come out to us. I wanted him to know he could trust me."

I like this woman. She helped the kid out. "His father," she says, "doesn't want anyone to know. He's ashamed. Worried about what other people will think."

I hate Barbara's story. I hate how I fear it is going to end, with everyone losing and distant and wondering. She looks like she knows too, like maybe she doesn't believe that the boy and his father are ever going to get things right. "I love him like he was my son," she tells me. "It's harder for my husband. Sometimes it's not so easy to be stuck in the middle."

"Are you eyeing my Oatmeal Creme?" I ask before I begin to natter on, saying a lot of boring stuff about how not everyone can make the leap into someone else's kind of life. I like to think my father would have made the leap, but sometimes I think my mother has hesitated, waiting at the boundary of ever really trying. I think probably because I was scared to lead her, scared of not being perfect.

Barbara asks me if it was hard for me, growing up here. When I cannot think of a joke to make, I tell her that it was maybe a little tough to be alone with it all.

"But I survived," I say quickly. She looks at me as if uncertain this is the case. Then she pops the big question, the one I hate most: "Do you have"—she eases into it tentatively—"a significant other?"

I tell her that I do better with insignificant others, but say I think I may be getting a dog, before picking up a paper and choosing the least expensive insurance plan; it covers an hour in a free clinic and a couple of cold sores. I am ready for Barbara to go now, but she has more of the form to fill out and begins to ask me more questions that get under my skin.

"Do you see a psychiatrist?"

"Yes."

"For how long?"

"Since 1983."

She looks troubled. I add, "He's grown dependent. I can't get rid of him."

"Do you," Barbara ask, "take any pharmacological medications?"

"Are you kidding? I was used for testing."

When she completes her questionnaire, I am certain that I will be denied coverage, but she is optimistic. "I have seen them," she says, "give it to people with cancer."

When I decide to take a nap, Betty, disgruntled over my indulging myself, slams doors loudly and stomps down the hall, raising every bit of racket she can to keep me awake. Unsurprisingly, I fail to doze. I imagine Mr. Dog in my room, tearing out strands of the carpet, stretched out beside me on the bed. I look for my pal outside, but our neighbor, who has seen us earlier, tells me that the police have taken the puppy to "Doggy Jail." I eye her suspiciously "It wasn't me," she says. "I swear. I didn't call them."

"I want to believe you," I say.

The city office says the dog will have to stay in custody for eight days, in case he has an owner looking to claim him. Opening my computer, I get on Facebook to type a plea for someone to adopt this dog. In a show of utter selflessness, I will give up my love to save him, like a biblical martyr or the baroness in *The Sound of Music*.

Betty asks, "What were you and Barbara talking about so quietly?"

"Her stepson is gay."

"Oh my," Betty says. "Oh my." She isn't negative, just goes quiet. Or say more. Or ask more. I don't know why I think she is going to this time. With us, the silences have always won.

I think I need another Oatmeal Creme.

8

My parents removed to Missouri in the early 'thirties; I do not remember just when, for I was not born. . . . The home was made in the wee village of Florida, in Monroe County, and I was born there in 1835. The village contained a hundred people and I increased the population by 1 per cent. It is more than many of the best men in history could have done for a town.

—Mark Twain's *Autobiography*

In the Paris post office, a mural, *The Arrival of the Clemens Family in Florida,* hangs, scrutinized occasionally by old schoolteachers in line for a book of stamps, gazing through their cataracts as they count out their change. Who else would stop to scan the nameplate? No tourists here, just hunters or fishermen passing through on weekends. Younger people have no inkling of the Clemens boy who became Mark Twain, or his birthplace, down the road, which no longer exists. Leveled when I was in high school, the place the Clemens family came to is underwater, the victim of huge road graders clearing the land for a lake project that did not, as it turned out, do much to boost the local economy. Stoutsville, Evie Cullers's hometown, is down there too. Maybe, buried in mud, is a fork or spoon, a cup or saucer or pair of glasses worn by someone she knew.

In winter, I drive out to see the vapor rising from the ice over the water, a sight that almost makes the season worth trying to get through.

This summer, the lake bottom is all but utterly dry with bare, spindly trees, vapor-thin themselves, rising out of the cracked earth. All a fisherman can catch near Twain's old town is a near-fatal sunburn.

When I was a kid, I wanted to enter the annual fence-painting contest held annually during Tom Sawyer Days in Hannibal, where I went once with Bill and June. We ate Kentucky Fried Chicken by the Mississippi, accompanied by a friend of June's who had terminal cancer. I watched the slender woman milling through the crowds on a cane decorated with what she said were bull's testicles, a decoration she was extremely proud of.

Glancing at the small dried objects, Bill eyed me mischievously and asked, "What do you think about that, Sport?"—a nickname no one had ever thought to call me. I knew I was no Sport. Still, it was good, this little clue that he had not realized what was true: I did not fit the nicknames other boys belonged to so easily they could pass them back and forth.

The lonely dog has been imprisoned two days. Worried about his surviving the heat, I take food and treats. My Facebook pleas on his behalf emphasize his most attractive features, minimizing his outdoorsy fragrance and yodel-like howls. In the picture I posted, he looks insane, curled up in a yellow bandana I arranged around his neck. I worked for seven years a few floors below *Vogue* magazine. I understand the impact of an accessory item.

The kid from the grocery store parking lot is mowing our lawn this morning, or what is left of it. Apparently he is part of our yardman's crew. Bare-chested, lawn-mower boy wears tennis shoes with no socks and a pair of filthy shorts his waist barely holds up. A few curls trail down from his belly button. He's twentysomething, but looks a teenager; his skin is clearly troubled. Nothing soothing has touched it lately. On his cheeks and shoulders are dozens of eruptions.

Boyd, the man he works for, apologizes for him, says he's trying to give him a break, help him kick drugs, a bit of info that snags my interest. "He's lost a lot," Boyd says. "That don't mean he can get away without wearing any pants." Meth, I guess, is the story, though Carol's son reports that people in Columbia are snorting bath salts. Maybe tonight I will throw down some Mr. Bubble, or a guest soap.

A woman I went to high school with, not long out of prison, is thin, about to crumble, and does not have Jenny Craig to thank. She is one of the women known at the grocery store as "Medicated Marys." Her eyes look ready to crack. Darting about the store as if on fire, she nabs this or that, mostly sweets, hand flying out like a bird's beak to snatch a worm. Before my arrival, because Betty was once a friend of her mother's, she got into the habit of stopping by to borrow money, explaining her emergencies in the half-assed way addicts do, throwing out whatever excuses will make someone want to get rid of them and dig into a pocket. I know the landscape. I never had to beg, but lost a few things I might have liked to keep. And people. People I liked a lot.

"No problem," I assure Boyd after his apology over the kid's clothes. In the course of ten years, my existence has gone from *Looking for Mr. Goodbar* to *Driving Miss Daisy*. A little skin is no tragedy. I have been away from New York a long time and am tempted to make love to a hanging basket. Recently, the discovery of the Big Wang Chinese restaurant at the Lake of the Ozarks has sparked my fantasy life.

This week Congress demolished bills to provide financial aid to veterans and farmers. This does not bode well for government subsidies for displaced gay book publishers whose personal trainers consume six to twelve small meals a day. I am not actually certain I qualify as homosexual anymore. A conversation about kidney outputs with Betty's physician's assistant, Ingrid Wilbur, a butch lesbian, is as close as I have come to intimacy in months.

Gradually, I have drifted out of the action.

I find myself holding out a Coke for the kid, who looks surprised and shuts down the mower. He says nothing, just reaches for the drink. "Are you from here?" I ask. He shakes his head as, trying a different gambit, I offer, "So what about those Cardinals?" He responds, "What about them?"

I falter. "Well, I guess they are winning or losing." He looks puzzled. No one gets me here, a problem as I tend to speak in one-liners. I try too hard, but as I tell my friends, it's better than not enough.

After making short work of the Coke, the boy runs a sliver of ice across his forehead and sets the plastic go cup carefully on the step as if it were something from Tiffany he has felt privileged to use.

An inside source (a friend of my mother's) has told me of a row at Monday bridge, where Betty was once an ardent, rarely defeated competitor. My mother, after consuming the entire bowl of mini-Snickers at her table, has apparently accused the hostess of a chintzy attitude toward snacks. Then, refusing to keep score, she slammed her cards down in a shocking manner that seems to have sent a woman named Maxie into a tizzy. "And Maxie has rheumatoid," the friend confided of the injured party.

"Do Snickers help with that?" I asked myself.

My mother's skirmishes, her irritability, threaten her social life. People don't get that she can't control these outbursts; a new aggression flares up in her at times.

Betty Hodgman, Big Muscle of the mini-Snickers circuit, is in the family room, staring down at her hymnal, frowning and looking confused.

"The oven's on. The oven's on," she keeps repeating. She won't take in the fact that I am trying to preheat it. I am busy strewing cinnamon around the kitchen, attempting to make the muffins she likes. "That looks nasty," she says when I pour the batter into the little paper cups, as if she had never seen anything similar before.

"Well, hang on."

"You have the oven on." She says it again. "I feel it heating up."

"I'm making muffins."

"Go ahead. Burn the house down."

If my mother is exiled from bridge, we are lost; the driver's license was a blow. This will be worse. She won't have anything. Mandy Winkler, just about her last remaining close friend, is concerned about being able to take her out to lunch anymore, at least on her own. Getting Betty in and out of the car is too much of a struggle; Mandy has a hip problem herself. Betty counts the days until she gets to see her, but she lingers less each time she visits. "She is so busy," Betty says.

Mandy's voice on the phone last week was grave. "You know, Betty isn't herself anymore." She advises, "George, I think you are going to have to consider assisted living." I wanted to respond, "Oh goodness. That has never crossed my mind." People mean well; they just aren't here enough to get what we are dealing with or what home means to my mother. Everyone thinks they know what should be done, and their suggestions make me suspect they must consider me an idiot who doesn't comprehend the situation. Actually, I don't, but never mind.

I get what makes sense; I just can't bear to do it. I cannot imagine the sorrow of dragging her out of this house.

Hours and hours I've spent on the Internet, considering and agonizing over assisted living and senior-care situations. One, particularly, Tiger Place, has many advantages, including sensors that can detect bathroom falls, a full calendar of social events, cocktail hours, movies with popcorn, a gourmet cook. Maybe I can convince her she's on a long cruise. We are to visit there at the end of the week, a feat it has taken months to arrange. I don't know if I can actually get her to make the trip. "Several women I know have died there," she said when we last discussed Tiger Place.

"It's for old people," I said. "Old people die sometimes."

"You just want to get rid of me."

"No."

"Someday something will get me."

"Probably your bladder."

Betty is determined to stay put. Do we literally, I wonder, carry her out of her own house? Will it come to that? Who gets to say? Me? *Me?* Betty, a woman who has lived her life in conventional clothes, possesses a will as strong as any man's. She has always seen herself as a bit above most women, silly ones prone to marital turmoil and cosmetic overdose, women easily taken in who mooned over their husbands.

One summer before we moved to Paris, the marriage of the Bucks, who lived just up the street in the late Blanche Mitchell's big old southern-style house, was a topic of discussion all over Madison. Willie Buck, a cattle buyer whose job kept him traveling, was having an affair with the receptionist of Arthur Fleming, a pediatrician. Arthur's wife, Evelyn, was my mother's best friend.

Betty and Evelyn conferred often. I eavesdropped. Evelyn said the receptionist had no shame. "She just parades it," Evelyn declared. "I know," Betty replied. She was not a woman to gossip, but did comment that Blanche Mitchell had to be turning over in her grave.

"She never should have sold them that house," Betty commented. "But who knew?" Evelyn assured Betty that "in situations like this," she was always "for the marriage."

Betty said she was for Lena Buck getting a lawyer and taking Willie for every cent she could locate along with every Hereford in that pasture. Lena, Betty pointed out, was raising four children practically on her own while Willie shorted her on money for the house and kids.

Something in me loved Lena. Perpetually tanned, she came from the Mississippi Delta and reminded me of the dark-haired queen who gifted Columbus with the *Pinta,* the *Niña,* and the *Santa Maria.* As a little boy, I spent long hours at the Bucks' house on rainy days, ordering their son Bobby around. At the slightest hint of precipitation, I would throw on my cowboy hat and pull on my red galoshes and head up there.

"When I look out and see you coming in that hat and those boots, I always have to take a nerve pill," Lena told me once.

When Bobby Kennedy was assassinated, I was playing with Bobby. "They killed another of the Kennedys," Lena announced to us. "Shot him dead. Now I'd like to know what they expect of you kids."

Lena was a fan of country music, especially Elvis. I did not care for the King, but Lena's soft sing-alongs to "Kentucky Rain" were an education in the realities of winter afternoons in a drafty old house bent over a sink of soap bubbles. I did my best to advise her on the matter of her wardrobe, a thankless task for even a zealous fashion adviser.

"Don't mix plaids," I told her. "My mother says." But Lena was stubborn—and no Twiggy.

"She lays it on with a trowel," my mother said to Evelyn.

Mother told me to keep my nose out of the affair business, but often we would wake to find Lena on our patio, trying to avoid her husband and seeking companionship. Or advice. There she would be, lying flat on her back on the top of the table, arm flung over her forehead in a gesture of romantic tragedy. I am not sure what my mother said to Lena on those mornings, but, watching from the kitchen window, I would see Lena listening and nodding her head. Sometimes I ran from the house with a warm honey bun for our visitor as Betty glared. "Get back in that house," my mother would say.

I would go to the window to spy, watching my mother patting Lena's hand or occasionally touching her shoulder. I had no idea that Betty knew what to do with a broken heart, but she was gentle with Lena and sometimes looked a little sad herself. So this was how my mother looked when she talked about love.

My mother never talks about love. What has always drawn her interest is money: Growing up without much extra has left her with the taste for seeing her name attached to significant amounts. She is careful with money and remains a firm advocate of the early bird special. I am afraid to ask about her funeral preferences, fearful she will demand a salad bar.

Betty likes to hear people talk about cash—who has it, had it, got it, lost it; how it might be acquired. She could have been a great deal maker; in another era, she would have ruled.

When her father died, a few years before I was born, Betty inherited, with my grandmother and her brothers, the four Baker Lumber yards—in Madison, Paris, Mexico, and Moberly. Sometimes on Sunday afternoons, in my grandmother's bare dining room, with its ringed but sturdy mahogany table, Mammy and her children circled to talk things out about the business, bent over paperwork. My father was never invited; he was not an official partner, but an employee, not in on significant decision making. Around the time I entered eighth grade, the Madison yard, which my father managed, started losing money. Mammy, always expecting financial cataclysm, looked agonized if it was mentioned; they all tried to hide what she would envision as the start of the family's inevitable journey to the poorhouse.

Eavesdropping as was my habit, I heard them make the decision to close the yard, and though they saw that times were bad for all businesses in the area, they blamed my dad, at least a bit. Bill assessed my father's performance with a jeweler's eye for flaw, said Daddy wasted too much time laughing with customers. Levity on the job was to him tantamount to embezzlement. Years before, during a painful, days-long session of labor, Bill, lying on his back on the top of a scaffolding platform, painted the tin ceiling of our hardware store, a grueling feat that damaged his back for life. Up at all hours, he never stopped; he basked in misery.

My mother, listening with a stony expression, looked furious at everyone, those in the room and, I was certain, one who was not.

After the yard closed in Madison in 1973, my father labored at the Paris yard with Uncle Harry, where I was forced to work too that summer. We were still living in Madison—our new home in Paris was still being built. Big George and I left the house every morning at 6 a.m. for the twelve-mile drive to Paris. "Time to make the doughnuts," my father said to me when he dragged me, reluctant and surly, out of bed for a Pop-Tart as he picked bits of Grape Nuts out of his teeth nervously. When we arrived at the lumberyard, he slammed the car door and headed in with his pocket full of pencils and a tape measure clipped to his belt. He never said much on our way to work those mornings; he seemed like a soldier heading into battle. He was different, disappointed.

In Madison, my father had whistled down Main Street in his dusty work boots, swatting the town's working women, all lipsticked and beehived, on their big, cheeky butts with his clipboard full of paint orders. I can see him standing in streaks of sun, slightly wobbly from a few beers and completely sweat-soaked with a hand-lettered sandwich board, accosting passing motorists whom he berated to buy chicken at the annual Lions Club Memorial Day barbecue.

Across town, in her darkened bedroom, my mother, who had long before ceased her efforts to control his antics, attempted to sleep away her embarrassment as he transformed the greater part of the Lions membership into a brazen mob of drunken boys who danced to a portable radio with bosomy, rouged-up women way into the night, in the parking lot of Del Miles's old gas station where they set up their grills.

"*Oh lay me down, in your big brass bed,*" my father would sing on these party nights. "*Oh lay me down, in your big brass bed.*" Hearing this favorite, I sensed scandal but didn't get the words: "*I'm going to Chicago to get my hambone boiled. Cause the women in St. Louie done let my hambone spoil.*"

One day it dawned on me what this all meant.

"That is a dirty song, Daddy," I said.

"Don't go blabbing to your mother."

The only secrets I didn't tell were my own.

Betty avoided the Lions events. "Is it over yet?" she would ask me wearily when she rose from her bed to confront me.

. . .

At the lumberyard, I pitched in as best I could. A special patience, I discovered, is required to dust a pile of nails. I did learn to use the paint mixer successfully, spending more time than some considered necessary experimenting with color combinations. Most I managed seemed suitable for the Caribbean. Within moments, I found myself streaked with more color than a Masai tribesman. When my father saw how much paint I was going through, he looked stricken. "That cost hundreds of dollars," he said, hoping my uncle was in his office, hunched over his papers.

"Don't you wish you had just sent me to summer camp?"

I accompanied some of the other workers on deliveries of lumber, paneling, whatever, though I was quickly exiled from the transport of windows and other glass products. I sipped Mountain Dews in the cab or rode on the back of the ancient, snorting flatbed truck as we shook and rattled our way down the freshly tarred roads with the wind blowing my sweaty hair. The drives through the countryside made me see, for the first time, the place I am from. It was not a dry summer. Everywhere, there was green, shade after shade after shade of it. According to the *Appeal,* Monroe County "boasts more rivers and streams than any other place in Missouri." Closest at hand, the thick Salt River runs slowly, drearily past the edge of town, flooding the banks when the spring rains come. Here, in the murky waters that mirror ancient overhanging branches, daring children, balanced precariously on fallen trees, are sometimes swept to their deaths, while farther upstream, blacks and Baptists held baptisms and sang hymns, their voices carried by occasional breezes drifting through the steamy mornings. Fifty miles east is Hannibal, where the passing Mississippi brings huge barges loaded with factory products and grain, stopping on their way from Des Moines before heading on to St. Louis and New Orleans.

On the day we moved from Madison, I was not there when the big trucks came to our house. Knowing my temperament, my mother stationed me at Mammy's where I lay on her bristly couch. My grandmother shut off the light and let me mourn. At noontime, as the fire whistle announced midday, Mammy, maneuvering now on a walker with an embroidered pouch stitched up by June, brought me warm homemade bread spread with some of her preserves and a 7-Up, the things she made me when I was ill. She sat beside me. She didn't want us to go, really. Paris was only a dozen miles away, but Mammy wanted Betty close, and not long after would come with us to stay most of the time, leaving the House of Many Chimneys where the summer kitchen had become a dumping ground for things left from the dead: Uncle Oscar's Smith Corona and boxes of photos and papers that belonged to Wray Chowning. He had died a drunken mess with only the loosest grip on anything resembling reality. Betty had been left to take care of his house. One day, I discovered a paper Wray had written at the university on Shakespeare's *Henry IV;* the title was "Harry in the Night." When driving downtown in St. Louis now, passing the old hotels that were once Wray's haunts, I tend to imagine him getting drunk enough to entertain the strangers passing through for brief transactions.

The day of the move, Aunt Winnie appeared with a chocolate pie for us to eat that night. She stood at the doorway where I lay and came to brush my hair off my face. "Things gotta change, kiddo," she said, "things gotta change. One day I'll be saying good-bye to Madison too, going off to live at Nahncee's when I can't keep up the house." But Winnie never had to say good-bye to Madison. She succumbed to a heart attack after a hearty meal at a function for Christian ladies. She had apparently been stricken suddenly, soon after arriving home, as she was discovered still in her Sunday clothes and best church hat, waiting—eyes wide open—for the savior she had been blessed to expect only briefly.

A few nights after my encounter with the lawn-mower boy, in the very early morning, I notice him, not in his usual place on the car at the parking lot, but standing in the middle of the lane at the empty car wash where I presume it is a little cooler. With him is the skinny woman I went to high school with, the addict who was after Betty's money. They look like they are dancing.

"Don't do it," I want to yell. "Watch out." But I think the damage is done. He isn't sober, and when Boyd finds out, he'll be out of a job.

I do not get a wink of sleep that night, no good at all because I have so much work to do. My laptop is screwy and I am certain I am under some form of cyber attack. Earlier, after reviewing her marked-up manuscript, my new editing client, a South American economist, has claimed I am not getting her sense of "humous." But what really keeps my eyes open and my head unable to shut down at all is our upcoming visit to Tiger Place. It is ridiculous to be a fiftyish man who cannot handle a ninety-year-old with narrow feet. For her sake, my mother should not stay here. I should not stay here, all bound up with my mother. I am not making decisions that are right for her. She needs to go somewhere where she can be properly looked after and fed. The only cuisine I have ever mastered was seasonal drugs. But I cannot leave. I will step up. In the morning, before the fog burns off, I will water the roses. I will get them through this summer. They will not wither on my watch.

9

This morning, Betty got up at 4 a.m. after looking at the clock wrong. I looked up from my work and there she was, confused, disoriented.

"Why is it still dark?" she asked. To calm her a little, I asked if she would let me comb the hair on the back of her head, which gets tangled when she lies with her head on her pillow.

Who says there are no advantages to giving birth to a homosexual?

I combed carefully, separating the strands with my fingers where her hair is matted.

"Don't pull it," she said. "Last time you did."

"I didn't mean to."

"My head is tender."

"I'm watching out."

"Are you going to make me wear those shitty shoes today?"

Her days are filled with little hurts. When I try to pat my mother's back, she says, "No, no." Her arms are as tender and reluctant: She gets angry if I take hold too tightly. When I make my most careful effort to rub some cream into her face, she winces, shakes her head, as if the tread of fingertips brings agony.

"No. No. No."

"Let me rub this into your forehead," I say. "It's amazing how few wrinkles you have on your forehead for a woman your age. It's smooth."

"Don't get it in my hair. Last night you got it in my hair."

"Pretend it's mousse."

She bruises easily now. On the underside of one arm, there is a trail of purple tracks. Across her cheekbones and forearms, the skin is nearly transparent. Fearing I am about to tear or leave a cut, she stares at me, steeling herself. I must be gentle, attentive. A prick is a stab that makes her jump. A careless touch is sharp as a prick. Everything is an invasion.

"No. No. No."

There is nothing that doesn't press too hard, or seem too tight, or feel uncomfortable. She is so sensitive. The tightening around her arm during the testing of her blood pressure is much too much to bear. She yells out, kicks her feet.

"No, no, no, no."

The space around her is all she owns, and if I come too close, she seems almost frightened, as if she fears what I might do. Yet on bad days, when things are rough inside her head, she wants me always in plain sight and follows me around, watching my every move. In the family room, there she is. "Where are you going?" If I go lie on my bed, she is right behind me, clearing her throat loudly in the doorway. "Where are you going?" If I walk into the living room to read, she is there, watching me. Even in my thoughts, where I retreat sometimes to escape, she appears, standing there with her purse in my mind's eye, waiting and demanding: "Where are you going?"

She does not believe I will not leave her, does not fully accept that I am not about to take flight, even though I tell her over and over. "No, no, no, I will not go. I'll just be out a few minutes. I have to refill your prescriptions." Maybe she forgets. Or knows by now how likely people are to change their minds.

When she is especially agitated over something that has happened (a broken anything, an unexpected change in plans) or is about to (a small obligation that seems a terrible challenge, an upcoming doctor's appointment, taxes), my mother's noises filter through the day until I have to escape, leave the house, take the risk. Mostly I go outside, sit on the steps or walk down into the woods.

There is a bottle of Xanax in the cabinet above the stove. I have to get out of this kitchen. Now.

Standing on our back deck, I hear the whistles blowing over at the high school at summer football practice. Every day, I see the boys tramping to the field in the heat. Freshman year in high school, Betty made me go out for football; she insisted. She set her mind to it. I had never played or watched the sport on television. When my father tried to interest me in the Tiger games, I begged off. I didn't care, though I liked the marching bands.

Betty did not see as an obstacle the fact that I had no idea of the rules. She was on a mission: to make me all right, to make me fit. I was an adolescent: She smelled sex in the house and wanted someone to pound it out of me before anything took root.

On the first day of practice at my new high school in Paris, I noticed that one of the boys was carrying a Bible in his helmet. This did not seem an option for me. Then there were the uniforms: They gave us strange long underwear things to wear under the pants and over our underwear with pockets for pads that protected body parts I did not seem to have. I couldn't get the pads to fit in right, so I just threw them down the pants. Every time I ran, a pad fell out one of the legs.

I told the coach on the first day that I had ruptured myself. I needed a specialist, X-rays.

He grunted, unsympathetic. On the second day, I said I thought I was having a heatstroke. I could not believe how hot it was in my special underwear, even though most of my padding was strewn across the field. No response.

"I have chafing," I whispered as he eyed me. His name was Quigley, a name that seemed right for a rabbit.

I could not believe the shit they were putting us through. It couldn't be legal. Large people were crashing into me—farm boys, strong from hauling hay. There were yells and curses. I had no friends. Not even the Bible carrier.

After the second practice, I was exhausted. I told Betty I had leukemia. She was skeptical. I told her I dreaded waking up in the morning. I fell into despair, tried to break my own arm on the side of the tub and knocked the shower door off its tracks.

On the third day, when my father came to pick me up, he arrived early and watched. "Damn," he said when we got in the car, "you are really terrible." I answered, "I know. I am the worst player in the history of Paris R-II High. Can I go to boarding school?"

He said, "Maybe your mother would let you off if we could think of some other sport you could play."

I asked, "How about bridge?"

One of the older boys was named Kevin, a junior or senior. He drove a noisy old car and taunted me. I imagined this automobile exploding, dismembering my most immediate nemeses and sending the Bible carrier flying toward the loving arms of his Lord Jesus. Every day after practice, as I waited for my father, Kevin drove by, and as he passed me, there on the steps, wondering if I was developing calcium deposits, he always screamed, "Fuck you, you fucking faggot. Fuck you. Fuck you." I braced myself for it every day, listening for his car to come around the curve, the crack of gravel under the tires.

I knew it was true. What could I do? It was the pure hatred that shocked me, the rage, the bitter face in the driver's seat. He began to do it more often. He did it every time we crossed paths on the field. He did it in the shower room. Some days, the heat was over a hundred degrees. One morning, on the field, sweat was running down my face and I felt the salt from it in my eyes. I had dropped balls, misunderstood plays, and been yelled at by everyone. Quigley was twitching. Kevin seemed to be everywhere with his usual greeting and I was tired, stripped bare; there was no pad in the world to protect the place where I was about to get slammed.

Kevin passed, kicked me hard, and yelled, "Fuck you, you fucking faggot," as I fell on the ground in front of what seemed like half of America. Picking myself up, I couldn't breathe. His words hung in the hot air and everyone turned toward me as, finally, it all became clear. I froze, could not move or speak.

I disappeared, just went away and returned in a moment, different. For a long time, for years, this scene came back and back again in my head—the air, my red-hot cheeks, his voice—in instant replay, like some champion's great moment.

On the football field, I thought I was going to cry, but I told myself that whatever came, whatever happened, I could not do that. Not there. I didn't. I swallowed my tears; I pulled them in. And they never came back. I cannot cry. Not since that day. Not ever. Not when Mammy died. Not when my father died. I joined my mother among the permanently dry-eyed. We have that in common. We do not cry. I think somewhere inside me my allotted tears are waiting. Maybe they will come when Betty goes. Maybe when it happens I will somehow be transported back to Kevin at practice, or keel over like Mama Cass eating that ham sandwich in her hotel room, waiting for her muumuus to come back from housekeeping.

Where do the hidden things go? Not away. Nothing goes away.

I think something happened at that moment on the field: Something shut down; something went into hiding, split off. Although it did not become clear for years, I suspect that from the minute I had that little break from myself, some part of me went inside and I began to watch myself, making certain to give nothing away. Nothing inside me showed. When people get sober they are told that they have to make their insides match their outsides. It sounded to me like something you would want in a Chevrolet.

I don't think a coming together will happen to me in this lifetime. I am not sure I will ever again connect up—the watcher and the other unfiltered part of me—in the way other people do. There has been a rupture, and here, in this house, on these days when the sounds my mother makes seem especially loud, I feel it, see the cost of long-lasting silences.

There are, I have learned, so many ways that gay kids try to cover up themselves. I can see I have on many occasions tried too hard to get a laugh.

"You're too clever by half," someone told me once.

"I know," I said. "It would be better to just be twice as stupid. Right?"

A joke, you see, can earn a place for anyone. People want to laugh, and when I realized I could do it sometimes, I tried to do it every minute. I became a performer, an artist skilled at distraction, control: *"Look at me, but don't see. Watch, but not too closely."* What I said to myself had nothing to do with what I told anyone. I went on the lookout for every word or gesture that might betray me.

A few years ago, a publisher read a draft of a book I was working on, something I was proud of. He eyed me, looked uncomfortable. "It's so *internal*," he said, as if naming some spectacular offense. Of course, he was a straight man. He never had to go inside. He was comfortable just where he was.

The thing about being a watcher is this: You are never really a part of things, especially if the person you must watch is yourself, always, just to make sure no one ever really sees you.

Earleen is raving about the dentist who screwed up her upper plate because he wanted to go play golf. The teeth cost $750. They have hurt Earleen's mouth for a year and she is going to take the dentist to a review board in Jefferson City. "We're gonna clean that jaybird's clock," she says as we watch my mother, hovering close as it seems her balance is off today.

Betty goes to the refrigerator to take out a bowl of pineapple that she drops on the floor and breaks. She yells out as if there has been a gunshot. I clean the sticky juice off the linoleum and wipe the front of her gown as she fidgets, then looks away. Finally, I settle her, distracting her with a pile of postcards from Europe from the end table as Earleen starts the vacuum in the back of the house.

"Where are these from?" she asks. "Who wrote these?" I tell her that she wrote them, note her handwriting, as it was, so familiar. She wrinkles her brow, as if trying to remember. "I never could write a pretty hand like that," she says. "Not now." It's true. Her letters look like shaky forgeries.

The cards were written on my parents' trip to Europe; it was a grand occasion, the only time they ever went there together. I was in New York by then; they didn't take that many trips, but came every Christmas to go to Radio City while I worked. They loved that Christmas show. They were so delighted by it. I never went with them. When they came to visit, I always took breaks from them. Partially because I had to; there were always deadlines. Partially because I could not bear to let our talk stray too far from what I was comfortable saying about my life.

When I let my mind wander back that far, what I see is how hard we tried to be our best for one another.

In Europe, my parents took some cruise on a river that streamed through many countries, the Danube or the Rhine. For months in advance they spoke of this trip as if they were teenagers. Europe: across the big wavy sea where luxury liners crossed, carrying queens with hats and heroes with medals. Europe: where the wars had been: Europe: where the mountains and landscapes were beautiful, and the food was rich and unforgettable and available, on the barge on which they traveled, twenty-four hours daily, in unlimited quantities.

"I'll just bet it's going to be very nice," my mother said before they left. She was so eager. "June loves to go on a barge. I hope your father will have a good time. He deserves a chance to relax after all these years."

"We flew into somewhere in Germany," Betty says, holding a card the sun streaks through, but she doesn't remember much else. "What is a beautiful city in Czechoslovakia?" she asks.

"Prague," I suggest.

"Yes, that's it."

And then, "What is a beautiful city in Germany?"

I suggest, "Berlin, maybe. I don't know how pretty it is, really."

She says, "No, no."

I suggest, "Munich."

She says, "No, no. That's where they blew up the Olympics. That nearly killed your father. They blew up the Jews!"

I say, "Hamburg." She looks a little excited, but even more, relieved. "Yes, that's it. That's where we flew in. I used my passport and your father kept looking up everything about the war . . . I didn't care about the war. I didn't care if they blew up the Olympics, to tell you the truth." She looks at me. "They go on *forever,*" she adds.

"I wanted to buy a new sweater or a dress and see some of the countryside. It rained a lot . . . I'm trying to think of another city, another place in Germany. Oh yes, it was Berlin. That's what it was. But his knee was hurting him and we didn't get to do much. The time changed, you know, and I never could sleep much. The time changed on us. The time changed. I think just once. It could have been more than that."

She looks good today; the new moisturizer from Saks is doing wonders for her face, though I am often surprised to find myself licking Estée Lauder products off my fingers. Her cheeks are pinkish, their skin softer, and it seems that the wrinkled places under her eyes have almost been smoothed away. Sometimes she even smiles back. She wants to give me a pleasant afternoon, but fears she has little to offer, so she hands me the cards, one after the other, and looks hopeful. She wants us to have fun, to share the experience, but she can't remember it. "The cities," she says. "They were nice and green."

Before the trip, my father took their passports to Kinko's and had the pages with the photos Xeroxed and enlarged. He taped them—not with Scotch tape, but with something used to hold heavier things together—to the inside of the suitcase top. There they were, George and Betty in black and white, ready to meet the world, ready to splurge a little after working, like everyone they knew, hard all their lives and doing their best to be good and do good. They were older now, but they still had innocent faces, faces that somehow suggested their times and America, their home.

"I remember a river," Betty says, "but there wasn't enough water. It was very dry. It looked a little bit like here."

"Do you remember the name of the river?"

"No, I don't."

"Was it the Rhine?"

"It might have been. What I remember is that it rained and I thought the water was finally going to fill up the riverbeds and when the next people got here it would probably be prettier." She goes quiet, then asks, "Can I help you anymore, George?" as if we were studying for a test and she was drilling me, like she used to with long division.

"Can I help you, George?"

"No," I want to say. "It is not you. It is everything that has happened. It is this sense that I have missed my chance and here I am." Maybe everyone feels like that.

"To tell you the truth," my mother confides, "I liked those Christmas shows in New York better than anything on that barge. I think your father did too. We always wanted you to come along."

"I'm just not a Rockette person, Mama."

I carried that suitcase with my parents' pictures for twenty years or more everywhere I went: to college, home, and back so many times, to Barbados, London, Paris, Miami, San Francisco, Los Angeles, to Morocco, where I stayed at a house in the Old City where every night we were awakened by the call to prayer and I searched for a gift for Betty in the souk.

People said I should buy something new, something bigger with wheels, something in leather. But I kept carrying that suitcase until the strap broke and one of the pictures inside got torn off. I carried them with me everywhere. I still have it. I keep special things there, stuff I want to save as long as I live. One day I imagine these postcards that are preoccupying my mother will find their way there, the postcards from their trip to Europe.

"What are you doing, George? What are you doing to your arm?"

"I'm scratching it, Mother."

"Why are you doing that?"

"I guess because I itch."

"I don't like it when you do that," she says. "It looks like it hurts to do that." And to her, it does. It would be enough to almost make her cry if she did that, ever.

"Is there anything I can do for you, George?" she asks again.

"You could try to remember the name of that river."

"I've tried," she says. "I can't remember, and why does it matter? I told you it rained and I couldn't sleep and I had to lay awake and listen to your father snore and I thought, here I came all the way to Europe to float down a river and listen to an old man snore.

"What can I do for you?" she asks again.

"What can I do for you?"

Neither one of us knows.

In the end my parents were just George and Betty, who always tried their best. That was enough. They weren't New York. They didn't have to be all the world or on television. I was different: Just me was never enough. Just me was something less than okay. So I tried to make up something a little better, too clever by half, I guess. I think I tried too hard. There were voices in my head, saying: "You have to do better." Then I fell down.

"Is there anything I can do for you, George?" Betty asks one more time, because perhaps she knows that the time when she can do anything for anyone is growing short.

"See me," I start to say. I don't know where the words have come from, and I stop before I utter them because I know it is too late anyway, too late for her to know all of me. I didn't discuss my sexuality with her until I was forty. She didn't ask. My father hadn't asked. We were all afraid. None of us knew how not to hurt one another. I made us all feel imperfect. I felt I was wrong. They felt they had caused it. No one said anything. They went to Radio City, said they missed me being with them. "Next year," I always said before heading off to the magazine.

I didn't feel comfortable when I was a kid. I didn't feel comfortable in my body. I didn't feel comfortable anywhere. I hated to have to walk across a room if people were watching; this was just a fear I had, something I did not quite know what to do about. In New York, all this made things hard.

"I never would have guessed you felt that way," a rare confidante told me once. "But I see it now."

Betty couldn't have known all the things I was feeling, back when I was a kid. She couldn't have known what to do. I didn't know what to do. I just knew that I loved them and didn't want them hurt by the fact that I wasn't right. That was what the world told me, what I always heard, that people like me weren't right. Gay kids hear everything. Because they are hidden in disguise or listening in silence. No one holds back. People will say anything about gay people. It still goes on. Pick up a newspaper. We hear so many terrible things about ourselves. People think it is their right. They just don't get what being different feels like, on the inside, for a kid and they don't care.

When I was not chosen for the football team, I was relieved, but there I was, at a new school; I was on my own. Before the first bell, I stood by the door of the algebra room waiting and watching. In Madison, I had friends, but in Paris there was no one at the start, and so I stayed in my head, imagining myself someone who lived in the city, the son of rich people, an actor on Broadway or in the movies. I made up lives and fell into them when I was alone. I just got lost, imagining myself as other people. You can make up a world and live there for a while, float down a river to someplace secret.

As time went on, I found another way: From movies and television, I stole lines and jokes, this and that, tried to stitch together an act that passed. Did I know what I was doing?

I know it now.

"Do you think you have trouble with intimacy?" they asked at rehab.

"Only when I try to get close to someone."

To fall in love you have to think you're okay, stop watching for clues you've done something wrong.

At school, I imitated teachers: an ancient southern belle with hair gone slightly green; the study hall monitor whose hair resembled the helmet of a Roman charioteer; the kids I was actually most drawn to: the different ones. I wanted no part of them and often aimed my harshest comments in their direction. I learned to make people laugh—and I always could. I had to, and when in conversations the topic strayed too close to things I did not want to talk about—sex, or girls, or whatever, whatever could trip me up—I learned to steer the talk away, subtly, without anyone ever realizing. Even me. It was an animal thing—camouflage. It has taken me so long to see it all.

Sometimes, on bad days, it would happen again. It did not stop. Walking down the hall, I would see Kevin coming in my direction: "Fuck you, fucking faggot." I tried to stay in my body and not to disappear. If I felt hurt, I cut it off as fast as I could manage. I mean, what I was feeling? I could never ask anyone for help because what he said was true and all I wanted was for everyone to ignore it.

On TV, I hear them saying these things that they say about people like me, not caring if we have to listen. They don't care if the things they say leave their mark. They are so brave they can make kids feel terrible, these perfect family folk, so certain their lives are all so fine. They stand

and say it is their right to say things that injure children who have learned to hate themselves.

Kids even have to hear things from their own families.

We grow up hearing everything.

"Shame is inventive." It can do so much and you never know.

A guy named Freddy often strolled alone through the crowds in my high school, and that first year, I tried to attract his attention, because he seemed to be on his own too. In class, he turned bright red at the slightest thing and had a kind of funny walk—from a back injury, I later learned. He didn't seem to quite belong with anyone. I sensed something familiar. I thought he did too, even from way across a room. I scared him, I knew, because I was different, just what he did not want to be. But I wanted to try to reach him if I could.

Sometimes he spoke or nodded when he saw me, but he kept his distance, even when people began to like me and almost everyone said hello. Though he certainly did not remember, we had seen each other before, years back, when we were kids. Granny was visiting from St. Louis and she, my mother, and I had come to Paris to the Home Market where Betty liked to shop for meat. It was a very nice store for a small town, like somewhere you would find in a bigger place. They gave out samples of cheeses, sausages, and new sorts of snacks. I loved Chicken in a Biscuit.

While Betty waited for the butcher, Granny and I pushed the cart. As we turned one corner, we encountered an enraged woman yelling at her little boy, whose fair hair—almost clear enough to see through—was slicked back with oil and combed so neatly that he looked like a mannequin in a store. His skin was very white, the sort that burned and never tanned. As his mother's anger, unexplainable to us, terrifying to me, built up, the boy looked like all he wanted was to fade away, to back into the shelves among the cans and disappear. Even then I knew she saw something in him she despised.

When the mother slapped the boy hard, as if she could just slap him away, my grandmother blanched, staring at the woman's face. I thought Granny was going to call the police or go over herself to try to help. We saw the red streaks from his mother's fingers come up on the boy's white cheeks. Granny stopped the cart and eyed the woman as the boy ran down the aisle, tears running down his face. Back in the car, my grandmother kept bringing up what she had seen. "That woman," she said, "that woman looked at that boy with hate. *With hate*. She looked at her own child with hate in her eyes. I have never seen anything like it."

I knew somehow that the woman was ashamed of her son; he was small and delicate. I just knew. In the car on the way back to Madison as Granny began to settle down, I watched Betty carefully, looking for signs that I might be in trouble too. I felt like I was in terrible trouble too. Like that boy.

"Aren't you glad," Granny asked, "that you are surrounded by people who love you?" For reasons I did not understand, this made me feel terrible; bad feelings flooded through me that day in that backseat.

Freddy was that boy in the grocery store. It was that pure white skin that made me remember. He had grown up to be good-looking—a cute guy, as they say in high school—but because of his back, which was often painful, he had not gone out for football. When he and his older brother, Earl, both started working at the IGA, Freddy was quickly fired. Because of his injury, he couldn't lift the heavy boxes. Every day, his brother gave him the twenty-five cents for lunch in the cafeteria.

In mixed chorus, Freddy was a tenor, like me. Sometimes we shared the same piece of music and he laughed at my jokes. We became friends. He never mentioned his mother, Wanda, who was known for her spotless house and her ire. How that woman could flame up, swearing, grabbing at those boys, seizing a collar or an arm wherever they were, even after they were older. Wanda would scream at those boys; the neighbors talked about it. Every night it went on. In the summer, people heard her while they worked in their gardens.

One afternoon after school, near the end of freshman year, Freddy rode his bicycle past my house where I was sitting on the step. Maybe because it was one of the first warm days, because it was spring, and we felt unburdened, just a little freer, he stopped to talk and I took him inside. Betty had fried chicken and it was cooling on a rack on the kitchen table for supper. I offered him a piece, and before I realized, he had eaten the whole chicken. For the rest of that year, he came over after school every day, always eating supper with us and never leaving until it was time for me to go to bed, something he never seemed to do. He roamed the streets till late, even when it was cold.

If a day went by without his visiting, I was lost. I needed him and wanted to touch him. So many times I had to stop my hands from forgetting what was acceptable. They knew what they wanted; I knew what they could not have. Even regular boys slapped each other on the back, roughhoused, and reached out occasionally to pat each other's shoulders. Yet if I came too near, Freddy moved away; he had a kind of radar, a sixth sense for when to take off, flee. If I sat on the bed in my room, he sat on the floor. If I came up behind him, reached out to tap him to get his attention, he moved. When my father cupped Freddy's head with his hands one day to steer him toward the table, Freddy looked shocked, and for a moment I thought he might hit my father, who was so surprised. He looked at me as if to say, "What can we do?"

I loved Freddy. He loved me. There was this feeling when we were together; it was so strong that, reaching out, I almost expected to feel something in the air between us.

Wanda slapped Freddy because she was ashamed of him. I didn't want anyone to be ashamed of me. All of this was a long time ago. Maybe people don't understand it now.

In a school play, Freddy and I were cast, fittingly, as best friends, two gentlemen arriving to call on some pretty women on the Riviera. It was a musical, *The Boyfriend*. During rehearsals, Freddy was, as usual, reticent, standing far away as he said his lines to me. Like almost halfway across the stage. Like almost in Cleveland. It was like he was doing *Hello, Dolly!* in another county. But on the night of the actual performance, there we were, in front of everyone. Something was going to happen. I watched the coach's face in the audience and the expressions of some of the other boys as Freddy threw his arms across my shoulders and kept them there, hanging on, drawing me closer to him and not letting go. It was just too much; there, in front of everyone, we were more than chums about to fetch some ladies for an airing on the plage. This was something else. Who were we now, so suddenly? I was suddenly very uncomfortable. My cheeks went hot, just like at football. Embarrassed, I tried to move, but his hand stayed around my shoulders. At that moment, something passed between us. I knew it. The people watching seemed to be aware of it. The other boys felt it. I thought the world sensed it. There was talk, I think. Later. For a while, I guess.

After that night, Freddy never visited our home again, barely spoke to me, moved farther down the hall when I approached. We were no longer close. By that time, I had many other friends; I was popular, a funny guy, a little bit beloved by some, part of things. At last. But I could not understand why there had been this rupture, and I felt ashamed, as if I had done something terrible. For years I was ashamed to think of it.

I ask Betty, who is just sitting with her cards in her lap, if maybe when it cools down she would want to go sit on the deck for a while. To get some fresh air. She shakes her head. She says nothing. There is much we have said nothing about, and, yes, it is too late now. I kept silent. I didn't tell them who I was. They didn't ask. We didn't know what to do about me. She would have helped me, if she had known how. She just didn't know. I didn't know what to ask for. I was scared. So was she. We never broke open. It was too frightening and we have all paid the price. My father never knew all of who I was. I never gave him the chance.

Betty never says anything, really—about me or herself. She has never told me about anything that ever happened to her. If I could ask her anything, it would be this: "What was it, Mother, that just shut you up, so tight and quiet?"

I hope there was nothing, that this was just her way from the beginning. I hope there was nothing that hurt her, back there someplace.

10

My mother is standing with her purse open, clutching one strap and staring at a framed watercolor of a field of flowers as if it were a window, as if it were her window. She looks as if she were home, surveying the yard and the roses, monitoring Alice's comings and goings, worrying that my aunt has been invited someplace she has not.

But this is not her window. This is just a picture in a frame; the flowers are not pink, not her roses, and this is not her home. This is something else to her; this place for old people to come to is giving up, whatever words I use. This is the stop where everything she knows is left behind and she won't go quietly. She won't let go of home. It is her most sentimental quality, one we share, our attachment to our place. She has not lost this longing: Her mind has not altered radically or broken in two; it's more that the surface, the coating, has been rubbed away a bit. You can see more of what is there, the hard and soft, but she is still my mother and she still does not surrender. Or maybe this is how I need to think about her—unconquerable.

I rush up to retrieve her purse, which is full of dirty Kleenexes, loose charge cards, and an old Vuitton billfold I bought her in the city when she came to see *The Lion King* and I left the tickets in a suit I spilled syrup all over and sent to the dry cleaners. We have argued for hours about this trip to Tiger Place, which I have characterized—to her and myself—as simply an outing for information's sake.

As she sits on the couch outside the administrator's office, she glares at me as if being sold into white slavery, gearing up for a battle I don't have in me. She knows that if she fusses enough, I will fold and give up this whole idea.

Waiting for our tour, Betty rummages in her purse, pretending to disregard the passersby, little ladies in groups, little birds in running shoes, who squint at her, assessing the new recruit. Betty just stares down at her old sandals, slowly pulls her feet back under the chair.

Last evening, Betty was on an upswing. Studying a newspaper column, she yelled, "You're too old" at the page, then looked at me. "She's seventy," she says, referring to a letter in an advice column. "Says intercourse is too painful. Fix me another gin and tonic."

"Please be quiet, Judy Garland."

I think she believed a hint of daring would change my mind about today's mission. She doesn't need to leave her home, not this cantankerous party girl. She looked at me expectantly. "I see through you," I almost told her, but instead let her carry on until it was time to sleep and she realized I wasn't giving up, that we would have to make this trip. All through the night, I got up, and up, and up again, finally heading up to visit the lonely dog who lay completely stretched out on the concrete floor of the pen, doing his best to cool himself. His yellow eyes shone in the dark as I splashed him with water from a pail I had brought for this purpose.

At the convenience store where I stopped for powdered sugar doughnuts to spruce up Betty's breakfast, I watched a man hand over a five and a one for cigarettes and a tiny Bic lighter. "I need thirty-two more cents," the cashier said.

"Well, you're gonna have to git it from somebody who likes you more than me," the man responded.

"Oh, quiet down. I'm trying to do three things at once here. . . . Do you like my new eyebrows?"

He just stared.

"They're tattoos."

. . .

Everyone thinks Tiger Place is Betty's best option. At the very least, even if she remains at home for a while longer or even permanently, we need a safety net, a plan in case she is suddenly beyond my care. The good places have waiting lists and she needs to be on one, to be prepared. She has always dreaded the idea of winding up at Monroe Manor, the senior citizens' home in Paris where Mammy lived before her death.

Run by the University of Missouri, Tiger Place is a cutting-edge facility that attracts retired professors or the parents of professors. For my mother, who does not see how lucky she would be to get admitted here, this cast is not a selling point. When Jackie, our guide, mentions the lectures by visiting scholars on fascinating contemporary subjects, Betty looks pained, bored in advance. She is not the type to sit and listen. At church, a few ministers back, she developed the habit of holding up her wristwatch when the old man got long-winded. A stimulating roundtable on *The Vagina Monologues* with a women's studies professor is probably not going to make her day.

"What is that?" she asks as I gaze at the lecture schedule. When I explain she asks if she will be able to get a gin and tonic.

She may not even be accepted for admission. Residents must show that they are able to care for themselves and become part of the community. There is a list of criteria that people admitted here must meet. Betty, inclined to fall inside herself, to just not register the goings-on around her, to refuse to do what she is asked, may be beyond assisted living here. But I don't want her to fail further and wind up somewhere dismal. Dementia or Alzheimer's facilities would be the end of her. Without the stimulation of active people, she would fall fast and fade. But I can't say these things to her and she won't see that I am just trying to take care, to be the strong one now. For her.

Last night, I heard her at the piano, when I thought she finally was in bed. The hymn she was playing was "Take My Life and Let It Be."

"Don't play that," I yelled out.

"Well, what do you want me to play?"

"Something cheerful."

"Wait for Christmas."

At Tiger Place, there are chairs upholstered in cheerful shades that make Betty grimace and carpet that, unlike our own, shows no spills. The residents are mostly younger and in better shape than my mother. Would she mix well, I wonder, try to socialize or hide in her room? Would she dress in the morning or just stay in her robe, as she does if I do not force the issue? Would the ladies, gathered in cliques, understand or shun her because of her eccentricities? I just don't want to see her hurt.

Dragging her feet down the hall, Betty looks a little sad, like the kind of old lady she has never let herself become, but steels herself, trying to get through this day, to cooperate a little. My cousin Lucinda has joined us to help out and Betty is more docile with her on hand.

No matter how I try to position Tiger Place as a fun-filled new lifestyle, as a relaxing relief from burdens, Betty will not participate in these fictions. She will not speak or comment as we are shown the studio, one-bedroom, and two-bedroom units that, empty for display, are okay but not especially inviting. "These rooms are empty," she tells Jackie, who says that of course she would bring her furniture from home. "I would *never* bring my furniture here," Betty exclaims. She doesn't want to break up the house. Maybe because there is no place for most of her things to go.

Our basement is piled with stuff. Late at night, I inspect everything as I listen for Betty to call out. I see what is ahead, picture the furniture lined up in the yard, all for sale—the antiques, chests with marble tops and tables, the candleholders, cups and saucers, the cloisonné, the brass tea set, the row of Japanese ladies from the top of the piano.

"Remember," Betty always says, "those are hand painted."

I see the silver butter basket, the love seat my father refinished, the pie safe, Granny's kneeling Buddha, the shiny cranes that Sade gave

Granny, the kitchen things: the canisters and plates, the silverware, crocks and pots, cookie jars. Everything is for sale. Off to others. Someday soon. All the old things that witnessed everything, all the days and nights of our lives. I don't have a place for them; this is a regret I have. The life that I've carved out is not equipped with extra rooms or empty cabinets. If Betty moves to Tiger Place, we may have to sell the house for financial reasons, depending on how long she lives.

I glance at Cinda, who has been the major reason for my maintaining a hint of sanity in the last few months. She looks at Betty and then at me as if to say, "What were you expecting?"

I don't know. *The Golden Girls*?

"Is she a craftsperson?" Jackie asks, but Betty, who rolls her eyes at this, does not knit or embroider. She does not tat or sew and is not the type to linger over the creation of a lap robe. She cannot see well enough, nor does she have the patience. She is irritable, and now sometimes a challenge. Though she tries her best, she cannot always remember names. How can she make friends if she cannot call their names out? Who will come and sit by her? She has no hobbies; she once had friends instead. But now the country club in Moberly, where the couples of her generation once gathered for dinners, is gone, torn down. Moberly is no longer a place where many people can afford a country club. My mother grieved for months.

I try to smile at Betty, but she looks away. I try to walk with her, but she won't let me be The Son. "Please let me do for you," I want to say. "Please let me help you. Maybe I can surprise you, make this all a little easier." But she has to do everything on her own or it is cheating, breaking a rule.

She suddenly looks tired and whispers to me that she just wants to go home, but Cinda and I guide her toward the exercise area. She looks dispirited and a fraction of her former height. Unwrapping a tiny Snickers square, I hold it out as Betty eyes an exercise bicycle as if it were a guillotine. Staring at me, perturbed, she shakes her head. Nor does the prospect of yoga in a chair arouse her enthusiasm. "What kind of thing is that to do?" she asks.

"I want to go home," she whispers to Cinda. "I want to go home." So do I, but we can't. We have to forge ahead. I have to lead; it's my responsibility.

She stumbles on a stair. She is wearing the terrible sandals, a concession I have allowed today. Braving her resistance to public endearment, I kiss her head, but she pulls it away. "You won't let him leave me here, will you?" she asks Cinda. I realize that she believes I have brought her here to abandon her. This is actually what she thinks. She believes I want to run away and leave her. Clearly I am, in her mind, the Joan Crawford of elder care.

"Tonight," I tell her, "we'll buy peaches; we'll go to the Junction for prime rib. We'll do whatever you want." But she will not listen. Perhaps because she feels I hold power over her, I am the enemy. When I turn to face her, she still refuses to look at me at all. She smiles at Cinda, her new ally, the one she considers persuadable, as I resist the urge to fold into the yoga chair and begin a round of chanting.

"Are you aware of the concept of being mindful?" Jackie asks my mother. Spotting a nearby men's room, I wonder if I can work in a quick autoasphyxiation.

We see the library, a movie theater where popcorn is served, a beauty parlor. The main room for gatherings is dominated by a huge flat-screen television tuned to a game show. "I hate *Wheel of Fortune,*" Betty says to Jackie. "Is that *Wheel of Fortune*? Every time I turn my back, someone puts on *Wheel of Fortune.*"

Watching Betty at Tiger Place, Cinda looks at me and seems for the most part amused. Again and again, she saves us: She knows the right questions to ask, makes a note or two as Jackie explains the walking tests administered each month, the bus for church pickups and shopping trips, the stages of care: Stage One, Stage Two. There are four stages. I think I may be a Seven.

When I manage to come up with an inquiry that actually seems on point—"Is there anyone to make sure she takes all her pills in the morning?"—Betty interjects, "I can take my own medicine." But she doesn't, and every time I hold them out she asks the same question: "What are these? Who said I had to take so many?" She acts like taking pills is some sort of hard labor.

Jackie introduces my mother to a woman with a fancy blouse passing by. "Do you play bridge?" Betty asks. When the woman, who looks a little startled, shakes her head, Betty turns away from her, stares at me coldly. I have promised cards. I want to ask the woman if she likes *Wheel of Fortune,* but Betty would tell me I am not as funny as I think I am.

"Older people eat small meals," says Jackie as we head into the dining room for lunch. "They don't get hungry like we do." Cinda is a little taken aback, as am I. My mother eats enough for a camp of lumberjacks in the Maine woods. Betty asks of the lunch, "Are they going to charge us for this?" Jackie overhears and assures us that the meal is complimentary. "Well," Betty says moments later, staring down at what seems only the suggestion of a hamburger, "it better be.

"Don't you offer to pay," she whispers to me.

After lunch, we sit for a while in a courtyard filled with flowers. Betty, dejected, reaches out to snap a deadhead off a geranium. I like the courtyard and preparations are under way for a party that evening. It is someone's birthday. Jackie tells us that she is so devoted to the residents here that she got married in the courtyard.

I would have chosen Chipotle. "Where did you honeymoon?" I want to ask.

The Tiger Place courtyard is a lovely place and some of the apartments have screened-in porches that look out onto this area. Sitting by the flowers, Betty rests, focusing on the blossoms. For years she has taken flowers to people from church who are sick and alone. Hour after hour, I have watched her standing by the kitchen table, arranging the stems.

"Who tends to these?" she asks Jackie. "It looks like they do a pretty good job." It is her one concession.

The trek through these halls has worn her down and lunch has certainly not satisfied. "Did you get a look at that hamburger?" she asks me. I say nothing. "No bigger than a half dollar," she adds.

Maybe I should just give up and let her be, I think, stay in Paris, see her through for as long as it takes. Then I tell myself I am an idiot for always going soft. That is not what the real Betty, who would have run me back to New York with a pitchfork, would have wanted me to do. She would have ordered me to live my life. Of all the changes that have transpired in my mother, it is this new belief that I should give everything up to stay with her that is the most surprising. This tells me just how worried she is, how much she cannot bear to leave her home.

"I know where everything is here," Betty said the other day, making her way down the hall at home. "I don't have to think about it. I just know. Even at night. I don't even have to see."

In my mind, I line them up for the auctioneer: the stubby pencils that say BAKER LUMBER, my mother's coats and scarves, Mammy's pins, Oscar's Smith Corona, Wray Chowning's family photographs, Granny's china, a jar from Aunt Winnie's porch. What will not make it? What, meaningful only to me, will be lost or burned? The years of photos, the family letters, touched by many, that said love or mourned a passing, the greetings from the war, the cards from many distant travels—the girls from Hawaii doing hula, the greetings sent from the Muehlebach in Kansas City during the lumbermen's convention, the vistas of the faraway Pacific that Mammy sent Betty, just married. What will become of these things? I feel like I should have made a place for all this. For generations—my father, grandfather, great-grandfather, and before and before—there have been George Hodgmans, and one day there will be none and it is a bit hard not to feel disappointed that I am the one to close the book on all of us.

. . .

Betty looks so woebegone when I explain to Jackie that I want us to go on the waiting list that I cannot look back at her. It is just a backup—I keep repeating this, trying to make myself believe this, to make Betty understand, but she just shakes her head as Cinda and I follow Jackie into the office to get the form to fill out and write a check. We have to do this. We have to make sure she has a pleasant place if she must leave home.

Betty will be number eight on the list; she can waive entry three times before she is taken off the list. Before she actually enters, she will have to undergo an assessment designed to test her level of self-sufficiency and "cognitive functioning." The application fee is a nonrefundable thousand dollars, which I do not tell my mother about.

As I turn the corner to do the paperwork, I catch sight of Betty. When she thinks no one is looking, she reaches out for another flower and yanks the brown top off with force. The sun makes her wrinkles stand out. When I return to her side, she says again, "I want to go home." She rests her hand on mine just for a second. "Please, George," she says. "Please."

"Mother, you've been so lucky," I tell her.

"Oh, you think so?" she asks, her tone implying that there are things I will never know, things she did for me that I cannot fathom.

I think Betty will never live at Tiger Place. She is falling too fast. Soon, I am afraid, she will be beyond movies with popcorn or exercise bicycles, though maybe she will remember flowers. Maybe she will find herself, on some future morning, running her finger along the glass of a painting in a hall she does not recognize, recalling in some corner of her mind the fat buds of her mother's roses growing in her old front yard. On Facebook, a lady wrote that the days she gets to be with those she loves are "gold-star days." I often tell Betty that these are our gold-star days. I have tried to make them special so she can carry pieces of these times in her memory. I am trying to pack her bag with things that might draw her back to herself someday.

I wonder if she will remember the cinnamon toast I make on Friday mornings. I wonder if she will recall Mammy washing her hair in rainwater from an old tin pan.

All the way home from Columbia, I break the speed limit. I want to check on the dog. I want to put an end to this day. My mother is mostly silent. She can no longer deny what is happening and she is plotting, planning her attack. As we travel, Betty's mood shifts. Suddenly, she is nice, so nice, too nice. Butter wouldn't melt in her mouth. She asks me if I need money. I turn the radio up. It is Reverend Lucius Love's gospel hour. I need some lifting up.

When I was in high school, a man named Harold Long preached at the AME church, across the tracks from the white part of town, even then. One of his sisters, whose first name I wish I could remember, was in my mixed chorus class. She was big; her feet bulged out below the straps of her shoes. Stepping up on the bleachers winded her. But I always listened for her. There were all our voices singing together, and there was her voice, full of church, and the people she had come from, and feeling. Her emotion changed the face of an ordinary day and I was drawn by it. Now there are only two black students at Paris High School, both mixed race. The others attend a school called Faith Walk run by one of the African American churches. "I don't know if it's segregation," says a friend, "or if it's more a matter of the black parents not wanting their kids around the shit the white kids are pulling."

If there was ever a time when I was convinced there was a God in the universe holding out his hand to me, it was when the Long sisters performed "I Believe."

"If you stayed in Paris, you could keep that dog," Betty declares suddenly, eyes glinting as if she has just been dealt a winning hand at the bridge table. She is playing for freedom. I have always enjoyed watching my mother in action. There is love and there is survival. At the moment, the latter can be her only concern. She will do whatever is necessary. Her independence is at stake. Her everything. Home.

I don't want to take away her home.

"Can't we just go on the way we are, just a little while longer?" she asks. "It won't be forever."

"You look pretty healthy."

"I could die tomorrow."

"I told you to get a flu shot."

The ensuing moments do not fly by.

"Mother, can't you see that I am trying to do everything I can to make you happy? Trust me, please. I'll take care of you. I will do right by you."

"I know," she says. "I know." And I think she actually believes it, that I can do it, that I can make it, somehow, okay. Outside it is so hot that steam is rising from the highway. When I was in high school, I brought Mammy, very old then and not far from her death, home from the doctor in Columbia on an old country road. Her eyes never left the window; it seemed as though she was watching something, though she could barely see. Whatever it was, it pleased her. Finally, outside Centralia, she spoke. "Look at all those pretty cows," said my grandmother, the old woman who still remembered the farm. The blades of the windmills still turned slowly in the breeze off the fields in her mind's eye.

"Look at those little calves," she said, directing my attention to the window. But the pastures we were passing were empty. There was nothing there but the strip of highway running toward Paris and the room at Monroe Manor where she lived by then.

11

On the table by my bed, I keep a picture of Mammy as a young woman in her hat with the side dented in, a heavy suit with a long skirt, a white blouse with ruffles, carefully ironed. Beside her, a suitcase; behind her, a railroad track and a boxcar with an open door. In the far distance, a long expanse of flat American land, a line of bare trees with thin branches dwarfed by the wide-open sky clear of clouds.

"Where were you going?" I want to ask her, but I'll never know.

I see her, decades later, reaching up to hang laundry on the line, clean clothes slapping in the wind.

The woman who will become my grandmother is alone in the photograph by my bedside and does not appear happy or eager to travel. She is a farm girl from a big family with a reasonable number of acres on the outskirts of a town called Clarence. Maybe she is leaving home, perhaps departing for the women's college—Hardin, in Mexico, Missouri—where she learned Latin. Maybe she is off to teach in another place. Her eyes are closed, perhaps because of the sun, or the fact that she is reluctant to be photographed, or because she is in tears.

A few years after the picture was taken, she would marry Joe Baker, back in Missouri after a few years in Alabama—Tuscaloosa, it said in his obituary—working in a John Deere factory. In photographs, my grandfather has shadows around his deep-set eyes. I never knew him; years before I was born, he sat down at the lunch table and died after a heart attack. During my lifetime he was never spoken of. None of them, not Mammy or Betty or Bill or Harry, ever told us anything about him. All Betty will say when asked about him is that he was "a very nice man."

The picture of my grandmother was taken almost a century ago, when hundreds and hundreds of small farms dotted this area and it was rare for anyone to leave home, especially a young woman. Today, most of the land around the county is owned by half a dozen or so families who pay hundreds of thousands of dollars for huge implements, large operations stitched together from dozens of the sort of little farms where Bill Baker once stopped on Sundays to deliver parts while June waited in the car, doing crewel embroidery.

"How cruel is it?" I asked her once, thinking myself extremely witty.

"It's a bitch," she said.

I did not leave home on a train. My father drove me in our blue Oldsmobile, and, riding in the front seat, Betty kept turning around to look at me. I thought she was giving me fond parting glances, but soon she offered a comment: "I cannot believe you did not get a haircut before you left."

When we got to the dorm room, she glanced at me, looking tender and a little lost, but left quickly. My mother and I hate good-byes.

The previous spring, the fraternities at the university had begun to host prerush parties for potential members. At an event at the Phi Delta Theta house where I had been invited by Jack Fleming—the son of Betty's best friend, Evelyn—I ducked out early. While others bonded over a trailer-sized keg, I was downtown watching Barbra Streisand in *A Star Is Born* for the fourth time. I just wanted Kris Kristofferson to go ahead and kill himself so Barbra could sing the closer. I believe she had the same idea.

At home, late that night after my drive back to Paris, I confessed ditching the Phi Delts to my devastated mother, who wrung her hands like a peasant woman told her village is burning. I expected a seizure. Glancing away, I saw my father down the hall, heading toward the kitchen. Taking a look at our expressions, he hotfooted it back to bed after mimicking my mother's scolding finger and making a face at me. I flipped him the bird.

"What," she asked, "am I supposed to say to Evelyn? This will kill Evelyn. She went out of her way."

I hate it when someone goes out of their way for me. It makes me feel guilty. "Please no," I say if someone wants to do me a favor. I pictured Mrs. Fleming, waxlike and stiffened laid out at the Theta house for viewing, dressed in an ensemble from the Tall Girl's Shop. I had known her since I was a child; now she would hate me. Proprieties were important to her. She was an elegant woman who, if I was eating at her table, always came up behind me to rest her hands on my shoulders. I liked it, but didn't want it to happen very often.

I wanted to please Evelyn, but I wouldn't change my mind about the fraternity. Despite Betty's repeated pleas, I refused to pledge, put my foot down for the first time. My mother attempted to stare me into submission, but found someone looking right back as determined as she was. I held firm; for me it was an emergency. No way could I be in that place; those guys would make my life miserable.

Freshman year, 1977, at the university in Columbia: guys throwing footballs in the dorm halls, running around naked, snapping towels. In my dorm room, I hung a giant poster of Monet's *Water Lilies*. Acquired on a high school trip to St. Louis, my masterwork had not drawn the praise I expected. A boy from Hornersville, Missouri, asked, "What exactly is that supposed to represent?"

"Floating flowers," I said.

"God Almighty," he replied.

The first week of school, the student newspaper, the *Maneater*, published a notice about a Gay People's Alliance meeting at the Ecumenical Center off campus on Tuesdays at 7 p.m. I figured I should try to go. I had to. I was desperate. I had to get my life going, somehow. By 2 p.m. on Tuesday, I was stepping into the shower, cleansing thoroughly before

Right Guarding myself so generously that I did not anticipate perspiring again until at least my midthirties.

What to wear? I sensed this a crucial, possibly life-altering decision. What did I have that was sexy? Nothing. Unbuttoning the top of my shirt, a white Lacoste chosen to show off what was left of my summer tan, I studied myself in the mirror before going to gargle again and brush my teeth more thoroughly. I had taken to smoking unfiltered Pall Malls after reading that they were the brand of my favorite writer, despite the fact that my lips stuck to the paper and any loose strands of tobacco. During my first month at the university my teeth appeared to be sprouting hairs.

Give or take Wray Chowning, the only gay people I had seen were a group of men in tiny swimsuits at the Chase Park Plaza pool in St. Louis where, a few summers before, I had gone with Betty and George for the weekend to go to the Municipal Opera, a huge open-air theater in Forest Park. Like a spy, I observed these men, but they ignored me, slathering tanning lotion over their already dark bodies and reading *After Dark* magazine as I struggled with a tube of Bain de Soleil, a product I considered luxurious and sensual that I had purchased at the hotel gift shop.

I couldn't stop looking at the men; I couldn't stop staring at their bodies, the sun pressing my skin as the children raced around screaming and I rubbed the lotion into my chest. I can remember its smell. Betty wore sunglasses. No one would ever know what she saw, though it was unlikely that she could have imagined the scenes floating through my head as I leaned back on my sun chair and closed my eyes.

That night, at *The Music Man,* Big George hummed loudly along with every number as if those gathered under the stars had come to hear him and not Eddie Albert. It was one of the moments when his desire for attention felt uncomfortably close to desperation. Betty, bored immediately by Marian the Librarian, mostly ignored the show, focusing on my father and whispering to me. "If he as much as sings one note," she began.

"Maybe he'll get discovered."

"Do you think we could leave at intermission? You could tell him you have sunburn."

"He likes the barbershop numbers . . ."

"That's what I'm afraid of. He'll give a concert."

"I'm hoping Marian gets murdered."

"She's not that pretty."

"She's bookish."

I didn't care whether we stayed or left. I was still back at the pool, lying in the hot sun, fantasizing about rubbing someone's smooth bare back with Bain de Soleil.

On the night of the meeting of the Gay People's Alliance, reeking of antiperspirant, I sneaked out of the dorm, nervous but able to find the Ecumenical Center in about four minutes. I sat down on a bench near some tennis courts. It was after 4 p.m. Hours to spare. I am never, ever late. Scoping out the parking lot, I checked for familiar cars, feeling under surveillance somehow. Evelyn Fleming, visiting Jack at the Theta House, might feel drawn to a discussion of nonviolence. I kept my eyes on the door of the center, trying to see who entered. I wanted to be touched; I had waited and waited. I wanted to be with someone.

Finally, I went in, suddenly tense, trembling on the inside. Scanning the room, I got more and more upset, so anxious I could barely move toward a chair. I did not think I could speak. If no one tried to talk to me, it would be a mercy.

I left my body; this had never happened. I felt about to break open. Part of me fled and I fell into a full-fledged panic. I had been so looking forward to this night, but it looked like none of this was going to work, and if it didn't I didn't know what I would do.

Larry, a bearded, thirtyish professor, appeared to be the head of it all. His haircut suggested an affiliation with the medieval period.

"Are you out to your parents?" he asked, and when I shook my head, he added, "Knowing parents are rare animals."

I was still panicked and could barely listen. I felt as though I had disappeared. This wasn't going to work.

A man in a wheelchair in a jaunty black beret gave me a look meant to be kind, but I was almost sick. When another man, Gene, held out his hand, it was impossible for me to accept it. I was frozen, felt bad, guilty to be thought unfriendly, but I just could not reach back.

It was hard to breathe.

I could not look at the faces. I could not look up at all. I was sorry I had come. It was just all wrong. It wasn't going to work. It was harder here than anywhere; I felt worse than ever.

Staring at the tabletop, I noticed my sweaty handprints on the table as, humiliated and ashamed of myself, I tried to listen to Larry talk about some Supreme Court decision.

The trip back to the dorm seemed to last for hours, but I didn't notice anything I passed. I was not there. I knew only that some part of my self went away, left me alone, ripped open in front of everyone. I had never heard anyone describe such a reaction to anything and was terrified that this would happen every time I went in public as gay. In my room, I sat down on the bed. I had soaked my shirt clear through and it hung on my body, so wet, as if someone had pushed me into the deep end of a pool.

A few months after my debut, I returned to the meeting. I felt I had to; I had to get a life. I needed help to get my bearings in this life.

A man named Michael, a medical resident, seemed to be sizing me up at the meeting as I tried to listen to the dialog. Feeling his eyes on me, I turned to see if he was looking at someone behind me, but there was no one. We looked a little bit alike and somehow I knew that this had attracted him.

Several months later, at a fish restaurant where Michael took me, my first date, it happened again, the bad thing. I started shaking again, leaving my body. I thought that Michael had plans for me for later on. I wanted this and didn't. Again, so tense, I broke into a sweat. He talked and talked about San Francisco, where he said everything was happening, but I could not speak. I was embarrassed. But it didn't matter. He took me to his apartment where there were textbooks and a pile of porno magazines. I felt so far away from home. I knew this man was going to give me nothing. I knew he wasn't going to help me out.

That night: a bizarre physical encounter, bargain-basement love, no kisses or hugs. Quickly after, Michael announced he was taking me home. It was maybe 2 a.m. I seemed to have misplaced several articles of clothing. Where my new pair of flesh-toned bikini underwear had lodged themselves seemed a mystery I was too exhausted to contemplate. Moving on to check out Michael's desk, I found a pad of paper and a pen. I wrote, "You're an asshole" on one page and moved quickly away from the desk when he returned.

Back at the dorm where he dropped me off, I realized that I was missing my card key. I walked back to the bench by the tennis courts and sat down, waiting for morning. A block away was the Phi Delta Theta house where Jack Fleming was probably prodding the new guys with a red-hot poker or forcing them to clean the basement in their underwear. What would Evelyn make of my night with Michael? I could not imagine she would approve. I figured that in the years ahead a lot of people would stop speaking to me.

On the day I went to the Ecumenical Center, as I started into the building, I thought of what my parents would think as I stood at the door I was trying to figure out how to open. I felt that if I stepped through that door I would be leaving them behind. I felt like I was losing something that connected us, something good. I felt like I was leaving behind the way I was taught to live.

. . .

A few years before I arrived at the University of Missouri, the gay organization that I attended later, at the Ecumenical Center, had sued the university for the right to meet within the official borders of the campus. The case went all the way to the Supreme Court, which ultimately ruled in favor of the gays. On the night that the group made its first entrance into the Student Union, I was standing on the sidelines, not ready to march through the streets in front of my friends or have Jack Fleming pelt me with a beer can. I could not quite take in what I was seeing: Dozens of frat boys were throwing rocks, rotten food, and water balloons at the marchers. I watched in disbelief. Where were the police? A woman with a guitar led the gay procession, which was far outnumbered by the crowd who had gathered to disrespect and disparage them. The marchers were not the type I had glimpsed in photographs from Greenwich Village or the Castro. They were, with a few exceptions, neither beautiful, nor well dressed, nor those who might have easily blended into the world of their persecutors. It seemed that at this time, in this place, it was only the loneliest, the most alienated who craved acceptance or affirmation desperately enough to risk a public stoning.

Mary Maune, head of the Association of Women Students, had a tape recorder. A journalism student, she was covering the event for radio station KBIA. She looked astonished when she—a student leader, a well-groomed, achievement-oriented sorority member—was hit and bloodied with something sharp by a beefy frat boy in chinos from Mr. Guy.

The man in the wheelchair from the meeting, moving the most slowly, was an especially vulnerable target. The jaunty black beret atop his disbelieving, shattered face did not fare well. I noticed egg yolks dripping from his wheels. The boys on the sidelines were screaming something like "Faggots die. Faggots die. Off this campus. Off this campus."

I was shaking, but I had to help him. Together with one of the other onlookers, we carried the man in the wheelchair up the stairs and into the union. I was afraid I would drop my wheel. He recognized me, put his hand on my arm, but I ran.

. . .

Although my mother has been consistent when it comes to discussing, or actually not discussing, my life, other people have surprised me sometimes. As it happened, Evelyn Fleming was my friend as long as she lived. After my father died, when I was back in the city, she called me up to find out how I was doing. Everyone else asked after my mother. She asked about me, took the trouble to find my far-off number. There is kindness, people who never fail you. There are others who do.

A few years back, Betty and I stopped by the Flemings' house when they were packing up to go to a senior community near Kansas City. Jack, who had married a born-again Christian from Oklahoma, would not as much as look in my direction. I tried not to feel I had been slapped in the face.

I don't get many unfriendly or judgmental vibes here in Paris, though a woman from church never, ever responds when I say hello. Every time someone doesn't speak or looks at me with an expression I cannot fathom, I think it is because of who I am. It has been this way forever; this kind of reaction feels to be bred in the bone, especially in territory where I feel isolated.

All through this afternoon, Betty coughs and coughs. When she dozes on the couch in the living room, glimpses of other women, her grandmother Anna, whose face I have seen in old photos; Bess; Nona; and perhaps others I never knew, drift across her face. The women she is from are there, in her chin, cheekbones, and slender nose. Mammy, though, is the one I see the most. Mammy is in her eyes. When my mother plays "His Eye Is on the Sparrow," on the piano, she always reminds me that this was my grandmother's favorite. "She couldn't sing, but she liked it enough to listen when she heard it." I see Mammy in her hat with one side dented in, that same old hat, sitting in a hot summer church, cooling herself with a paper fan with the image of Jesus rising on one side and the name Thompson-Mackler, the local funeral parlor, on the back. Clearing her throat—my mother's family has waged a decades-long battle with phlegm—she looks about to doze.

Mammy's family were farm people. Sometimes it is simple to imagine them, those who lived here once, all the good people, crossing the river, coming in from the country for church on Sunday mornings with clean, coerced hair and their best clothes. Think of wrinkled faces, mischievous eyes, hands in immaculate white gloves, wistfulness, innocence, worry over money, or crops, or sickness.

Think of the men, itchy to get back to work; mayors and merchants in their hard-pressed white shirts, tight collars, and stiff coats; lacy girls in ribbons; stoic boys, uncomfortable in their finery, confined in rarely worn shiny shoes; big-boned farm women with ample bosoms in dime-store brooches; old, milky-eyed codgers, freshly shaved with a few hairs still peeking out of their ears and noses; mothers with careful glances, pulling their kids away from puddles, holding their hands, smoothing their hair, and wiping their cheeks.

I picture them all moving across the land, the days, through time, crossing Main Street, clutching their crosses and Bibles, trying to stay pretty, trying to look pious, walking together, traveling in their snorting, hard-to-start cars, or heading toward town in their buggies or on horseback to bow their heads and pray together to Jesus, who, in the stories I read, stood for love, charity, and kindness offered every day to others, even those unlike ourselves. Kindness may be the most difficult of virtues, but when I have encountered it, it has meant everything to me.

12

Sunday is frying eggs and trying not to break the yolks; getting Betty off to church; *Parade* magazine; big men streaking down Main Street on Harleys with their hair blowing from their helmets; the long, silent afternoon. August is beginning to wane. I don't want to get up; it's barely 6 a.m., but I hear my mother in the living room, playing the piano.

Last night, strange news: A young man whose family sold tractors in Madison—a jolly-looking kid with a belly and bushy beard—was shot and killed, apparently by homeless people staying with him. The murderer or murderers are still at large. Taking all this in, I saw that a friend of the dead man had posted photos on Facebook, including one of the scene of the crime. "We had real good parties here," the caption said. "RIP."

I knew the place. It was Mammy's house on Olive Street, remodeled now, with a wishing well where her garden was. Apparently not long ago a meth lab in the kitchen where my grandmother rolled flour for bread blew a hole through the roof.

I chased lightning bugs across Mammy's yard on nights in the summer as, across the street, the old ladies in the neighborhood—my grandmother, Bassett, Dolly, Mary Virginia, and Virgie—chatted away on Dolly's porch in their nightgowns, taking in the cool air.

Betty said nothing when I told her of the murder. We'd had a bad scene and she wasn't speaking to me. For days I had searched for an old clipping—a story about Ella Ewing, the giantess circus performer whose shoes hang at the state capitol. I thought maybe I could try to write hing about her, and the article was loaned to me by the historical society. But nothing ever stays put here, and finally Betty admitted to throwing it away. She wouldn't say why. It wasn't the first time something like this had happened. What is mine is hers.

"Dammit," I yelled. "You won't throw away your Kleenexes. But the one thing I need, you throw away. It wasn't mine. Couldn't you have asked? It was in a Ziploc bag. Didn't it occur to you that someone was saving it?"

Betty, who never yells, looked back in disbelief, so upset, rising shakily from her chair, not able to cope with this. She began to make her sounds, as if trying to maintain some sort of equilibrium. Clutching the sides of her gown, she fled the kitchen as if attacked, making her way down the hall as fast as she could to her room where she closed the door. I thought I had made her cry and lay down on the couch shaking, knowing I had gone too far. On the rare occasions when my anger comes out, it's a river that can't be easily dammed up. I pressed my lips together hard, hoping my mouth would not fly open again.

I found Betty in her room, sitting—as she always does—at the far edge of her high bed, about to slide off, her hand cradling the side of her head. I tried to apologize, but couldn't make it right.

"It's the first time you've ever sworn at me." That's all she could say. She looked shocked, as if someone had died, passed away from her. I didn't know whether she was angry at herself or mourning the son who never raised his voice to her. She would accept no apologies and now it is Sunday and I still feel terrible.

I can't seem to get out of bed, though I need to make breakfast. "What's wrong with you, Betty? What's wrong with you? Why did you do *that*?" Betty is upset, talking to herself at the piano. She has played the wrong note. Later she is to accompany the choir at church and, scared of embarrassing herself, has gotten up early to practice. She still drives herself when she is scheduled to perform. The music stops; she coughs. I hope she won't make more mistakes. A fragile bundle in pink flannel, she is sitting at the piano in the living room as the sun begins to fall through the lace curtains she says will crumble if washed once more.

"It's imported," she says of the fabric. "Switzerland. Somewhere."

Betty is making her way slowly through "Take the Time to Be Holy." Not as sure or certain at the keyboard as she was, she hits a few clunkers. Each one hurts us both, tearing into our pictures of the woman we remember, shoulders held stiffly erect as she played, never hitting a wrong note. "Hold up your shoulders," Mammy always told her. "Hold up your shoulders." If her posture sagged, her father walked up behind her and struck her between the shoulder blades.

"Why did you play that?" my mother asks herself. "You know better than that." I get angry along with her when she makes a mistake. I get mad when she is less than she was.

Every time she plays, it's more of a trial. She will no longer allow me to accompany her to church. She does not want me to hear her.

The piano has been my mother's instrument since she was a girl taking lessons from Miss Elizabeth Richmond in Madison. Trudging through the street with her music books, she probably dawdled a bit, stopping to look at the windows of Chowning's Dry Goods, run by Wray's father, Scott, or stopping at the Rexall if she had the money for a stick of candy or an orange slice. "We weren't poor poor," Mammy always said. "But we were poor."

Betty's gentle touch at the piano, the soft way she rests her fingers on the keys and makes the music flow, remains. There is such sweet feeling when she touches the keys. The piano is where she hides a certain part of herself that must be kept covered up and safe.

I don't want her to have to stop playing in church. I don't want her to stop trying. I don't want to lose the part of her I feel when she makes music, that softness. Betty has always been a little tough on me; to her that is a mother's job. When I notice who she becomes at the piano or, on occasion, with other people, I find myself a little envious.

. . .

Every year after my father died, I came back in late August to check on things. About ten years ago, I arrived in the midst of a summer blooming everywhere, blessed by rain enough to fill the rivers and please the farmers. On the way home from the airport, I could do nothing but stare out the window. In the early mornings, the branches of my father's trees looked to be floating in hazy green clouds.

For weeks, I had gotten surprising reports from my cousins. Betty had a beau. I was the last to be told. Maybe she had always wished I would confide in her and this was her response to my silence. Maybe she thought the subject of love was off-limits, since I have never shared anything. Maybe she had been hurt by this.

Perhaps she believed I would think her disloyal to my father, but I didn't. I loved seeing her this way: happy, purely happy, and not just for a moment as a wave of enthusiasm passed across her face.

Her boyfriend was a former postman and recent widower named John Hickey. His wife, Charlotte, always wore a fishing hat, decorated with tackles, to church and sat on the side where we do when Betty doesn't play. She was formidable and, like Betty, was gifted at the piano. John was briefly adrift after Charlotte died before falling into the arms of another strong woman: Betty. More than eighty years old, he remained the little boy lost, dependent on a woman to handle what he couldn't or didn't want to. So Betty took control. She ran the show, as she often had with my dad. From what I could see, my mother had taken over John's life, helping him with everything that Charlotte took charge of. Betty and John stepped right back into what they'd had before with others, the unspoken arrangement of things that couples come to. Maybe I was jealous.

"You could let him make the occasional decision," I told her.

"I make what he wants to eat."

"He's sluggish. He goes to sleep. Last night I looked over and thought he was dead."

"He's not dead. He carried the mail."

"Can't you find someone a little more lively?"

"It's not so easy," she said, laughing a little, "after eighty." After she started seeing John, Betty began going to St. Louis to get her hair done. Out of her crazy, messy drawers came a foggy bottle of L'Air du Temps. Spritzed onto her wrist and neck, it scented her room, and sometimes I stuck my head in to smell the fragrance that settled comfortably into everything. Granny's bedroom also smelled of perfume. I remembered the old days back in St. Louis when, escaping from the others, my mother and I sat in front of my grandmother's vanity with its silver combs and brushes. I studied my mother's face in the mirror as she shyly reached out to try a bit of Granny's perfume, which she dabbed on her wrist and held out for me to inhale. "Don't," I told her, when she sprayed a little on my skin. "Granny will see."

That summer when John arrived in our lives, a coating of pink polish mysteriously appeared on my mother's fingernails. The weather seemed to inspire our sense of a world working out as it should, at its best. Betty called me out to the deck to see the mother deer and her fawn who emerged every night from the woods behind the house around the time the sun set. She was so warm that summer, my mother. She touched everything gently, including me.

John had a catfish pond, and sometimes we drove down there in his golf cart, my mother beside him, me sitting on the back and usually falling off. Betty laughed as I ran to catch up, and all was well. She and John had gone on one date in high school, which he had forgotten, though Betty remembered. I suspected that she had been hurt when he hadn't called again. It was clear that she had always been attracted to him, but I had never heard her as much as mention his name.

"I guess I wasn't pretty enough for him to ask out a second time," she said to me as John listened.

"Maybe you was too bossy," he said. Now and then he rose to the occasion. He had been a great baseball player and, he claimed, almost made the Cardinals.

When he spoke of his prowess on the field, I rolled my eyes at Betty. "Shut up," she mouthed silently.

John had a dog called Bob he had found as a puppy by the side of the road. I thought Bob was just some kind of bird dog, but John swore he was a genuine German shorthair and vowed there were "papers on him somewhere" as Betty looked slightly dubious. Bob had purplish spots—liver spots, I think they are called—and a head that reminded me of a jockey in a cap, his long ears falling straight down like flaps. He was an impressive creature, so alert he seemed to zip in a straight line to his destination like an arrow in flight. When he ran through the yard, one could see how perfect was the curve of his chest.

Betty adored Bob, maybe even more than John. I have rarely seen her so taken with any living creature. He ran toward her, jumped up to greet her every time she came around. Betty knelt to pet him, to stroke his soft ears, to contradict whatever John told him. She laughed when he approached, and saved him scraps from the table. "Don't touch that," Betty would say if I tried to throw something away. "That's for Bob."

Not long before my trip home, Bob had gotten sick and was hacking away, spitting up. Worried, they took him in the Cadillac to Monroe City to the vet. He sat up front, wiggling and squirming, with my mother in back trying to calm him down. "Here we were," Betty told me, "these two old people trying to get this crazy dog who wouldn't sit still, who was just all over everything, who I was just waiting to see spit up all over that Cadillac, to Monroe City to the doctor's. It was like a little adventure. I like to think we saved him."

Bob came along when John took Betty and me for rides through the country in his Cadillac. Because he had carried the mail, he knew all the back roads, the way to the covered bridge and to places by the Salt River where the breeze was cool. Betty loved sitting up in the front seat and waving at the other widows who got together at each other's houses. "They play dominoes," she remarked.

We went to Hannibal to gaze over the Mississippi. We went to prime rib night at the Junction. John helped my mother plant rows of daylilies along the side of our driveway. Watching him trying to stoop over to plant bulbs, I found myself liking him more than I ever had before.

"Are you going to marry him?" I asked her.

"Are you kidding? I get enough of him."

"He doesn't want to?"

"I don't know. Not exactly. He's too cheap. He's afraid I'd spend all his money."

"Is he rich?"

"If he was rich, we'd be married . . . That was a good one. I made you laugh." She looked surprised. "I made *you* laugh."

Betty is pretending to be mad because it distracts her from thinking about how nervous she is to perform at a church where people have heard her play the piano for twenty-five years.

"How do I look?" she asks before I take her to church.

"You look lovely, younger than you have any right to." I put my hand on her shoulder. I try to touch her gently as I am sometimes awkward.

"Can I please help you?" I ask.

"No one can help me . . . the forgetting," she says, conceding, breaking the silence for the first time. Her hands are shaking; she assesses them as if they were trapped inside a pair of ugly gloves. I don't know if she can play the piano. I don't want her to break down in front of everyone.

Suddenly, she looks exhausted; I go to hunt some makeup. When I return, she is glaring at a commercial for a new burger from Hardee's. Called the Jim Beam Thickburger, it is made with whiskey and appears to be larger than the head of the average construction worker.

"Look at that man eat that hamburger," Betty says. I want to kick the television because it is so unfair that everything she has is being taken away.

13

After I have Betty tucked away at church with the hymns marked in her book, I start my errands and ask God, if he is listening, to help my mom. Please. At the convenience store, the boy who mows our lawn bends over the sharp rocks around the bushes, hunting something. His jeans are too long and baggy. He wears his gray parka with the hood up, even as the heat builds. It is hard to see his face; it's just a pale blur. Paying for my gas, I see that he is holding a Band-Aid box and ask the man at the counter, "What is that kid doing?"

Looking for cigarette butts, the man tells me. "He does it all the time."

"Do you know him?" I ask. "He's from around the lake," I am told. "What lake?"

"I don't know," the man says. "One of them."

At Hickman's IGA, Earl Davis—Freddy's brother—loads groceries, as he has for decades. I think he is wearing the same clothes he wore in high school. The last time I saw Freddy, he was standing in the parking lot behind an insurance office that he cleaned on weekends. I was in college then, lucky enough to have parents who could afford to buy me a little freedom. That summer, I had interned in D.C., where I met someone who meant something to me. Of course I would never have admitted that to anyone, him especially, though in my mind he had become my boyfriend.

"Is it wrong?" Eric asked as he reached for my hand. "No," I said. "It's okay. I like it."

Eric loosened my tie and draped it over the back of the chair. He made me feel taken care of, an unfamiliar thing.

I was working with one of our senators as part of a program for college kids. Twenty years old, I was a little drunk. Eric, who helped supervise our group, was from Cape Cod and looked like a Kennedy. Assessing me, he said I should buy a dark suit. Mine was baby blue; he said I looked ready for the Easter Parade.

I said I was not taking wardrobe advice from anyone in shorts with spouting whales. After deciding I came off as too earnest, I was trying for some edge. He laughed, touched me for just a moment. In his hand, I felt everything waiting.

I had amused him; I saw that, in his opinion, this counted for something. We were suddenly complicit; I wanted to make him laugh again and reach out to me. I always want more of anything good. Immediately, I found myself craving his approval. There was something a little wicked about him. He had a bemused way of looking at people. Like me.

"You're from Missouri," he said. "Show me."

It was a fun game, this exchange, but he was straight. His girlfriend, Binky, from North Carolina, changed the bands of her wristwatch—yellow, blue, pink, and green—to match her outfits. One evening, she led a delegation of southerners in a rendition of "I Like Calling North Carolina Home."

At a cocktail hour at the Watergate, Eric hovered, brought me a drink, refills. When he touched my arm to guide me through the crowd, I wanted him to leave his hand there. Later, my friends and I went for dinner and to the bars. Eric tagged along. At every new place, I hoped that I would find him by my side. "Sit by me," I kept thinking to myself. He did. At every stop.

Binky was gone for the weekend. Since the debacle with the doctor, I had avoided dating, studying nonstop. Huddled over textbooks, I thought of myself as an intellectual, madly highlighting pages in yellow. Sitting in an uncomfortable chair at my first Introduction to Poetry class, I had experienced an epiphany when the professor entered the room and began, with no preamble, to recite a poem by Ezra Pound about a Chinese widow who lost her love. The story begins with the two as shy children pulling flowers, sharing blue plums, "two small people, without dislike or suspicion." As the years pass, they are drawn together, into an arranged marriage that becomes much more.

At fourteen I married My Lord you.
I never laughed, being bashful.
Lowering my head, I looked at the wall.
Called to, a thousand times, I never looked back.

When he departs on a fishing boat, she is filled with sorrow, an emotion that grows year after year when he does not return and her silent mourning increases as the mosses grow over the sidewalk. Finally, an old woman now, still waiting, watching the currents of the river from a widow's walk, she offers a quiet invitation:

If you are coming down through the narrows of the river Kiang,
Please let me know beforehand,
And I will come out to meet you,
As far as Cho-fu-Sa.

It was the holding back, the longing I recognized. Something in me connected to the widow, her sadness, to what had been lost. That day, in that class, I learned words, what happens when they are said out loud, how feelings became real when set against the silence of a clean white page. Something in me broke open, a crack.

I was a journalism major, a would-be reporter who could not bear the thought of calling up grieving widows with questions. As soon as the bell rang, I went off to see my adviser and explore a double major that would allow me to take literature classes.

. . .

Eric took me to his friend's empty dorm room. "I like you," he said as, tentatively, I laid my head on his chest, just where it had wanted to be all night. His smooth, soft neck smelled aftershavey and seemed, when he opened his collar, the most private of places.

He was gentler than I expected, big brothery, and I was surprised by who he turned out to be. He kissed my hands. Lowering my head, I looked at the wall, like the widow in the poem. Suddenly there were too many feelings. I was overwhelmed and wanted to run.

As the hours passed, we became more emotional and connected as we cared for each other. After we finished, we lay there in the hot summer night. When he walked to the closet, I was scared he was about to kick me out, but he made no move. When I had to go to the bathroom, I put on his shorts and took off. His clothes felt good. I ran down the hall excited, jumping up to swat a light fixture; this just seemed like something that needed doing. It seemed like things might turn out okay.

"What's up with Miss North Carolina?" I asked him.

"Just kicking the can," he said. "You know."

Actually, I didn't.

"My parents wouldn't get the gay thing," he said, continuing. "They aren't softies."

I realized that in my haste to make him my protector, I had failed to acknowledge that he wasn't much older than I was. I laid my head on his chest again as we started to fall asleep, but in the morning, I woke up alone. We had moved the beds together, but Eric had scooted his away in the night. The space between them didn't look crossable, but I decided it was okay to hold out my hand. He did not take hold and I started to prepare myself. I knew how it was going to be.

By the time I was out of the shower, he was dialing Binky on the hall phone. I should have known it was coming. Looking for love in the gay world of the late 1970s meant dealing with two things: (a) You are a little fucked up. (b) So is everyone else.

"Sooner or later," he said, "I will have to get married."

"It's okay," I said that morning before we separated. "Don't worry about it."

Later I learned that Eric had a rep for sleeping with many women *and* men. When I saw him around the dorm, he looked and turned away. Our connection scared him, the chemistry. What we had was intense and I wanted more. Intensity was my first addiction. It's like a drug; it takes you out of normal life. I miss the rush of it.

In the days that followed, I showed nothing, barely acknowledged him. One night, he came to stand by me at a gathering where "Miss You" by the Rolling Stones was playing. Mary, a wild girl from Milwaukee, and I sang along every time the line about the Puerto Rican girls *"just dyin' to meet ya"* came on. I thought I couldn't get any cooler, and then Eric—whom I had been doing this whole performance for—was right beside me. "You know Eric, don't you?" I asked Mary. "He dates that girl with the watchbands."

He looked a little wounded, but grinned. Later, when we were leaving, he swatted me on my rear, but he ignored me the rest of the month. I hated it. He was someone who kind of got me.

At the end of my summer, my father picked me up at the airport and hugged me as if I had spent the summer in Arabia. His love was so big and open, but he made me feel guilty and uncomfortable. I didn't want to be back there. When he hugged me, I felt myself going stiff.

On the way home, apparently desperate for tales of pretty girls, he tried to pry me open. I fished for something, but he seemed less interested than me in Binky's watchbands or Jamey—a rich girl from Beverly Hills—and her dazzling array of Diane von Fürstenberg wrap dresses.

"You'll find someone," he said. "You'll get a girlfriend." He was doing that thing, those lines. Of course he would; this was how it was with fathers and sons, but I didn't want to hear it. I didn't want to hear any more about girlfriends. He had to know it wasn't true. But he didn't. It hit me that we were always going to miss out on each other.

He would be disappointed when he discovered that there would be no grandchildren and bereft over what I was giving up. "Having children," he always said, "is the best part of life."

He wanted me to have all the good things. He would be sad to think I was missing out. I would just be one more thing that had not gone quite right for him.

For the rest of the summer, I worked every day with my father at the lumberyard. Until it was time for me to return to school, he seemed to try to reach out when we were alone, but couldn't wrap his fingers around someone so elusive. He tried to find some different way for us to be with each other, but I couldn't go in that direction.

One afternoon, Big George—in a confiding mood—told me that before he met Betty, after he returned from the army, he had been in love with another girl named Betty whom he had planned to marry. She was "a beaut," he said, like a guy in a movie from another time.

But she broke it off. And then he met his Betty, our Betty, the one he drew the sketch of, that young and lovely girl, tentative and uncertain. For years I have searched for that drawing he did as I watched, but it has long been missing. I think she may have found it and disposed of it or tucked it away in some secret place.

On their first date, they went to the old Busch's Grove in St. Louis. He knew that night that he would marry her, he said. He made it into a sentimental story where everything turned out just as it should. "There was something," he said, "a sweetness." She ordered the cheapest thing on the menu. She was nervous. He was glad he had found the right Betty.

My parents married on a scorching St. Louis day in August 1948. A small gathering with a cake from the Lake Forest Bakery. Bill Baker brought Mammy to St. Louis for the wedding in one of his crazy old cars, which broke down around St. Charles. Mammy said she was so hot waiting for Bill to fix that car she thought she was going to "upchuck," a term I have never known used outside my family. Betty was twenty-six, too old, she said, for too fancy a dress or too lavish a ceremony.

Afterward, they went to Chicago for the weekend. Sade Sizer took them to a restaurant with phones on the tables: the Pump Room. Betty called up Mammy and told her she was just about to eat a lobster.

I am standing in front of the church, hoping my mother is doing all right at the piano, that she won't wind up hurt, that she will come out of that church looking like she did when she was younger. At a wedding of a daughter of one of Betty's friends ten or fifteen years or so ago, my mother was maybe seventy-five or a bit older, but looked sixty or less. Big George was gone by then, and Betty, who no longer drove at night, refused to go "in a carload of old widows," so I came home to be her escort. I was having a good streak, making lots of money at a publishing house where my books were hitting big.

So I got on a plane, though I don't much like weddings, which make me feel out of place, especially single.

I told Betty that she looked better, more beautiful than she ever had, but she could not accept this, could not take it in. At the entrance to the cool, candlelit church, she reached out to touch the fresh flowers, in awe at the perfection of the preparations. "Hazel has outdone herself," she said, "spared no expense."

My friend Lauren, who thinks she is Margaret Mead, says that weddings and funerals stir all kinds of things up in us because they are tribal occasions. I am not sure I have a tribe, though I think I have always longed for one.

That night at the wedding, my beautiful mother wore a suit the color of key lime pie, her favorite. She actually seemed to want to have a good time. At the reception, after a few glasses of champagne, she took off her shoes and wandered through the crowd in her stocking feet, greeting old friends. She was swaying, but just barely, when no one was looking, almost dancing to the music. She touched my elbow once to steady herself. "Have you had some champagne?" I asked. "Mind your own business," she said.

"You are my business," I said, as she had always said to me, all my life, in similar exchanges. I wanted her to feel as I did when I heard those words: protected, aligned with someone, connected.

I want her to feel this way now.

Betty always says she misses my aunt June more than almost anyone. I miss her too, and can picture her standing up at her table at that wedding reception, rearranging some flowers in a centerpiece knocked askew, tucking little sacks of rice into her purse. She couldn't walk well anymore, but pushed herself to come, wanting to be part of the occasion, more lavish than most held around here now. Bill had stayed home and June had on a diamond-encrusted brooch in the shape of a large turtle along with her other major gems, the jewelry that Bill rarely allowed her to wear in public.

I wondered if June was imagining what Mary Ann, the daughter she lost, might have looked like as a bride. She looked left out, a little sad. I sometimes avoided my aunt, as she was the type to make reference on such occasions to my unmarried status. Or say something mortifying. I have always hated direct references to my way of being. Betty takes the easy way. Betty asks nothing. I prefer the easy way too, the approach that allows one to ignore every feeling until you are strapped in the back of an ambulance, screaming all the way to Silver Hill.

"I would like to go to your wedding someday," June said to me that evening. I knew it was coming. "I am truly grateful to have had love in my life. I hope you have love in your life." She meant it all with caring, but I couldn't take it. I hoped that no one would ever, ever again make me take them to a wedding. "Don't make me uncomfortable," I wanted to say. June was never one to pick up cues, not surprising. I am often subtle.

The architect who married the guy with the Mohawk, the guy I was crazy about at this time, was on my mind. He had designed a farmhouse near a town on the Hudson for a friend of mine, a fashion writer. I had told her how talented he was, introduced them, essentially convinced her of his talent and got him the commission. I wanted to see the house. I want to see his work, maybe let myself imagine how it would be to live in a place he built, up by the river. I hinted. But he never invited me. After that, my search for companionship just stopped. I shut down without ever realizing it had happened.

For a little moment, I wanted to tell June about this man, wanted to let her know that I had tried to find someone though I really never wanted to be married. That night at the wedding, because I knew the wishes she had for me made her sad, I wanted her to understand that for some of us there is nothing bad in having a less conventional life. I wanted to tell her things I wish I had said to my father. But all I could say was that Hazel wanted her to take home one of the centerpieces.

All around that night at the wedding were people I had grown up with—friends of my parents, our lawyer and accountant, a judge or two, the bridge club ladies, people we had always known from church, those who used to run things around here. All my childhood was gathered around me. This was not just a collection of the elders of Paris, Missouri; it was more to me. It was Bettyville, my mother's home, her place, with most of its surviving souls, those who had known her as a girl and who had been kind to me and watched me grow. They were older suddenly, much older, my people—men in white shoes fit for a bandbox, striped suits from other decades; women in outfits that looked to have been stored away and worn only occasionally—and all I wanted, all of a sudden, was to stay with them forever. I love my town; I love my home. I went from table to table to hug them as the younger guests spilled out of the banquet room into the summer night to dance on the patio. I thought of asking my mother to dance, but did not. My father would definitely have been dancing. But probably not with her. He had given up on things like that many years before. Betty was not a dancing girl.

That night at the wedding where Betty was young again, the bride and groom headed out into the world. Hazel cried, big tears falling on her big, bountiful corsage. "She'll have a hard time letting that one go," remarked June.

"That's the way it is," Betty said. "We're old ladies now."

Overall, the evening seemed a kind of farewell to two women I loved who were leaving nights like this behind. Betty sat beside me, a row of silver bracelets on her wrist, surveying the scene, holding court as people came to greet her. She let some kiss her on the cheek as, behind their backs, she rolled her eyes at me and wrinkled her nose.

On the way home, June praised the festivities, said Hazel had always been the type to "do it up."

"Didn't you see their faces?" June asked my mother. "I know that look," she said as I noticed in the rearview mirror, as the headlights passed, Betty looking amused but fondly at her sister-in-law.

"What do I know?" Betty asked. "I was an old maid."

"But you were so pretty," I reminded her. "Lots of men must have asked you out."

"I didn't fall into all of that so easily," she said.

When we pulled into June's driveway, Bill's face was in the window, waiting, on guard for the arrival of his wife, eager to help her out of the car and usher her safely back into their home. Bill didn't like to let June out of his sight after it got harder for her to get around.

"You okay, my dear?" he asked as he opened the passenger door, looking at me as if I could barely be trusted to get anyone back from a wedding without broken bones.

Bill Baker, when discharged from the navy, was unwilling to pay for train or bus fare. He hitchhiked from San Francisco to Missouri with the mumps. My picture of Bill is a young man, sick and running a fever, sticking his thumb up by the side of the road in some unfamiliar place.

Bill Baker was never satisfied that he had properly appeased his lord, the God of Hard Labor.

In March or April, ten years or so ago, one of the first warm days: Bill was clearing away things at an old building he owned. June, a few blocks away at home, was cooking his lunch when, without Bill's noticing, the fire from the trash hit something flammable. A blaze began, spreading rapidly. Bill started to choke in the smoke; he couldn't see clearly or get out. During his attempts to escape, his hands and arms were badly burned. The fire even singed his face, and as he lost his balance and fell, he suffered a heart attack and died. I went to the funeral for June's sake. Bill and I had barely spoken during the previous few years. He had stopped addressing me at family gatherings, wouldn't look me in the eye. On the phone, when I tried to engage him, he said almost nothing. Once he told me explicitly, "You don't have to come to my funeral."

I didn't, in the moment when he said that, feel anything. I was a master at monitoring reactions, not having them. I wished he hadn't said it, but I knew why he did. When I was driving June home from somewhere, she pointed out the home of friends, people who had done business with Bill for years. "Their son died of AIDS. Bill wouldn't go to the funeral," June said, "but I did."

In his casket, Bill was outfitted in white gloves to camouflage the burns on his hands. After his funeral in Mexico, we went to Madison, where he was to be interred, and all the cars on the other side of the highway turned on their headlights to salute the hearse, something that is always done here. It was a rainy day and there was more than the usual traffic and it seemed to me that the trail of passing headlights went on for a mile or more as we drove past the fields, too wet and muddy for the farmers to get in and plant yet. In Madison, as June stepped out of the hearse, a man who had worked for my uncle for years at Mexico Equipment told her he thought he would never hear tell of Bill Baker riding in back of a black Cadillac with white gloves on.

I carried in the centerpiece for June, that night after the wedding. She had grown attached to it, as if it were the bride's bouquet and she had been the one to catch it. All I could think of that night was what would become of my mother and aunt. That the time was coming. It was my turn to step up. I told myself that whatever happened, I would do this one thing right, better than I had ever tried to do anything. Because even though my life was different, I wanted a place in the tribe. I still do.

Across the street from our church is the undertaker's. As I wait for the end of the service to go into the sanctuary and help my mother gather up her music, I realize that the boy who was murdered in Mammy's house may be lying inside. In the house on Olive Street where the shots were fired and the young man died, Mammy and her kids played cards in the kitchen and ate popcorn. They loved a game called rook. According to Miss Virginia, Betty had a fit if she didn't win. "No one could tell Betty Baker what to do. She'd fly out and slam the door hard enough to be heard all over the neighborhood. Then came Harry, running out to chase her with Bill running behind him. Then came Marge. All four of them would be chasing each other around the house and I'd think, 'Well, I guess Betty didn't win the card game.' "

A few years ago, it became apparent that my mother's boyfriend, John, a diabetic, couldn't really take care of himself and Betty couldn't see to everything. He moved to Monroe Manor, and although I took them out for steaks when I came home, Betty knew that their time was over. Last winter he had a stroke and died about a week later. My mother said his death was a blessing, a mercy. Bob, his dog, the beautiful German shorthair that my mother had fallen in love with, had gone to live with some people on a farm on the highway outside town. Betty worried about him, out there on the highway. Dogs that live by roads don't fare so well here where the cars and trucks whoosh by without paying much attention to animals in their way.

Betty took him bones and scraps, even on bad winter days, and never complained when he jumped up to greet her with his dirty paws. Then one night, after John was gone, in the midst of a terrible winter, my mother called to tell me that Bob had died. He had gotten loose from his pen and wandered into the woods and somehow frozen to death. There we were, my mother and I on the phone, not crying, but knowing that if we were people who cried, we would be doing it at that moment.

"They say that freezing is the easiest way to go," I told her.

"Maybe," she said, "I will just lie down in the snow."

After John died, Betty told everyone she was okay, but she could not seem to rouse herself. Maybe he was more to her than I realized or than she could ever admit. Gradually, she went to the couch, stopped getting dressed, lost heart. In public and at family dinners, she had nothing to say. She was simply not herself. When I saw her begin to change, to leave us, I started coming home on visits that became more and more extended.

After waiting for a few minutes, I see people coming down the church steps and I go in to gather up Betty's music and help her to the car. On the way back to the house, I ask how it went, and she shakes her head. "Fine," she says. That is all she will reveal. "Fine." But she is subdued and I can't tell whether it's because of how she played or whether she is still upset about our battle over the newspaper clipping the day before.

I apologize again to her. "Do you want me to just treat you like some old lady who no one can hold responsible for anything or get mad at?" I ask. "Is that what you want? You have your struggles, but you have to realize there are other people. I'm here too, you know."

Her eyes widen as she takes this in. "No," she said, "I have to be held to account, I guess. You're right to hold me to account."

I am still not convinced she didn't throw away the clipping on purpose. I know she hates me sometimes. How could she not? I am the guard at the prison she will never get out of. Sometimes I am just as pent up and angry. I loathe her too. Just a typical American family, torn between love and homicide, but united in our way.

"I'll bet you did fine," I tell her. "I'll bet you sounded great."

But I cannot be certain if she did okay and I don't want to hear if she has had trouble or hit a lot of wrong notes. I don't want to lose the part of my mother I hear when she is playing the piano, her soft touch, the sweet music. I think that when she pulls the cover over the keys for the last time, all of this will be very hard to find.

14

Headed to the dog pound—a small, fenced-in area with a couple of cubbyholes for shelter and room for a few animals—I pass the spot where the city pool was, near the place where they hold the county fair, complete with livestock shows. I groomed no cattle, but was a life-guard at the pool, which twenty or so years back was filled in because of filter problems. I ruled from my elevated chair, watching the boys and sending girls to the penalty box if I disliked their swimwear. *"Do not come near me, young missy, in that little poncho with happy faces."*

For the lonely dog, I have brought a stewlike concoction, but they have mended the hole in the fence and I can't slide food or pie plates under the wire. The animals are not actually supposed to be fed; people poison them sometimes. I throw turkey dogs over the fence. Next the Milk-Bones go flying.

My car has become a canine supply station. In the event of disaster, I could feed and nurture a pack of huskies. At PetSmart, I couldn't resist a winter coat for dogs made from bright orange fabric that glows in the dark. It reminds me of an ensemble worn annually at Christmas by one of my high school teachers.

In the backseat of our old Infiniti, sacks of rawhide chews are stowed alongside shopping bags overflowing with balls and treats, a huge sack of grain-free puppy mix, and a bunny toy that reminds me of Wesley Brown, who used to help Mammy in her garden. A strange man with a speech impediment, Wesley lived in a shack with an overgrown yard and kept hundreds of rabbits in battered hutches. Some of the creatures were older, big, and menacing. But my stuffed fellow does not look threatening and I may keep him. He doesn't deserve to be chewed.

The dog is dancing, making his yodeling noises, madly scurrying about. As he vomits up large chunks of turkey dog, I tell him things are looking up. Marci Bennett, who I have known forever, wants to take him. I am relieved, but resentful. I love this pup and he should be mine. Before Marci popped up, I could keep my fantasy. But it had to end. We would never work. I can't commit. Not the way my life is now. He knows that I am about to desert him, barks and barks, eyes me suspiciously, particularly after the turkey dogs. Or perhaps it is the fact that I am clutching my bunny.

My friend Lauren says that people who are emotionally reserved—frigid and icy, I believe she is implying—often lavish their feelings on dogs. She cites the English, well-known canine enthusiasts, and points out my English heritage. I feel like Camilla Parker-Bowles. *"Charles, don't worry about making it back tonight. Mummy's having gin fizzes with the corgis."*

I want to hug my dog, but suddenly I am angry, so mad at him, and want to get out of here. Nothing upsets me more than feeling myself lacking. "Shut up," I yell. "Shut up, shut up, shut up." As he looks at me, astonished, I stomp back to the car with my bags of animal products and my bunny. I do not say good-bye. I cannot keep a dog.

As far as relationships go, I have a small, checkered past that began in college when I tried and failed to do what people do: come together in harmony and then learn gradually to ignore each other.

Senior year in college, I moved into a small apartment with my first real boyfriend, Steven, who trimmed his beard meticulously each morning, listening to the *Evita* sound track and pretending to address the people of Argentina from a balcony. He cooked all the time, fed me like a mother. Sourdough bread was his specialty. He gave loaves to everyone. He was so giving. It made me sick sometimes. "Enough with the bread,"

I thought. It embarrassed me. Nobody else seemed to care, though Betty winced at his neatly wrapped loaves, handled them as if they might explode. She always thanked him politely, but there was a hint of something else. "It's sour dough, you say?"

"It's one word, Mother."

Steven seemed oblivious. He never bowed down to win over my mother. He never appeared to care so much what others thought.

"Try some of this," the person doling out samples at the supermarket asked Steven, innocently holding out a plate of something, sausages or couscous. Whatever.

"George would never eat that. George is finicky," Steven would respond as, a few feet away, I braced myself for what was coming.

"Who's George?"

"George is my LOVERRRRRRRR!"

They could have heard him in Cleveland.

But no. That wasn't really how it was. He was warm; he was friendly. He was proud to be with me. And no one looked up, or noticed, or really cared what we were doing together. It just felt like that to me. Because when you have a secret, you think the world is watching your every move, trying to discover it, and that changes everything—the way you think, and look at people, the things you are willing to do, the places you can go, the reactions you expect. You aren't quite there. Hiding the secret is what is always on your mind, somewhere. You feel better alone.

I felt better alone, but I was with him, and that made everything complicated. There was too much going on inside for me to really be with anyone. Always something ticking, ticking, ticking inside me, almost drowning out everything else.

The little stuffed bunny, perched on the dashboard of my car, has turned malevolent, like a toy in a *Twilight Zone* episode. It eyes me. "Take the fucking dog," he seems to say as I roar away from the pound in a cloud of dust.

. . .

I wasn't ready to be so public. Steven was. Approximately twenty thousand hearings of a double-disc soundtrack featuring Patti LuPone does not lead to diffidence. It seemed to me that he told everyone everything. The mailman knew if we were fighting. The landlord got an earful. Thinking himself in store for a pleasant morning of toilet repair, the unsuspecting man was showered with details of our meeting, our backgrounds, the fact that we were both Aquarians.

And then he got a loaf.

Every time my mother came, I fell into a state of anxiety, just waiting for him to blurt out something to Betty. Probably about my troubles with sex. I was nervous. I was messy. If I managed to successfully uncap a tube of lubricant, the entire household was ready for penetration in about five minutes.

Steven was concerned that I wasn't out to my parents. It was an affront to him, to truth and honesty, to "the movement."

"Shut up about the movement," I told him. "Be still. Listen to *Evita*. Argentina is crying."

He was loving and sweet, giving and generous, but it always felt like he was pressing against me, too close. He wanted me to tell him I loved him; every day he needed it, sometimes more than once or even twice. I saw the statement as more of a specialty item to be bestowed a few times yearly, perhaps at birthday time or during the excited unpacking of a Christmas stocking.

I felt bad most of the time, cold and heartless. What I really wanted, I told myself, was out of the relationship. But I knew that word he made me say, the one that began with *L* and ended with my feeling hemmed in and embarrassed, was not just something I was dredging up to please him.

During part of my time with Steven, I was employed on campus at the career counseling center, where my boss, Mary (aka Pinky), was completing a doctorate in psychology. "Do you have an issue with this?" she kept asking me. "Do you have an issue with that?" Narrow-shouldered and small-breasted, Pinky tried so hard to get next to me. "I just want to feel you out on this," she would say. "I just want to feel you out!" I often felt violated.

The center was staffed by psych majors and other kinds of counselors who wanted us to learn to communicate effectively with the clients and one another. At retreats, we talked things out with empty chairs as our colleagues listened. Even my chair wanted more from me than I could give. Folding chairs: They had some nerve. I could have taken criticism better from a recliner, even an ottoman.

It was a touchy-feely place, but I was only touchy. I failed to mention to Pinky that I was gay, though of course she knew. It wasn't that I thought her unsympathetic. I just didn't want to talk about it. Our absence of meaningful communication was working beautifully until the day Steven bounded through the doors, looking for a résumé critique. He spotted me, gave me a hug.

Pinky's head, small in size to fit with the rest of her upper body, popped up as if from a burrow. She spotted Steven. Like Evita and Juan or Masters and Johnson, they came together as I saw the future and cringed.

Pinky said she found their chat "illuminating." Steve began to ask about how I felt about everything. "What does everyone expect of me?" I asked over and over. Finally, I just asked Steve, "Why do you care about me? What do I give you?"

"You always make me laugh," he said. "You even make the bed funny. I come home and see the way you've tried to push the sheets up under the mattress and, I don't know, I want to hug you."

Wait, I thought, until you see the ironing.

He was so good. I was so hard. I vowed to try. I talked to Pinky and to almost all her office furniture. The couch and I got down to brass tacks.

But Steve began sleeping around. Monogamy was for heteros. It was 1980. The gays in San Francisco were getting it on in supermarkets.

Steve wasn't going to be left out. I knew that I was. People approached Steven; men were drawn to him. I was harder to approach and wasn't good at instigating a pickup.

Pinky called me into her office one day and closed the door. I thought I was being fired. "Are we going to do the chair thing?" I asked. "No," she said. "Honey, I want to go personal." She reached out and put her hand over mine. "I think," she said, "that you have some self-esteem issues. I don't think you like yourself so much." From here on out, through decades, from the lips of many well-intentioned others, these words would come back and back and back.

"I didn't know I was supposed to like me. Isn't that like being arrogant?"

She stared at me.

"I'm sorry," I told her.

I have worked myself into a state about the dog. I need a brownie. Last night I made a panful, but they are all gone. Every one. Betty has given them to Earleen, she tells me with a glint in her eye. She is afraid I'm getting fat. The brownies have joined the ranks of The Disappeared. It started with the clipping. What will come next?

I retaliate. When Betty goes to the bathroom, I grab a spoon and last night's chocolate pie from the refrigerator, go into my room, shut the door, and lock it. She may magically materialize. Sometimes I think she can walk through walls.

I eat the pie like someone is going to yank it away, straight from the dish, wiping the last bits of chocolate from the dish with my fingers. She has eaten the lion's share already, but my taking the rest will be seen as a serious offense. All her life, Betty was a fashionably slender woman. For decades she held back, didn't touch a dessert or a slice of bread. Now she eats ravenously, especially sweets, which she craves like an addict.

Midmornings, I catch her standing at the window in front of the sink, gobbling up whatever she can find. If someone mentions food, she wants some. If I get something from the refrigerator, she wants some too. "What are you eating?" she asks repeatedly. "What did you have to eat?" She must know. We are ravenous here.

I am gaining weight. This morning I awoke with a bee in my bonnet over the bare torso selfies the gays post on Facebook. In my opinion, if you post more than three photos a week of your naked chest, you had better be part of some emergency rash-alert squad.

My new girth angers Betty. It reminds her of my father, who got heavy. I've started drinking some powdered greenish stuff that you mix in water, which Carol sells. Called moringa oleifera, it is supposed to suppress appetite and provide super-duper nutrition. African villages apparently swear by it. Today, so far, I have had four packets and six cups of coffee. I am in the mood to build some huts, or perhaps shoot a wildebeest. Later I may barbecue a missionary or two for the tribal elders.

I can't stop thinking about the dog. I am tired of having nothing.

Against my better judgment, I once brought Steven home for the weekend. He had demanded it, wanted to get to know my parents.

Before dinner, I smoked a joint in the basement while he, ignoring my amorous inclinations, perused everything stored there. Earlier he had complimented Betty on her antiques, on her upholstery, on the chairs in our living room that, thank God, said nothing to anyone.

From anyone else, she would have liked the attention.

Him she just ignored.

At the supper table, Steven and my father talked beard maintenance. Daddy had recently grown a beard, which Betty hated, a fact that pleased him. During this chat, Betty banged pots and pans like a drunk in a truck-stop kitchen. "Steven made this bread," she said as she plunked a platter of it—not sliced but yanked apart—on the table. I worried that she had connected the dots about Steven and me. How could she have missed it? But they seemed to know and not know, accept and reject. I tried to find some tiny place between honesty and comfort where I could just be peaceful.

"It's sour dough," my mother said of the bread, breaking, as I recall, the word into two, like always.

"It's one damn word," I mouthed to her silently, but she was off and running.

"You know, Steven," she said, "I never eat bread and neither should my husband. I have to watch what he eats. He has a heart problem. It is extremely serious"

"It's just undiagnosed," I explained to Steven. Whatever her apparent diffidence, my mother had long been the protector of my father's vulnerable heart.

That registered.

"Later," my mother mouthed silently across the table. We have always had our best chats like this.

My father grabbed hunks of the bread, one after another. He wouldn't stop eating the bread. As my mother stared, he stared right back, savoring every bite.

After dinner, we adjourned to the guest room where Steven was to sleep on one of my mother's most uncomfortable antiques—a creaky bed with a wafer-thin mattress dating back to the Civil War. I was embarrassed. Late that night, my father, in his underwear and demonstrating my family's continuing tendency to appear out of nowhere at the worst possible moments, caught us making out on the couch in the family room. Adopting our usual stance toward anything out of the ordinary, he had said nothing as I waited, anticipating the cardiac event that Betty had predicted.

At breakfast the next morning, after he saw Steven and me together, Daddy was quiet, not especially upset or especially friendly.

He was just blank, as if a lightning strike had left him . . . absent.

A few months later, all four of us were together again, on the afternoon of our graduation, drinking champagne at the apartment Steven and I shared. Before we left for commencement, my father kept getting up to look around the apartment. He lingered in both bedrooms, the one crammed with stuff with its double bed and the other with the tiny, narrow bed where, I hoped they believed, Steven slept.

My mother was calm that day, almost sentimental as she brushed crumbs off the shoulders of my suit and looked at me as if she could not fathom the speed at which I was traveling away. She smiled at me tentatively, as if expecting some sort of rejection, as if she were about to discover that I had somehow moved beyond her. She always believed that people who lived in other places or traveled more were bound to reflect her. That fall I would go to Boston, to graduate school. When I had told my mother about this, she was quiet, just shook her head. "Well then," she said. "Good. You need to get out of here. I can send you a check now and then."

That afternoon, after commencement, my father just could not stay in his chair. He seemed interested in every detail in our place, determined to uncover any clue he could find to the life of his son. When I walked into the bathroom, Big George was there, spraying a bit of Steven's Royal Copenhagen cologne on his fingers. Rubbing them together, as if he were wary of actually taking a sniff, he caught a glance of me behind him in the mirror over the sink. My face reddened as our eyes met in the mirror that Steven always kept so clean.

That night we had dinner with some of my friends and their parents. There was the feel of a festive evening, though I was nervous and just wanted to get it over with. We arrived at the restaurant, the best in town, before anyone else, and my father went to the bar. As my mother headed toward the bathroom, he began the process of slamming down four gin and tonics one after the other. He drank quickly, downing each in an instant.

At dinner, my mother sat up in her chair, growing stiffer and stiffer, her hand occasionally wandering to her head to secure an errant lock. The restaurant was filled with laughter, the cheerful noises of special occasions. In the corner of the room, a young man played cocktail piano. Not songs, just riffs. Before the dinner was over, my father, less gregarious than usual, got up, red-faced, and threw off his jacket. Then, moving to the side of the piano, he began, to the astonishment of his unwitting accompanist, to sing his song: "Old Man River."

He sang as if the restaurant were his. He sang as if all the guests at Jack's Coronado Steak House had bought tickets for this occasion. He sang emotionally, his waves of feeling flowing through us all. The river rolled on and on, like time and change and all we might hold back if it were possible.

My emotion built with his every word and breath. The song, it seemed, lasted forever, my father's voice growing louder as he held out his hand, I believe, to me. Betty looked down at her unfinished food. When he finished, the room exploded with applause. That evening, my father was the star. Steven stood up to clap and my mother kicked him—hard.

It was a mysterious performance. I didn't know whether to consider it a blessing, a resentful usurping of the prominence of others that evening, or a crying out as the river's waters swept me from his world, his extended hand, the place where it was possible for him to try to save me.

15

When you think about your mother, what do you remember?" my therapist asked. "Do you think you disappointed her? Do you ever feel guilty?" I told him this story.

When I was a kid, before I went to sleep, before she turned off the light, Betty reached for my book and closed it, took my glasses off, folded them, laid them on the table, and took my hand.

Then, closing our eyes, we said the "Now I Lay Me" prayer out loud, adding a list of blessings for those who needed them. Together, we named the names, always beginning with Mammy, Granny, Aunt Bess, and Aunt Winnie. We turned it into a sort of game: Making our way through Madison, from one street to the next, we asked for help for those suffering in this place or that, for people who were poor or who had lost someone, or those who had found themselves in trouble. We traveled through town, saying name after name.

"Just think of all of us together, all over town, asking help for each other," Betty said. "Try to think of the people who have no one else to remember them."

"Does it work?" I asked.

"It is something we can do for each other. Bow your head now, bow your head. Maybe there is nothing else, but we can do this for people. We can remember them when they are sick and remember them when they go. We have to understand we are all together here. We have to try and help people."

If there was a time when I heard my mother say what it was she believed in, what she stood for, it was at these moments. Betty always wanted to try to rescue people who were sick or alone, to do whatever she could for those who had no one. She called and checked on those she barely knew when they came out of the hospital or if they were ill. She worried about people who were out there on their own. The worst thing she could imagine was being sick and alone.

One night, I decided it was time that I said my prayers without my mother. It was after one of her eye surgeries and I was scared she was going blind. I wanted to ask God to look out for her and it seemed she should not be present. I didn't want to make her think of what might happen to her. The idea of praying for her in her presence was embarrassing to me.

When I told Betty that I needed to say my prayers on my own, her face changed. She dropped my glasses on the table and looked down at her lap before pulling away. I wanted to take it back, but it was too late, she was gone. She left so fast. She didn't bring it up, but the next night she did not come to my room. Never again would we have our special time. She would not risk being sent away again. I grew up to be just like her. Like my mother, I flee at the slightest suggestion I am unwanted.

I was twenty-four, finished with grad school in Boston, new to New York, with no job. A few weeks before, I had found myself sitting in the lobby of a building on East Thirty-second Street, about to meet this man, this therapist who could supposedly help me. My friends were all employed and my afternoons were hard to fill. It was late fall 1983. I was living in Carroll Gardens, a Brooklyn neighborhood that felt like a small Italian town. Sports bars played Connie Francis and Sinatra singing "Luck Be a Lady." Our landlord was named Carrado Carbone. There were dozens of bakeries that sold beautifully decorated cookies that all tasted terrible. In the apartment I shared with three Californians, a previous tenant appeared to have done engine work in the bathtub, which was smeared with black.

I wanted to be an editorial assistant at Knopf or Random House. Dressed in my suit and scuffed wingtips, between interviews I set up a sort of office in the lobby of the Waldorf Astoria, where instead of proofreading my résumé I found myself scoping out the bar to see if any of the women were prostitutes. My first interview was at Random House, where a senior editor named Joe Fox, a gentlemanly sort, asked what subjects I intended to make my specialty. I said, "Fiction and nonfiction."

He smiled and said, "No, that is too general. You are supposed to say something like sports."

I was crestfallen and beginning to perspire, fearful of leaving sweat prints on the upholstery. I said, "Not sports."

He said, "I do sports."

I said, "I swim like a fish."

He said, "You remind me of Truman Capote."

Although I had in the previous weeks spent hours in front of Tiffany with a cinnamon roll or two, I considered this a private matter.

"Does Truman swim?"

My interviews were all failures. Every time I tried to impress someone, I left myself, abandoned ship— the old problem, and it still happened on dates. At a party, a friend gave me the card of a gay therapist. She said I needed help adjusting.

"To what?" I asked.

"Everything," she said.

Aside from Pinky, I had never been counseled, though my handwriting had been analyzed by the mother of a friend of mine, an extremely slender woman from Los Angeles who practiced something she referred to as grapho-therapeutics.

"There is fear here," Mrs. Asher had determined after examining my signature.

I just could not get a job. "Come home," my father said on the phone.

Not Betty. She held firm. She knew how much I wanted to make it in New York. "Don't be a quitter," she said. "I'm putting my foot down on this. Do not come back here with your tail between your legs. Something will happen. I have told everyone at bridge you are working there. When was the last time you got your hair cut?

"Don't give up," she whispered before hanging up the phone after my father had already gone off to bed.

My counselor in New York, Paul Giorgianni, asked about my family, my life, my feelings, sex life, vices. When he asked if I used drugs, I said only when they were available. He asked if they were a problem. I said not for me. He said I should not use them as an avoidance. Why else I would use them?

"You don't have to entertain me," he said.

"Then what are you paying me for?"

"You are hiding from your feelings."

"Can you teach me how to hide a little better?"

"Why did you come here?"

"Lobby art."

"Why did you come here?"

"Because I can't get a job." I explained that I could not get through an interview and that I kept making a fool of myself on dates. "I lose myself," I told him. "I go away. I can't be there when I need to be. I go away."

It all came out. "You know that cat in the cartoons that gets scared and winds up clinging with his paws to the ceiling? I feel like I am up there, upside down, barely hanging on and there is just the shell of me in the chair, looking desperate. Can you help me not go away?"

He was Freud. I was Dora. He was Dr. Wilbur. I was Sybil. He gave me a discount, and, considering my estimated neurosis-per-dollar ratio, it seemed a deal.

"How long will it take to stop this from happening?" I kept asking him. He didn't know. "Can't we please hurry?" I asked.

Just before Christmas, I actually got a job at a place called Yourdon

Press where they published books about systems analysis. When I read the ad, I thought that was health-related. Something to do with kidneys.

My job was writing advertising and catalog copy. My computer went down about every fourteen seconds. In the corner of my screen: a tiny picture of a tiny man in a tiny boat. When things were purring along, he smiled. When technical disaster struck, he frowned. It seemed that every time my fingers neared the keyboard, his expression changed to that of a *Titanic* passenger. Constantly I found myself on the phone, pleading, "Please send the fixer man!" The IT specialist and I became so well acquainted we could certainly have adopted a child.

At night I wrote letters, sent résumés to real publishing houses, got some interviews, and finally secured a new job, not in books, but writing pamphlets for a Wall Street firm. My boss—a young Harvard guy from Cleveland—was good to me. "Why did you hire me?" I asked one day. "I don't know a bull from a bear." Looking out of his glass-partitioned office at the collection of middle-aged men on the other side, he said, "Look at them. They are boring. Your job is to talk to me about the movies. You are interesting."

"Sometimes I think so," I said, "and sometimes I don't."

At the beginning in New York, while my roommates, who were straight, had dates, I went to Uncle Charlie's, a gay bar on Greenwich Avenue. Although the guys still laughed and drank; although Madonna kept on pushing her love over the Borderline, it was the beginning of AIDS, wartime. The newspapers were filled with photos of men with lesions from Kaposi's sarcoma. Reality had turned on us; we were very young but it didn't matter. At Yourdon Press, a woman joked, "Who will do my hair?"

"Maybe," I replied, "it's your chance for a makeover."

By the time I heard the fourth or fifth person my age say they did not expect to be alive in a year, I had stopped going to Uncle Charlie's. For a while, I avoided all gay men. As the disease got closer and closer, I began once more to pray before I went to sleep every night. I said the prayer that

Betty and I had said, way back. It was just a child's prayer, but that was how I felt, like a kid far from home.

It was a fast shot to this new place; it was such a fast shot from being young and hopeful to young and thinking about dying. I was twenty-three years old.

The disease was all we talked about and all we didn't talk about. I didn't know if I was sick, but all I could think of was George and Betty finding out not only that I was gay, but also that I was dying. It would kill them and they would be disgraced: I was not even certain that the people in Paris would hold my funeral in the church. Someone told me that back in Missouri, in Columbia, where I had gone to the university, a woman had circulated a petition to drive some gay men from her neighborhood. In the newspapers, there were stories of parents who sent their sick sons away and religious groups who screamed of God's wrath. I knew my parents would care for me until I died, but every day, every minute, looking at their faces would be worse than dying alone. I decided not to tell them if I got sick. I would write them a letter for them to find later, a message saying I did not mean to hurt them, that I loved them.

Again and again, I tried to start this letter, just in case. It would be easier to write beforehand than from a hospital bed. When it was finally finished, I left the envelope on my bureau, glanced at it some mornings as I thought of my mother at home, sitting at the breakfast table reading the bridge hands in the *Globe-Democrat,* adjourning to the bathroom for a secret cigarette. Reopening the letter many times, I subtracted, edited, threw in some jokes so they would think I was able to laugh in my last days. I wanted to leave them something to keep. I wanted to remind them that I was more than someone who died of sex.

I thought of my father; he would have no friends to talk to if I died. There were the men he played golf with, the women who sang with him in the choir at church. Maybe they would be kind to him. More likely, they would not know what to say. There would be no one to help him understand. When I thought about my parents, I felt ashamed. They suddenly seemed so vulnerable to me. I did not want to cause them pain, but all over the city of New York, mothers and fathers were crying.

My friend Ned, who was older than I, seemed to know only dying men. Visiting a friend of his, Kevin Hayne, in the hospital, I held Kevin's hand while the nurse tried and tried to find a usable vein for his IV. The needle hurt every time she jabbed him and he cried out. His thin white arm was a long history of sharp, hasty stabbings. When she finally succeeded and hit a vein, he screamed out loud and it seemed to me that his pain flowed through his fingers into me, like a shock wave. I yelled too, and ran to the bathroom, trembling. I wanted to get out of there. But he could not. So I could not. I hoped he would not die that night with just the two of us there. I had no idea who to call.

It was a Sunday night. On the subway, the 2 or 3 train, I remember black women in their church hats coming back to Brooklyn from uptown, Harlem. In the Clark Street station in Brooklyn Heights, a row of grimy homeless men. At home I threw up and did not close my eyes until I fell asleep in my cubicle at work the next day. My boss just let me be, and when I woke up, everyone was gone except him. He was there, at his desk behind the glass, waiting to ride back to Brooklyn with me on the F train. I never outed myself at work, never ever talked about my personal life; I did not think that this was considered appropriate. All around were married men with shiny shoes who talked about women and money, rich young guys from Long Island who did coke and got quiet when I appeared in the doorway. But my supervisors understood who I was and what was going on out there. They were kind, but that confused me. I have always felt immediate reciprocation necessary with every form of giving. Never have I been willing to owe anything to anyone. People being nice made me uncomfortable.

Rapidly, Kevin was transformed into an elderly man with a curved back who always seemed on the verge of tears. He referred to his mode of transportation to and from the hospital as "My Beautiful Ambulette."

When he died, I didn't have much time to take it in. Steven, who had also moved to the city, had found out he was positive for HIV. If he had it, I thought it inevitable that I did too, but I felt nothing for a while. I was numb. As I had on the football field in high school, I disconnected somehow, put the feelings somewhere they couldn't get me, ran from the pictures that came into my mind, shoved it all in a box in my head that I tried to keep sealed. But every time I did anything, I asked myself, "Is this the last time I'll see a movie?" or "Is this the last time I'll eat roast beef?" I told no one because I could not imagine anyone who wanted to know.

I didn't want to know. I tried to avoid going home unless it was Christmas. Parents and family were not people I wanted to gaze upon.

Steven's new boyfriend got him into one of the best doctors in the city, but I still called him every morning, to make sure he knew I was on his side and to make certain that he was still there at his desk, where he should be. He had to stay in place. I could not watch him fall. Things were going so fast, there was no way to take in what was going to happen to Steven or what was going to happen at all. Kevin was down. Tim went down. Bill went down. Jim went down. Richard went down. He was the nicest man I ever knew.

There was nothing to be done. We just watched them disappear. I had heard of the Catholic tradition of lighting candles for the sick and to bless the dying. After work every few weeks or so I went to Saint Patrick's, paid a dollar for each of the flat round pieces of wax, and lit the candles in the dim light of the huge church. As Betty and I had walked through Madison naming names, so now I walked through Carroll Gardens, and Park Slope, and the Village, and the Upper West Side, asking for help for my friends.

In Missouri, almost every gay man I knew went down: John, who sold me button-fly Levi 501s; John, the hairdresser with an A-frame overlooking the river; Jim, the one everyone wanted. Maybe the biggest shock to some of my friends was the fact that even beauty was no protection.

Before I came to New York, I had taken a summer course in how to get a job in book publishing. The man who ran it was shy, extremely closeted, and eccentric, despite his great desire to be interesting, a quest that took him to many of the world's less traveled places. Maybe he could be himself only when he was far from home.

Two years or so after we had moved to New York, he came to a party in Carroll Gardens. It went on late and I went to bed before some people left. In the morning, I woke to find him sitting on my bed next to me, his warm hand on my bare back. Not long after that, he disappeared. We asked around, but no one could ever discover what became of him.

In the spring of my first year in the city, my parents arrived for a visit. I wanted it to be as memorable as I could make it because I didn't know what the future was going to bring or if I would ever make it home again. For weeks, my mother called to find out our plans so that she could pack the right things. She worried over her outfits, planned to bring her best suits and jewelry. There was discussion of blouses, bracelets. Although my father didn't seem especially excited, Betty asked me over and over where we would go, whether we could see the Plaza or the place where they did *The Today Show,* if we would make it to Barneys, which someone was always talking about on television. After I told her that the women in New York tended to wear black, she purchased a chic raincoat in that shade.

At the airport, standing by the baggage claim in that coat, she looked like a New York lady who could hold her own with anyone, a Wall Street woman or someone successful, just back from a business trip. But when we stepped out into the taxi line, the clouds opened and it poured. Betty was frantic. "But you have a raincoat on," I reminded her.

"I know," she answered, "but I don't want it to actually get rained on. You didn't tell me it was going to rain."

"I predict the weather now?"

"You knew."

That night we went to see, appropriately, *Sunday in the Park with*

George, and before the theater met Steven, who wanted to see them. He had taken up with an anesthesiologist and was living on the Upper West Side with him and a remarkably large Tamara de Lempicka. He couldn't wait to tell my parents that he lived with a doctor. After he had shared the news, my mother looked down at her hands and said, "Well, that will be handy if you get sick." Steven stared across the table, looking frightened for a second. "She means like with a cold is all," I said.

My parents weren't crazy about the show, but at the end there was an extraordinary song called "Sunday," sung by the entire cast. It was the real thing, the goose bump experience, hitting somewhere between jubilation and sorrow, instilling a little of both. One voice—a woman who it seemed was trained for the opera—soared over all the rest, and the first time I heard her, bringing the humor and its emotion further, I took my father's hand and squeezed it. Leaning over, I whispered to him, "This would not be the time to sing along."

During the two previous hours, through all the songs and the changing of the sets, and the intermission when my mother watched the many glamorous people, I wondered if we would ever sit in another theater together or if there would be another trip, or if they would ever recover if I died. I wondered if my father would ever sing again.

The next day they visited our apartment in Brooklyn. On the subway, I told Betty there were hookers at the Waldorf. "What did they look like?" she wanted to know. "I'll bet there are some on this train right now. We'd never know." We met my roommates, had coffee and sweet rolls. The blackened tub was a concern. I said it had been painted after a gangster was shot there.

Basically, they thought the entire apartment seemed like a potential crime scene. My father, always concerned about my living in New York—a place where he felt certain I would get hurt in some way—looked around and asked, "So this is how you want to live?"

Betty was less concerned. "Things are different here. Let him go," she said. "Let him go."

She glanced at me as if he just couldn't understand city people like ourselves. She was in an excited, festive mood and wanted to get out of Brooklyn as soon as possible. She was determined to shop. That afternoon at Saks, because I wanted her to have something to remember the trip and maybe me, I bought her a blue St. John knit sweater with black-and-white stripes on the collar, paying with money she had sent the week before. She bought me some Giorgio Armani pants. "The way they're cut," she said, "you won't want to gain a pound."

At Saks, Betty stopped at every floor, looked over what seemed like every piece of women's apparel, eyed every New York woman as if she wanted to know everything about her life. My mother always loses track of time in department stores, but this time it was worse. "I just want to see everyone. It's Saturday afternoon. That girl looks like the one on *L.A. Law.*"

"I love a tall woman," a clerk told Betty as she lingered over some dresses. Betty was ecstatic. I didn't say that my mother had spent her whole life trying to look shorter, hated being taller than all the women and many of the men. "The models are all tall," the clerk said.

"I've heard a lot of them are foreign," Betty replied.

When my mother shopped in St. Louis, at Stix or Famous-Barr, or Montaldo's, or Saks, Mammy was in her mind as she searched for hours, hunting out the bargains, looking for outfits. Time and again, Betty brought home clothes from the city, unwrapped and carefully unfolded them, tried them on in front of the mirror, frowned at herself, walked through the halls in them, looking kind of guilty.

Mammy would always look up and say something like, "What did you pay for that?" or "How are you going to get any wear out of that?"

The dresses and shoes and blouses and skirts would wait in their boxes, unworn, until my mother's next trip to St. Louis, where she returned them, ready to begin the whole process again. Every trip to St. Louis began with the returns. It still does.

. . .

When my father and I were ready to leave Saks, Betty said, "Go, I'll get a taxi home." She wanted to stay, I think, to be there alone and wander the aisles and see the people and imagine, as I did in such stores, buying the best things and taking them home to a fancy place. She wanted to be on her own in the city for a little bit, to hail her own taxi, to see what it would be like if life had led her somewhere far different than her home. When she returned to the hotel, she was especially cheerful, as if she had pulled off something extraordinary. She had fallen into conversation with a woman in the shoe department. A woman from New Jersey. Betty said she was nice, but she would never go to New Jersey for a haircut. "It did like this in back," she said of the woman's style, waving her hand and rolling her eyes.

The next day, I took them to Barneys, where the movie stars shopped. Just inside the door, before we could decide on a place or time to meet, Betty disappeared into the crowds, as she always did when the three of us went shopping together at someplace nice. "Wham," my father said, "and she's off."

He looked around a bit but quickly stationed himself near what for him was the highlight of the store: a large tank of large tropical fish shimmering magically under a special light in brilliant colors—red and black, blue and yellow. They were exquisite, these fish, and my father's eyes followed them as they darted and undulated. I had read somewhere that the collection had cost more than seventy thousand dollars. It was a stunning assortment, and I stood with him in front of the tank, looking at our reflections in the glass tank as he tapped occasionally to draw the attention of the extraordinary creatures. He was transfixed; they would not let him turn away, but moments later as he surveyed the rest of the floor, he looked sour, put off by most of what surrounded him. He looked at me and said, "Except for these fish, this place is all bullshit. Strictly swindle. I hope you won't fall in with a lot of phonies."

After an hour or more, my mother suddenly appeared, looking upset, like someone had slapped her or hurt her feelings badly.

"I've looked and looked for you," she said. "I couldn't find you. I was standing there by the scarves and someone took my purse. A woman next to me tried to help and I talked to someone in security who let the police know, but the man behind the counter was rude. He made me feel like an idiot." She was broken, so crestfallen. She took us back to the counter where it had all happened, and the clerk—a sexy Puerto Rican queen in eye makeup—kept saying over and over that it was all her fault, that she should have watched her bag. "We have women with ten-thousand-dollar purses here. This place is crawling with thieves. You can't just set something down."

My father did not seem at all surprised or taken aback by what had happened. It was just the sort of thing he expected to occur in New York.

"That son of a bitch looked like a fool in that getup," my father said of the salesman.

"God, he was good-looking," I said. "They'll probably fire him when he gets older and doesn't look so good." What I actually was wondering was if he could keep working in this fancy store if he got sick and could not put on his eye makeup, or go to the gym, or mousse his hair to perfection.

My mother's face was red, a shade it rarely showed, redder than when she was moved or furious. Embarrassment brings its own regretful shade. My father looked uncomfortable too, especially after hearing me refer to the haughty man's handsomeness, but said nothing. As I stood with Betty, who was shaking, Big George returned for a last look at the fish. We were eager to go, but he was bound and determined to get another look at those fish. They were the only thing on the trip he really enjoyed, and he wasn't going to let anything spoil it. He returned to say that some had come from as far away as Brazil. Someone had told him. Those fish had come all the way from South America and Japan. My father appreciated genuine beauty. I think one of the things he loved most about my mother was that she was never anyone but who she was.

Betty said nothing on the walk back to the hotel; the store windows she had assessed so eagerly no longer seemed to hold much appeal. Her black coat hangs now in the front hall closet, next to Charlotte Hickey's old mink, in a clear plastic garment bag, like a museum piece, a reminder of the injunction she was raised with: "Don't ever think you are anything special."

That was never her message to me. She was prepared to lose me if my success took me away from her. She would have gladly taken any hurt if it could put me forward.

"Go on," she always said. "Get out of here. Live your life. Don't worry about us."

On the Monday morning my parents left New York, I called in to work, said I was sick, and I was; I was almost nauseated, thinking about their leaving, thinking about what might happen to us. I rode with them in a taxi to the airport and stayed with them until their flight was called and they boarded, despite my mother saying I should go on to the office, that my boss was going to be angry. I wanted them to remember me staying, waiting with them until the last minute. I cannot remember how I got back home, but for the rest of the day I was in bed, willing myself to feel nothing, trying to hold back the feelings. My room was dim and I lay there even after it was dark outside and I heard my roommates home from work, not realizing I was there.

In articles now about AIDS, there are always the photos of the crowds, the men in combat boots and T-shirts that say SILENCE EQUALS DEATH. I believed it. I believed in every act of protest, taking action, every instance of someone standing up, speaking out, and venting his rage. Yet for me those years were not about the silence of repression or cowardice, but other silences: the stillness of the room where I found myself, hiding, hearing Italian words filter through the walls; the quiet of neighborhoods in the Village; the faces of men in the windows of clubs that were often empty; the rooms of apartments hurriedly cleared out, their contents left on the street because no one could quite bear to sort through them. Silence did equal death to me, but not in the way that the protesters meant it. To me it was the silence of empty, the silence that arrives when there are simply no words to cover the situation, the silence of retreat. I wasn't trying to figure out how to live anymore; I was trying to figure out if I would die and how that would work. The silence I heard was what surrounded what could not be expressed, the sound of shutting down because there was only so much we could take in.

We were young and I wish I could have been one of the ones who went to the barricades, but instead I went to work very early in the mornings and stayed late at night and tried to avoid all the sadness, to push it away, because it was so unfathomable. Other people screamed in rage. I got quieter and quieter, and when it came time, as it always did, to talk about those who were sick, I excused myself because I had to, and if someone's parents were mentioned, if there was some story of so-and-so's mother or father flying in, or not coming, or leaving with ashes, or maybe staying until the moment when it was over for their son, I went out the door and back to my room, that bed, that silence. I excused myself, as my mother would have, in the face of this. For me, AIDS, those years, was that room where I read books and felt scared. At Easter, that first year it all started, when the Italians came down the street with their crèche in its long glass case, I mistook the celebration of resurrection for a funeral for someone who had grown up in this neighborhood that was really so much like the village I might never return to.

When the AIDS tests came out, a friend and I went to take our place in line. Contemplating the signing of a living will, I moved slowly through the three-week wait time after they drew my blood, but registered negative when we got the results. My friend was negative too, but because the test's effectiveness was uncertain, he was not relieved. He had been with a lot of men and could not shake the belief that he had AIDS, whatever the test showed. For years, he dissolved with the discovery of every mark or pimple. It turned out that he had also written his parents a letter, and when he found out I had too, he gave me his to hold on to, just in case. It already had a stamp and I wondered why I had not thought of that. It was a city of letters waiting.

We are getting on a bus to go to the AIDS march in Washington. I remember the trip. Almost everyone I knew from New York was going. It seemed for many a necessity, a last chance to have all their friends gathered around them before they got really sick.

Thanks to Steven, I rode on a bus with the Gay Men's Chorus, which he and the doctor had joined. All the way they sang. When I looked at Steven and made a face, he looked offended, but I didn't care. It was too early in the morning for anything from *Sweeney Todd*.

From a friend, I had learned that Eric was back in D.C., working for a senator. From directory assistance I got his number and called him up. He agreed to see the AIDS quilt on the Mall with me on the afternoon before the march. I didn't know what to expect, but after I had settled in at the hotel I made my way to Dupont Circle, where Eric had an apartment. When he came to the door, he looked skinnier than I remembered and I thought he was about to tell me something terrible, but he said nothing about being ill and I assumed I was just paranoid. I thought everyone was sick. Of course, everyone was.

Things were a little awkward. When it came down to it, I did not know Eric well, despite the full and interesting life we had led together in my imagination. Unable to hide my curiosity, I asked if he still had girlfriends. He replied that he was a "full-time homosexual" now, as if it were a difficult job he has accepted somewhat reluctantly.

"Great timing, huh?" he said.

I thought he might come to me now. Afraid of dying, men suddenly wanted to be in relationships. He was friendly, but distant, melancholy, like everyone. What was missing was his enticing spark of mischief. It was harder to make him laugh and I tried too hard. Now and again he was gracious enough to smile.

Outside, as we walked to the Mall, we said little to each other. I wanted to fill the space between us, but could not and got more and more anxious. I had felt so good with him before, but not this time. This time it was harder.

At the quilt, there were names and names and names, patches that signified lost lives with trinkets and photos of faces sewn on. I watched a woman who looked to be from out of town gazing at the quilt, as if she could not tear herself away. She took off her scarf and pinned it on. She became my picture of our lives at this time. She became my mother.

I did not want to go to the Missouri section—I didn't want to see for sure who was there—but Eric navigated us toward the Massachusetts panels, where he cried, and on to D.C., where he cried again. I did not look but heard him, surprised that he was so emotional. I wanted to cry along with everyone, but could not, so I pretended until I realized that no one was thinking about me.

"If you had died, would your parents be here?" I asked Eric. He said nothing, but looked back at me, as if to pose the same question. I shook my head.

"It just isn't something they would know to do. They wouldn't have anyone around to tell them to come."

Later, when my mother finally spoke of AIDS, she asked if I knew anyone who had it. I nodded, said nothing more. I didn't tell her about Steven's HIV status. It would have terrified her. My father never said anything about it. He was retired now. After the trip to New York, he purchased an aquarium, and though his fish were much smaller than the ones at Barneys, they were colorful and looked good under the light of the cylinder that shone over them as they darted through the water to ride in the waves of grass. He kept it all immaculately, and recently I found the tank neatly packed in the box it came in under his desk with a book on tropical fish inside it. He had circled the photos of the most glorious creatures. His fingerprints were still on the tank. When his health first worsened, he gave the fish to a neighbor boy whose parents were getting divorced.

As we left the quilt that day, a fat woman standing by the entrance with a lot of Christian literature had looked at Eric and said, "I will pray for you." He said, "Pray for yourself."

I had never seen him angry before. As it turned out, I shared that feeling, but it took awhile to know. I never knew what was going on inside me or how it might surface. It took a long time for me to lose my habit of disappearing at important times. Eric was special to me because with him I was able to be present. It was mysterious; I never knew why he made me feel comfortable when no one else could. With him I could be there, not just watching for my own mistakes.

We did not come together that day, even though I wanted to. It was not that kind of day. I left him standing alone by a window in his apartment.

As it happened, I saw my parents again, rather soon after they came to New York. Not long after my trip to Washington, I found myself arriving at a hotel in Sarasota, Florida, to meet George and Betty for a long weekend. They had torn down the old lumberyard building in Madison and it had been a draining few months for the whole family. Betty had said that on Main Street it looked like someone had ripped out a big tooth. It was the building her dad had built after he came back from the war. My parents wanted to get away from businesses closing and stores shutting their doors. They were old now. The funerals where my father sang were for friends.

When I arrived at the hotel in Florida, my dad was standing alone on the curb in the golden sunlight, bending over to touch a colorful, exotic flower. He was waiting for me, my arrival, and when he saw me there, all there, unchanged, safe, he wiped his eyes with his sleeve and rushed toward me to take me into his big arms.

16

Today was supposed to be my day off. I was going to drive fifty miles to Columbia to see the movie *The Master*.

The plan was to go buy the Sunday *New York Times,* read it at Lakota Coffee Company, see the movie, and go to Taco Bell (secret, disgusting vice) for dinner. But when Betty finds out about this, she decides she has to go. I guess she has been longing for art house fare. She will not take no for an answer, is raring to take off. I sense looming disaster, but she is actually ready to leave by my scheduled departure time. She has put on her new blouse, a little snug, a little formfitting now.

"I look so buxom," she says as she glances in the mirror on her way out, as she always does.

"Betty," I say, "you're ninety years old. If you got it, flaunt it. Now would be the time." She looks at me quizzically, pulls her shoulders back, and heads out the door.

My mother and I rarely go to movies together, a situation stemming from the fact that forty years ago I somehow manipulated my parents into taking me to see Jane Fonda in *They Shoot Horses, Don't They?*—which was "Suggested for Mature Audiences"—one Easter Sunday. (The sacredness of the date was emphasized for decades as an essential part of the horror of it all, when the story was told.) Unfortunately, the movie, which dealt with a group of doomed participants in a 1930s dance marathon, turned out to be the most depressing film ever made.

My father, who seemed to be expecting something spicier, registered disappointment as we walked to the car afterward. Betty, significantly more aroused, was appalled by the fact that the movie was ever shown in America. Or anywhere. She couldn't believe I had lured her into such an experience. Jane Fonda, previously a "reprobate," a "Communist reprobate," or "an unmarried, topless reprobate," became simply the woman "in *that* movie, that movie you dragged us to *on Easter Sunday*." Some years later, when Gig Young, who won an Oscar for his role in the movie, committed suicide, my mother read it in the paper and flung the article across the table at me.

So, *The Master:* I know she doesn't even want to see the movie. She has another motive altogether. My mother, reluctantly and rebelliously, takes her prescription medications—morning, noon, and night. But she is kept alive—and this is an absolute fact—by regular Dairy Queen Blizzards, which she acquires at the Columbia DQ. Her entire interest in the trip is the Blizzard. My plan is to get the tickets to the film, go get her the Blizzard, and then come back to see the movie, where, I hope, she will doze.

But when I buy the tickets, I realize that the film goes on a half hour before I thought. The Blizzard has to be postponed. Not happy, but a good sport, Betty allows herself to be temporarily placated with popcorn. But the Ragtag Cinema in Columbia, too hip and healthy for its own good, does not have butter for popcorn. They have olive oil. Starting on the popcorn, Betty eyes it suspiciously after a few bites, then glances at me ferociously. "What is on this popcorn?" I answer, "Olive oil." She is furious. "What right," she inquires, "do they have to do that? Are they *Italian*?"

Finally, the movie begins. I know, in about four seconds—certainly by the time Joaquin Phoenix drinks his first glass of turpentine—that I am going to hate it. Worse, I know that she is going to really hate it. I sense a potential *They Shoot Horses* situation in the making. I pray for sleep to wrap its gentle arms around her. But no. She is wide awake, rustling and squirming, sighing dramatically about every ten minutes. At one point, there is a scene where all the women in the room are suddenly nude. My mother sits up. "Good night," she says. (Both my parents talked louder in movie theaters than anyone I have ever encountered.) "This is *terrible.*" I whisper in her ear, "Stop talking or no Blizzard." Immediate silence. This continues for a half hour.

Then a loud exhalation and a comment that seems to be nearly shouted: "Why in the world would anyone make a movie like this?" Our neighbors in the theater turn to my mother, who begins to rummage loudly through what she calls her "pocketbook." I lean toward her, whisper, "Blizzard." She settles, but I no longer can pay any attention to the movie.

High on Blizzard, Betty is alert as we head toward home. I switch on the radio. It is Bartók night on KBIA. Betty, whose last favored tune was the love theme from *The Titanic,* flicks off the switch militantly. The miles pass. She leans over to check my speed about every fifteen minutes.

At some point, she fixes me in her gaze.

"Rachel Maddow," she announces, "is a lesbian. I read it in an article. And I'll tell you something else. I think Ingrid Wilbur is a lesbian too." Something in her tone suggests that I am the executor of a Watergate-style conspiracy designed solely to bar her from this revelation. Ingrid, the assistant to my mother's physician, stands five feet tall, wears cargo pants, and is topped by a head that bears a near-perfect shave.

"Ingrid Wilbur," I say, "was there when they invented it."

Although it is far from chilly, Betty turns on her heated seat, as usual. She encourages me to do the same. When I resist, she reaches over and flicks mine on. My ass soon feels like the site of a barbecue. "If you don't turn off my seat," I tell her, "I am going to burst into flame." She stares at me, but does not make a move to ease my pain. "These seats are the best thing about the car."

And then it happens: Whenever we go out at night, my mother, with her uncanny sense of speed and, despite her failing eyesight, sonarlike skills of detection, is always on the lookout for deer, the curse of drivers in these parts. She is always petrified we will hit one of the apparently suicidal animals and can repeat a list of people she knows who have had this experience over the last few years. We use Route T when we go back and forth to Columbia because a friend of ours, a judge, whom she respects as an authority on every topic, says he has never seen a deer on Route T.

But tonight, there is a deer on T. I barely see it as it leaps across the road, into my path. I am driving too fast, with my mind on other things. Its eyes glare at me as it stands, immobilized, just before the point of collision. Then I hear a huge thump and see the deer, at least part of it, flying through the air. I envision my lonely-dog-related karma hissing out of those antlers.

I get out. A large part of the deer, most of it in fact, including the head and antlers, is still in the highway. What is the proper etiquette in such a situation? Is one expected to move the deer off the road? Is there some authority to be called? A game warden? A wildlife emergency team? I don't want to move the deer. If I had a gun, I supposed I would have to shoot it to put it out of its misery. But I don't. Maybe I should choke it?

"I have to go to the bathroom," Betty shouts from the car as I eye the deer, oozing dark blood, feeling horrible. Its head seems larger than is fitting for display in a studio apartment.

I consider trying to move it, but I tell myself that I could easily contract some sort of germ or infection that could kill me, and Betty, before basically destroying the universe. The thing will have to stay in the road. I am sorry, oh creature of the forest. I meant no harm and have no gun to send you heavenward. I hope you don't have children. I just wanted the Arts and Leisure section and a taco. I am a peaceful man.

No way I can move this thing. It will have to stay. Maybe a highway patrolman will come along. Or perhaps someone burly and hairy will arrive, someone adept at the removal of large carcasses on the way to an NRA confab. "I have to go to the bathroom," Betty yells again.

I check out the car. There is the smell of burning antifreeze. The front is somewhat mangled, with the grille badly dented in. This, I realize, will not go over well with my passenger.

"I knew that was going to happen," my mother says. "It was just a matter of time."

Screw the deer; I wave good-bye as I peel out. "You never should have dragged me to that movie," Betty says. "But the deer was not your fault. I was watching out and didn't notice it. I didn't notice it. It just came out of nowhere."

"It was deranged. It hated its life," I say. I am collateral damage.

Betty is animated but calm, ready to take on at least part of the responsibility. It was her watch. This is a woman who can treat the transmission of a common cold as a tragic twist of fate, but crash into a creature whom you fear is Bambi's papa and you will encounter a soldier prepared to storm the beaches of Normandy.

"How's the car?" she asks.

"Kinda banged up." I imagine an estimate from our mechanic that will send her into cardiac arrest as he jabbers on about tanks or belts or vaporizers. Or whatever. My mother loves this car because, I suspect, she knows it will be the final automobile she will ever purchase, her last ride. It gets us back home, though something loose on the front scrapes the road all the way and the smell of smoke does not fade. I fear I may have snagged a smoldering piece of deer flesh. Maybe I should throw it in the Crock-Pot.

Inside, I fall into a state of near breakdown. I have spilled innocent blood and am contemplating the arrival of vengeful animal spirits.

The next morning, I find Betty staring out the garage door at the car. I call the insurance agent, deal with the paperwork. I do the kind of thing that I normally put off until crisis threatens. Miraculously, I pull it off. The insurance man is nice and helpful. The check will arrive without delay and the Infiniti is destined to fly once more, in search of other prey.

My mother seems rather astonished by my crisp, businesslike efficiency, and I am too.

"I thought we were going to have to get a new car," she says. I feel, suddenly, competent. I have braved antlers, paperwork, possible renal failure, and emerged triumphant. Maybe, if I can keep it together, I can save the ranch. Betty says, "The next time you see a movie, go by yourself. I have better things to do with my money."

17

On Fire Island, where I went for seven summers in the 1990s, one of my housemates planted flowers in wooden barrels on the deck of our place on Sky Boulevard every season. I watched him smoothing the dirt with his fingers, wishing I knew how to make things grow like my grandmother, who until almost her dying day squinted at plants as if they were children in need of care.

In the early mornings, home after a night of drugs and dancing at the Pavilion, I stretched out exhausted on the deck in a recliner and those blossoms would glower at me, blaring colors and chastening. They made me feel lost. This morning, the survival of our roses in the midst of the heat makes me feel better, like maybe I am doing okay here.

The lonely dog is being released today and, except for errands, I will have little reason to get out of the house so often. I am already picturing his empty pen. As I try to get Betty's bed changed, she watches closely. The old spread and her thin yellow sheets have been washed too many times. "They'll last me out," she says when I suggest replacements. My back is giving me trouble and, in the mornings, I wake with hands gone numb. Lately I have been obsessed over getting old, though there are gay nursing homes now. I see myself amid a group of old, tattooed codgers comparing waist sizes at Villa Fabulosa while I—wild-eyed in the Liza Minnelli Wing—grouse over the late delivery of my laxatives.

My barber on West Twenty-third Street in Manhattan and I have been together for fifteen years. Sometimes I think he is my most significant relationship. He is Russian, a remarkable fashion presence. During my last visit to the city, I stopped in for a haircut and found him in a bright red shirt with button cuffs. The buttons were covered with matching material. The yoke of his shirt had little cutouts that revealed swirls of coal-black hair. He looked like the best man at the wedding of Satan.

After all these years, our relationship has evolved into a very similar routine. He always greets me in the same way: "How you feel?"

Whatever I reply, he always says the same thing: "No way to be!"

Then he takes me through the changing group of photos of movie stars and rock stars taped to his mirror. Their coifs represent his current range of hairstyle options. Over the years, I have been through a range of celebrities, culminating in George Clooney. On the day of my last visit, he was offering Anderson Cooper, Justin Timberlake, and Adam Levine. Taking in this gallery, I felt that I had perhaps aged beyond his area of specialty. I wanted to say, "Adam. Please, I wanted to be Adam." But I dared not. I am middle aged, not a tattoo to my name. Suddenly I was sad. What to do?

I tried to level with him about a recent problem that has really been bothering me and that I hoped he could help camouflage. When speaking to him I tend to fall into that blend of broken English and demanding assertion that characterize his speech.

"I have fat face. How to hide?"

"What you mean?"

"Fat face. Head huge. Elton John. Help!"

He scanned the photos on the wall, finally fixing on one that seemed to have been there for decades. It has been adhered to the wall and is in tatters. I glanced. I was afraid, but there was nothing really scary. It was a picture of a clean-cut middle-aged man, a stockbroker type. It appeared to have been plucked from a Sears catalog. I had not even noticed it.

"I do this for you," he said.

I felt ancient, but just nodded. Whatever. I just wanted a clean neck and nothing puffy.

He inspected my head. "You don't come anymore. Who do this to hair? Bum."

"My mother is sick. I have been away."

"Turrible."

In a few minutes, he was finished. "You want product?" he asked, hand sliding toward an endless row of hair fixitives, including some lugubrious-seeming gels. He is a man who loves mousse.

"No product," I said. "You know I hate stuff in my hair."

"You need."

"Stop."

He looked at me "Why you frown. No way to be!"

"I want to be rock star."

"The governor's father, you know, my friend, the old Jay, has written a book," Betty begins. This comes out of nowhere and at first I am only half listening.

"Jay says," she tells me, "right in the book, that I was the most beautiful woman he had ever seen. When I was young. He says that, *right in the book*. That I was beautiful. When he knew me." She isn't bragging. She is surprised and a bit reluctant to mention it.

"What kind of book?" She replies: "I don't know. Bob Thompson read it. He got it in the mail. He called yesterday when you were with that darn dog."

"The father's name was Jay, right, like the governor's?"

"Yes. You remember Bob, don't you?"

Bob Thompson is a retired lawyer in Shelbina, a town that burned almost completely a few years back. His home is a local landmark, one of the houses where my mother used to imagine living. Betty always wanted to find herself in one of the mansions with columns, mostly haunted-looking and decaying now, that dot river towns such as Hannibal, Louisiana, Boonville, and of course St. Louis. In the city, Granny took us to walk by the huge old houses once owned by river merchants on the old gated streets—Portland and Westminster places. "Aren't they grand?" Granny would ask my mother and me as we walked past the enormous mansions, under the oldest, greenest trees I will ever see.

"Why would anyone publish Jay Nixon's book?" I ask in a little while. "I don't think anyone would publish a book even by the governor himself."

"Jay Nixon was the mayor of De Soto!" Betty is emphatic. "He had three children. One is the governor. One is a game warden, and one, Bob told me," she says, her voice becoming almost a whisper, "is obese. Bob read the book. He read every word."

Jay Nixon Sr., the father of the governor of Missouri, was my mother's boyfriend before my father. This was revealed years back, after my dad's death, when Betty—very excited—handed me an envelope that she would keep on the coffee table for a year, a blue invitation to the son's inaugural in Jefferson City. Pressed for a reason why she was invited, she confessed, "I almost married the governor's father."

I tried to take this in, but she refused to elaborate. She did not wind up going to the inauguration, or the ball, though for weeks she considered and reconsidered it. I offered to fly home to take her, but she wouldn't let me and didn't have a ride. It was January and freezing. She didn't complain, said it was hard to go out at night anymore, that she would be afraid to fall, that she couldn't see well, that it was silly to even think of going. But when we spoke on the phone I could hear the hangers scratching on the pole as she looked through the dresses in her closet. She kept bringing it up and up and up. Every time I called she continued, though she kept saying she was not going and that was it.

"It's crazy to think about it," she claimed. "I'm an old woman. I'm not going unless there's a radical change."

"In what?" I asked.

"My hair for one thing," she said.

The summer after the inauguration, when Betty could still walk easily, we were in St. Louis, staying at the Chase, and Betty asked me to take her somewhere. She had found the address of the governor's father and wanted to see the apartment building where he lived on Lindell Boulevard, just across the street from the hotel. It was an exquisite old building and we looked in the glass of the front door, which was locked. The walls of the entry were marble or granite, and at the top there were scenes carved out of the stone, tableaux of what looked like Greek gods rising from what I took to be the Mississippi River. Inside, in the main lobby, coach lights flickered softly. It reminded me of New York, of places where I had hoped to live before my life became a disaster area.

"He wound up in a nice place, didn't he?" she said.

"Mother," I say this morning as I finish up the bed, "I wish you would have let me come take you to the inauguration. You could have seen him."

"I didn't want him to see how I look. I look like something the cat dragged in."

"He said you were beautiful. Maybe he hoped you would read the book and know he remembers you. Fondly. You know. It was a little message. Would you like to see him?"

"I gave to the son's campaign," she says. "I sent a check. I guess I should have gone. In a way, I'd paid for the dinner, but I thought I'd be cold. My feet get cold even with my boots, and I couldn't wear my boots to the ball. My feet look big enough anyway."

"Why didn't you marry the governor's father?"

No response.

"What is the capital of Portugal?" she asks.

My cousin Mimi and her husband, before leaving for a vacation in Portugal, purchased a condominium in Scottsdale. Betty is trying to keep track of it all, but forgets where Mimi is traveling as well as the location of her new home. So she drills herself:

"What is the capital of Portugal?" she asks again.

"Lisbon," she says in a minute or two, answering her own question. "You ask now."

"What is that place where Mimi goes in the winter?"

"Scottsdale."

"We went there one Christmas."

"I told your father I thought it was overrated."

This is what my mother does now, night after night: Walking past the living room on her way to bed, she says, "I have to stop in here a minute," and pauses at the piano, picks up the hymnal. Sitting at the edge of the bench as I wait for her to slip off, she studies the pages for a while. After brushing her teeth or putting in her curlers, she returns to the hymnal, turning more pages. Sometimes after she is in bed, after I have turned off the light, she will get up—once, twice, sometimes three times—and go back to the piano, then return to her room to jot things down on the back of the envelope she keeps by her bedside.

Time and time again, I ask, "What are you doing?" Time and time again, she will not say. Finally she concedes, "I am trying to remember the names of the hymns. I cannot remember the names of the hymns anymore."

Under her bedside table a conglomeration of things—empty eyedrop bottles, used Kleenexes, coupons, and tiny notes she has scrawled on index cards—are piled in a crazy heap, which I call the bird's nest. "That is my spot. You are not supposed to look there," she tells me if I refer to it. "Sometimes you make me feel so embarrassed."

She doesn't want me to see the papers that fall from the end table by her bed, the lists she keeps of words that will no longer come that she is trying to keep track of.

On one I found she has written, "eggnog, eggnog, eggnog, eggnog."

Sometimes I turn to the hymns whose numbers she writes down; I read the lyrics, wonder if they are clues to what is on her mind, but they don't reveal anything to me. Sitting at the piano bench, I take in the paintings she commissioned from an artist in Moberly for our new living room when we moved to Paris. They are little oil renderings of pink roses.

. . .

The lonely dog just stares at me, as if he knows I am sending him away with a stranger. I look at him, wave a little, but do not leave the car. I am not budging until Marci arrives to take him. I always liked Marci; in high school I made posters for her bid to become homecoming queen. She lost, but was gracious. I was not; it was as if the tiara had been ripped from my own head.

After she arrives, the pound man frees the dog, who rushes out—a few flashes of fur and madly wagging tail—to shake himself. If that dog who has consumed more than a hundred dollars' worth of my food bounds up to this woman who couldn't even win a queen contest before he licks me, I am going to give the orange jumpsuit to a church auction.

Marci waits expectantly—entirely inappropriately, I believe—for the dog to come to her. I hold my breath.

Love is a battlefield.

But there is a surprise. He runs to me. Whatever happens, he is really my dog. I pick him up as he thrashes around, licking my face. Marci takes pictures of us with my iPhone. The dog looks rabid and I am no ad for Slimfast, but they will do. Marci tells me what her grandsons have decided to call him, a horrible name that I immediately repress. In my fantasies, I have named him Nicky, which suits his warm nature, but which can be shortened to Nick if he gambles or is drawn toward organized crime.

In the trunk of my car there is the crate I have purchased and lined with lots of my old clothes. I want him to breathe my scent and mourn the man who got away. I ask Marci if the dog can ride with me to her house. She agrees; transferring the crate to her car would be a pain anyway. Nicky bounds into the front seat of the Infiniti, sniffs indiscriminately as he surveys everything, his nose poking over the dashboard and his ears fallen back. It is exactly as I had imagined. He drools on the seat, as I do often.

"Don't be a stranger," I tell him as I back away toward the car, before

I can change my mind. As he zips off toward another part of the yard, he whips his head around to look back at me and half his body turns. It is maybe my favorite thing he does.

On the way home, I keep my eyes peeled for the lawn-mower boy. Sometimes I spot him walking by the side of the road on Cleveland Street, carrying a white trash bag. He doesn't cut our grass anymore and I worry he has been fired. I always wave. He does not.

Lonely dogs roam empty streets everywhere now, even in this town where all of us once had a home—a husband, a wife, a father, a mother, a place. This boy who hides his face under a hood: No one will take him in or stop to ask how things are going. Never before did kids like this, young ones with no connections, show up on these streets where, this summer, flowers burn in the sun. On sidewalks everywhere, small brown petals are scattered.

In Madison, in the oldest part of the cemetery where my father and all the Bakers are buried, the names on the tombstones are impossible to distinguish. Mammy always took flowers to a boy who died very young who was buried there. He was either an orphan or his parents passed quickly after he did. I think he was taken by diphtheria, or whatever was in the air, or maybe in an accident, far out in the fields, where no doctor could come in time. Mammy knew the family. She never let the place where he was buried go unadorned. Bill knew the place too. He and June always took flowers after Mammy died.

At home, I check Facebook where a woman I know has written: "I don't need to be home alone all day with nothing but my little Havanese and my ferret to keep me company only to be subjected to someone's being a prick when he gets home." I like the ring of the line. The dog, I imagine, is really missing me.

"You remember Bob Thompson, don't you?" Betty asks me after a little while. She seems to have forgotten our earlier conversation. "I thought Bob was dead," she goes on, "he thought I was too. I told him we both ought to be. He says Jay Nixon's father, who was my boyfriend when I was trying to finish up college, has written a book. He says, right in the book, that I was the most beautiful woman he had ever seen."

"Why didn't you marry him? Why won't you tell me?"

She pays absolutely no attention, begins to sort through the bills on the coffee table, and then, when I think I am going to learn nothing, she begins and I am taken aback.

"We were just out of college. He was going to law school. I would have had to support him and Mammy said no woman should do that.

"Men," she assures me, "always leave women who get them through school. That's what Mammy thought. And I, well, I wanted to do what she said. She had worked so hard to get me through college. She worked all the time and had a lot to do already. She said she wanted me to see the world.

"I went to William Woods that first semester, but I had to come home. We didn't have the money. But Mammy got busy and got me into the university. I went stop and start, when we could afford it, but she was determined. She got me through, eventually. She didn't want me to be ignorant."

"How did she make the money?"

"She sold milk."

"You had a cow?"

"I guess so. I know she sold milk and vegetables from the garden and in the summer she wouldn't let up. She grew what we needed and she grew stuff to sell. She really worked. I had to do what she wanted.

"She said he'd just leave me, and then what would I have?"

"Did she not like him?"

"She never met him."

"Never?"

"I never brought him home. She never laid eyes on him. It wouldn't have mattered."

"So she had no way of knowing if he was nice?"

"I told you," she says. "I never brought him home."

"Why?"

"I was ashamed."

"Why? Why were you ashamed to have your boyfriend come home with you?" I ask my mother.

"I was ashamed," she says, her eyes falling to her lap.

For a while we do not speak, and then I brave it, I go in: "What were you ashamed of?"

She does not speak, just keeps eyeing the bill on her lap. She has scrawled words on the back of it: Lisbon, Portugal, Scottsdale. Finally, she admits it.

"We didn't have an indoor toilet. We had an outhouse. I didn't want him to know."

"You didn't have indoor plumbing?"

"My father was so careful. We didn't have a spare nickel. He hated to spend money. We were some of the last people in the city limits of Madison to have an indoor toilet. When we got one, Mammy wouldn't let anybody put paper in. She thought it would break. Winnie put paper in the toilet once and it overflowed."

"Did you want to marry him?"

She says nothing until, moments later, "What is the capital of Portugal?"

"Lisbon."

"I would like to get away one last time," she adds, "but it's too late. I know. My walking's not that good. After I'm gone you can travel."

"Probably to Mayos." I like the name of this hospital. It sounds like a destination in the Caribbean. *"Two tickets for Turks and Mayos, please, and do not stick me by an emergency door."*

"What is the capital of Portugal?" she begins again, determined now not to let the words slip away.

"Lesbian."

Mammy sold milk to get Betty through college. I have never before taken in that they had so little to spare when they were growing up. As a very old lady, Mammy wandered our house, turning off the lights to save on the electric bill even if I was reading or my father was working with his house plans.

"Turn off the light!"

This is my mother's stern command every night when, after the dishwasher is loaded, I come into the family room. "Turn off the light!" she cries out all the time. Just like Mammy.

"Just go," my grandmother told me on the day I left Paris as Betty and George waited in our Delta 88 to take me away to college. "Just try to act right," she told me. She could barely see, never looked quite at me anymore, but only in my direction. I wondered how much of me she could really take in by that point. With her mind as it was, with her sight as it was, I never knew who she was seeing anymore.

When I first went away from home, Mammy wrote me often, her handwriting revealing, more and more, her descent into confusion and blindness. Words left her, and in her notes she would scratch out the ones she feared were spelled wrong. Her letters were full of black marks. She couldn't trust herself, though she had been an excellent speller and a prizewinning student of Latin.

When visiting at my grandmother's as a boy, I slept with Mammy in a huge wooden bed she won after discovering a prize ticket in a Quaker Oats box. Her foot always stuck out from under the blanket, too stubborn to be covered up. Since birth, her little toe, surprisingly long, was bent over the others, as if to keep them in place.

Mammy snored loudly, but that is not what awakened me on the night of what I considered our greatest adventure. My nose was stuffed up; allergic to everything, I could not breathe and my nose drops were at home. I watched the snow fall over the houses of the neighbors, wondering if Bassett Humphrey, an elderly friend, was awake across the street. During storms with thunder and lightning, she always came to Mammy's, bringing her own pillow.

In the middle of the night of the falling snow, I woke Mammy to tell her that I could not sleep, that my nose drops were at our house, that I was sure to suffocate. She squinted her eyes at me, dubious, but put her winter coat on over her nightgown, along with her shoes and the plastic galoshes she pulled over them. From the closet she plucked the dented-in hat she wore to funerals. Her braids hung over her shoulders; she didn't bother to put them up.

Outside, as the snow came down, Mammy—expressly forbidden to drive—carefully negotiated the porch step with me helping all I could. The trip to the garage, where Bill kept one of his old cars, a yellow-topped Chevy with sharp fins, was a major expedition. The two of us drove slowly down Olive Street in the quiet of a town at rest under snow. Mammy could make out little, but she kept driving. Though it was less than half a mile, the trip seemed to take us far from our known world. It was freezing; the world was white, and when the car swerved, Mammy, confused, slammed the brake and we slid, almost off the road. But I had faith. Mammy would get us home. She was a pioneer and we were making our way across the plains.

When I visited my grandmother not long before she died, she was holding her head, too heavy to lift up by then. She was tiny, faded, a scrap of thin cloth. "Take care of my little girl," she said.

I am trying.

Mammy rarely left home. She went to Moberly, to Mexico, to St. Louis to see Nona or the eye doctor. Once, though, with Nona and Wally on a car trip to California, Mammy saw the swallows at San Juan Capistrano, some big ships bound for all the world. She saw Grauman's Chinese Theater, the Farmers Market, the Pacific Ocean. I have her postcards.

The ocean, which she had never seen before, was her favorite.

"It was quite the sight."

She took her shoes off and waded in.

"Nona kept her eye on me. She thought the waves would sweep me all the way to Hawaii."

She always said she hoped she would get to see the Atlantic too, but she never made it.

I did. I lived by the ocean for a while. It began in 1990 on Fire Island and I had never felt so free.

I was working at Simon & Schuster, where I started off as a copywriter. The place was a gallery of characters. Sandra Soliman, an editor perpetually in search of glamour, brought her hairdresser in mornings for a quick office shampoo. She stalked the halls in the wee hours with her hair in towels and kept pink bulbs in her lamps to soften her look. At a dinner with an important author, I watched Dick Snyder, the CEO of the company, charm everyone and ventured one comment that no one seemed to listen to.

"Don't say shit in front of the talent," Dick told me afterward.

As the years passed at Simon, I was promoted from nonentity to senior editor. I lived in the office, worked hard, rode the service elevator up at 5 a.m. I believed that if I worked and worked, I would have something to offer my parents to make up for not having children. At a party on the Upper East Side, I was introduced to Lauren Bacall, who put her finger in my cleft and said, "Where'd you get that chin?"

When I called Betty to tell her, she said she was going to go to the nursing home to tell Mammy right that minute because my grandmother always vowed I had her chin.

An acquaintance at Simon asked me to join the house in Fire Island. I didn't have much social life. I thought it was time to try again to enter the world of gay men. Tom said you could hear the ocean waves crashing in the morning when you awakened.

This is how you traveled: You packed an old white carpenter's bag you got from the lumberyard when it closed. You left from Penn Station, changed at Jamaica, got off at Sayville, rode on a bus to the ferry, which crossed the water to the island, the Pines.

You stopped working every weekend, and for one, two, maybe three years, the island was your favorite place, the best place you had ever been, the happiest time.

Then, gradually, things changed. You began to lose your way, knowing you were suddenly in trouble, but just going on, figuring that later you could get it together again if you did not get arrested on the Long Island Railroad for passing a vial of cocaine among you and your friends.

It was our first summer in Fire Island, late in the season, late at night. We were walking from our house to board the ferry in the harbor of the Pines to go to a big party at the Ice Palace in Cherry Grove. The night was known as the Invasion and had been talked about for weeks. At the party, I was chemically enhanced; we took ecstasy, mescaline, bumps of this and that. I danced, bounced around. The air was filled with sparkles. Men in boots, shorts, and jeweled cross necklaces floated by me. Leather henchmen stalked about in chaps. In a corner, a fierce black queen in a turban, sunglasses, and long rhinestone earrings read everyone to filth.

David Geffen stood by the door, checking out every man who came through it. He had redone Calvin Klein's house that summer and was everywhere. Madonna and her brother came in on the seaplane for lunch one day.

"Vogue, Vogue, strike a pose." I tried to. I stood in the mirror before every party. My face was okay, but my body wasn't marketable. The impressionable gays of New York go through phases when certain things are desirable. I am not cut out for chaps. Nor am I a piercing type. There was the long decade of the muscleman when the great beasts, bulgy-veined and orangeish from their steroids, lumbered down the avenues. There was the period of lean, the summers of sculpted, the days when dating participation required the complete absence of body hair. Black men were for a while the favorite. Then Latinos. At no time, in my memory, have Midwest Protestants been the flavor du jour. A year or so ago, when someone on a dating site asked me to Skype naked, I decided I would do better at Christian Mingle.

At the party at the Ice Palace, I was wearing a pair of five-hundred-dollar sunglasses. I had splurged. I didn't want anyone to get a look at my eyes, to see how messed up I was.

For hours and hours, we danced that night in Cherry Grove. When I looked down at my feet, they seemed to be miles away. The night seemed to go on and on. "Do we live here?" I asked someone, barely able to speak.

My housemates were gathered in a pile on a banquette, holding one another and talking. They reminded me of wanderers gathered in a forest around a campfire in a strange, dark forest. The dance floor was the shifting, changing mating place, the ritual. Our comrades were home bases. We went out to seek and then returned to fall back into the arms of our own people. The music played and the hours flashed by and it seemed we had stepped out of time into some safe, warm place where no one was dying or ever alone.

We walked back to the Pines after the Invasion party by the ocean, all together, taking our shoes off, trekking through the shallow waves as, under our feet, the sand and tiny shells sparkled and changed colors. We were so high.

I was happy, but scared too. I was going out too far; I knew this, but it was worth it. I needed these people to feel close to. I was tired of being on my own.

Back at our place, sitting around, laughing with everyone, I just closed my eyes and did another little hit of something when I looked at the flowers on the deck.

"Doesn't it feel a long way from home?" my friend Leo asked me one morning after everyone else had gone to bed.

In her last years, when Mammy was living at Monroe Manor, my mother brought her food several times a day, and in the summer took her rosebuds from her bushes wrapped in damp newspapers. I was in Fire Island when I heard that my grandmother had had a massive stroke. She was ninety-six. On the day of the funeral, as we were getting ready to leave, I went to check on Mother and there she was, sitting on the edge of the bed. She had already turned the lights off in her room. She was just sitting on the edge of her bed, still, with her eyes closed.

"What is the capital of Portugal?" Betty asks over and over all day long.

"Lisbon."

"What is that place where Mimi goes in the winter?"

"Scottsdale."

"Will you let me help you?" I ask my mother as she tries to navigate herself toward the bedroom. "Will you let me help you?"

"I am trying to remember the names of the hymns. I cannot remember the names of the hymns."

I sit on the bench and take the piece of yellow legal paper she is holding as if it were currency. There is a list of numbers.

"Number 519," I read.

" 'Something Beautiful,' " she says.

I write it down.

"Number 451," I read.

" 'O Master, Let Me Walk with Thee,' " she says.

I write it down.

"Number 324," I read.

" 'Come Celebrate Jesus.' "

"Number 465."

" 'In His Time.' "

"Number 256."

" 'He Is Here.' "

She is trying to hold on.

In Fire Island, I was letting go.

18

The ocean in South Carolina had smooth pebbles on the bottom, and maybe because there had been rain that spring, the water was murky and gray. When my father rose up from it, I noticed his face was the same color. He was in his midseventies. He didn't look well. I watched him attentively as he chased the birds—terns, gulls, pelicans—though his knees were bad and he rarely moved fast enough to photograph them before they flew away.

Always, on whatever beach we visited, he roamed until he sat reluctantly to see the sun fall, following the birds and their eccentric doings and picking up shells on the sand. He bought cheap plastic buckets in which to bleach his acquisitions, polishing his conchs with a toothbrush as he lay back on the bed with a cocktail balanced on his belly, checking to see if he had gotten them shiny enough to display on his desk at home.

If my father knew how I had been spending my time on the island and elsewhere, he would have been brokenhearted, and that bothered me so much in South Carolina that I couldn't enjoy myself and was not disappointed when I was called back to New York.

In the 1990s, I worked at *Vanity Fair,* a magazine so slick that its pages were perfumed. Finished copies tended to send me into sneezing fits. At the office there was always drama, some kind of crisis—a writer in the midst of a breakdown, a must-have piece on an heiress who had axed her in-laws. I left my parents with their disappointed looks in the rented house they had been proud to show me and ran out quickly when the taxi came.

Graydon Carter, the editor in chief, was apologetic about the interruption of my vacation, and as we sat in his office he offered me a Marlboro and told me how much he appreciated my work. Soaking in his flattering words, I noticed—as I always did—how remarkably his hands and thick fingers resembled my father's, though his were tanned, whatever the season, and always acquired whatever they reached for.

My father's hands did not.

Graydon was on the rise, and usually had a bespoke suit awaiting pickup in London if a writer happened to be there. At the beginning, he had a way of making me feel brilliant and talented in a way no one had before. I took it all in eagerly; I was a little desperate. With Graydon, I was still just a hungry kid.

"I don't like the way you sound," Betty would say on the phone. "I don't like the way you sound. Are you all right? Are you all right?"

"I am fine. I am fine. What about Daddy?"

She never answered. She was worried too, but that was the sort of thing she never said out loud. I think she believed that the sound of her voice articulating her concern was enough to provoke the worst to befall us.

At *Vanity Fair,* the contributing editors included a roster of killer reporters: an English aristocrat ("Lady Kitty's daughter") who had hung in Mustique with The Rolling Stones; a fashion director who muttered imprecations in various languages (*Honi soit qui mal y pense!*); an assortment of devious Brits; the Marquis de Torregrosa; an elderly Italian doyenne who referred constantly to the preferences of Count Laszlo, whom I believed to be an aristocrat until I discovered that he was actually her aging pug. Before the parties and dinners thrown by Graydon, tears over the suitable position of place cards were not uncommon. The seating of Edie Wasserman or Mrs. Reagan within a mile of the kitchen at Morton's was an offense worthy of capital punishment.

Every morning I rode up in the elevator at 5 a.m., hoping the day would pass without some disaster in which I would be implicated, and there was always dread before I walked through the doors. People who passed through these halls monitored one another, carefully assessing whose stock with Graydon had risen or fallen, who was in or out. Some left his office with smiles and Prada bags; others exited in tears. Anyone could plummet out of favor.

When the stories I supervised put me in Graydon's good graces, I was jubilant, but after failure, when it was possible to wait endlessly outside his office for a brief and chilly audience, I could do nothing but worry and obsess over the rejection.

I lived with a succession of bizarre stomach ailments, always in terror of failing. For weeks I disappeared from polite civilization for trips to East Hampton to wage war during at-home editing sessions with a political reporter whose name drew readers despite her indifference to deadlines.

It was Condé Nast. It was big-time, an environment hermetically sealed to block out signs of aging; the poor, charmless, and unslender; and any vestige of reality. I bought new clothes, edited pieces on presidents, movie stars, murderous heiresses, and warring Hollywood executives. I worshipped Graydon for his creativity and eye for the subtle treacheries of Manhattan's stylish power brokers. He saw the hidden strings that held his world together, but he was boyish and mischievous, delighted by glamour and fun, the first to pummel the pretentious. An effortless raconteur, amusingly ironic, he was also surprisingly vulnerable, judgmental in the extreme as he tallied up style offenses, lapses in etiquette, imagined slights from employees, sushi deliverers, or celebrity handlers. He was, I still believe—outside of Betty Hodgman—more attentive to hair-related error than any human I have ever known on Planet Earth. "After thirty," he told me, "a man should never change his hairstyle." I took it in.

I craved his regard. I wanted more. A little bit was not enough. I wanted what those hands could deliver, what my father's shaky fingers could no longer give me: a place that felt certain. I hated it when they were occupied with pursuits beyond my sphere.

. . .

On the island one summer, I kept running into a nice-looking man—a cheerful-looking guy of the type I thought I should find. We smiled at each other when we were out with people, or buying groceries, or lying on the beach. His appearance was reassuring; he didn't wear Lycra or spandex and looked like someone who had grown up in a leafy suburb and had his insurance policies in order. He seemed comfortable in his skin. I needed a rock. There was something; I sensed it. It was one of those times when something sparks without a second of conversation, though—because I was high every time I saw him—I thought it was probably something going on in just my head, the kind of private show that occurred there, confusing me and making me reluctant to believe that any attraction could ever be mutual.

One night, at an AIDS benefit, I felt a hand on my shoulder at the bar, a hand attached to a classic monogrammed cuff, and there he was, the man from the island—maybe a lawyer, or someone who worked on Wall Street, or a businessman, the old-fashioned type who never got flummoxed. As it happened, he was in advertising, his wardrobe a way to offset his industry's flash. I discovered all this during the course of the evening when I received every second of his attention, though the room was crowded with others easier to engage than me, someone too uncomfortable to converse while standing and hyperconscious of my inability to meet his eye.

Flattered, I felt drawn to him, and was happy to return to his apartment where, after discovering my unwillingness to engage in unprotected sex, he threw me out. It was fast and unexpected, but these things happened in these times. My friends spoke of the same experience. I wasn't the only one and they let me know I didn't really have the right to feel so badly treated. I had no right to linger on this. People were dying. They were right.

After I left the apartment, I went back to my place on East Tenth Street and, though it was very late, got high, wishing I had checked in with Missouri earlier that Sunday because I felt that there was something my mother was not telling me. This made me need to get even higher. They never told me if anything was wrong, but there was nothing I could do at that hour, with the sun rising, so I did more drugs because there wasn't time to sleep and I needed to be alert in a few hours.

"I don't like the way you sound," Betty said on the phone. "I don't like the way you sound. Are you all right? Are you all right?"

"I am fine. I am fine. What about Daddy?" I answered.

"He's okay," she said. But I didn't think he was and felt terrible receiving attention that should—with his increasing weakness and difficulties getting around—be aimed in his direction. My problems were easier to focus on; she could always tell herself she was only imagining them. He was right there, failing indisputably in front of her eyes. She hated to see him weak and pushed him to get up out of his chair and do more, get out of the house.

"Get up and let's do something. Get out of that chair."

She wouldn't see what was happening.

"But what about Daddy? I don't think he looks too good."

"You don't sound right," she said.

"I'm fine. I'm fine."

There was a song we loved on Fire Island, a song they played when the crowds on the dance floor thinned and the breeze from the ocean blew in. Morning music, they call these soft, late-night songs. This one meant something to us. When it played, we came together and did not let go. It was called "I'll Be Your Soldier" and was about standing with, staying with your friend or lover through whatever happened, whatever trouble. It seemed to sum up our days and for years I have tried, unsuccessfully, to find it, though I don't think I really want to. Hearing it would be too bittersweet. None of us who danced together ever speak anymore. Several in our house on the island were HIV positive, and this lent an undercurrent to every moment. So we danced together. You didn't ever have to speak. I learned to love to dance, for that reason specifically. Late at night, we guided one another's trips to abandon. When someone flew too high or low, another was there to scoop him up. If you found yourself, in the middle of everything, lonely or afraid, a friend would appear to sit beside you until it was all a little better. But nothing lasts forever; the breakup of our camp was inevitable. There were tensions festering. Men compete.

I really did not want to feel this. I had gotten a taste of closeness and wanted more. But as more members of our group tested positive, a division between the haves and have-nots became more apparent. And then there were the drugs—at the beginning a diversion for all, but gradually a danger that some could draw away from while others grew more and more attracted. I was in the latter party. I could not stop if I started. I never wanted to go back to feeling merely ordinary.

At High Tea one weekend, I recognized a familiar face—Eric's. There he was, standing on the deck in Topsiders, leaning against an older man who did not rate as likely boyfriend material. The man's hair was gray and it seemed as though he was looking after my old friend. I sensed the situation immediately. He was older and I knew that he was Eric's soldier, the one who had hoped to love him but had settled for steering him through everything we had never imagined happening. Eric didn't look sick yet, just drawn, tired, and older than he was.

When we began to talk, Eric apologized for being so quiet on the day we visited the quilt, but he had just a few days before tested positive for HIV. He said he had hoped we would run into each other. He actually said he always thought we might wind up together. I looked at him. He had sensed my little dream of our getting together all along. And here he was, dishing up the fantasy I had come up with and serving it to me for his own benefit. He was just as bad as that man who threw me out. He was just the same, I thought, feeling that he was trying to use me. He wanted me to come back to the place where he was staying, said that it would be all right, that I wouldn't get sick, that I didn't have to worry, but I didn't want to be manipulated. I was dubious, having been through a few confusing battles. I didn't want to find myself walking back home along the beach feeling bad about what I had or had not done.

I think I wanted, this time, to be the one with the power, the one to decide.

The man with the gray hair, who had been looking bereft, seemed relieved when I disappeared.

Later, I wanted to go back, change it, the way it turned out—my coldness, his disappointment, the look on his face as I hurried across the room after just a few minutes. But I could not.

When I left our house on Fire Island, when it all fell apart and everyone was harboring little grudges and telling tales, I was a full-blown addict. It took a lot of drugs for some of us to feel free. I boarded the ferry back to the city, carrying my carpenter's bag from the lumberyard with cocaine tucked into the inner pocket and little sense that my departure was regretted by anyone. I started to go out on my own. I didn't ask for much, didn't want it. No longer drawn to the college-boy type, I was not interested in anything like a relationship. "Would you just go?" I had learned to say, even to those who might have been willing to linger. My love was drugs.

After my father collapsed after a coronary, the doctor discovered that he had suffered two silent heart attacks. No one had known, though I suspected one had occurred that day we arrived in St. Louis to see The Music Man *when, angry and put out, he had carried all the bags up by himself and collapsed on a chair.*

His heart had been so badly damaged that there was no operation possible to repair it. The diagnosis was congestive heart failure.

I went home, stood by his bed in the hospital, listened to the doctor talk, but his words were so carefully chosen and so buried in detail that I wasn't sure my father was definitely dying, and it wasn't like I could ask him if he had heard what I heard. He acted like nothing had happened.

My mother was waiting for us to come back from the hospital. She didn't ask me what the doctor said. She didn't seem able to take in what I was trying to tell her, didn't want to find out what she suddenly realized she couldn't quite handle: losing him.

"I'll be all right, Betty, I'm okay," he told her. We were all fine—fine, fine, fine.

I felt like there was something I should say to my father and every time we spoke, I tried to, attempted to let him know that I loved him in some way that didn't feel like some kind of parting gesture that would be too hard for us to manage.

I kept waiting for him to reach out to me too, to say something, to let me know that I was okay, that I was all right as far as he was concerned, but there was nothing in the end like that. I guess he had stopped trying, or maybe he had seen enough of who I had become to just go quiet.

He had looked up the Fire Island Pines on the map or read about it in some kind of magazine or tour book. "I know what goes on in that place," he said to me on the phone. "I wouldn't think of you there."

My father's hands were letting go of me.

Late one afternoon at *Vanity Fair,* the phone rang and I heard my mother's voice, excited, in a kind of unusual, keyed-up way. At a Christmas luncheon, she had met a woman with a piece of jewelry unlike any other she had seen, a bracelet purchased in Istanbul. She had to have one too. It was essential. Oxygen. She was racing, too driven, too wound up.

She wouldn't talk about my father. I could tell she was on the extension in her bedroom. She didn't want him to hear.

I was editing a piece centered on an interview with the mistress of a national political leader. Her quotes were mainly one-syllable words. It was a challenging effort to make it all seem revelatory.

It was not long before Christmas; Graydon had gone to dine with a writer whose daughter—Graydon's assistant—would, in the not too distant future, set the Dior-draped fashion closet partly ablaze while sneaking a cigarette.

All day long, the company mail conveyance, which looked like a train in a children's zoo, had delivered gift after gift to Graydon's office. A photo by Annie Leibowitz of his family was propped up by his office, displaying the cherubic children in Santa hats and holiday pajamas, et cetera. So perfect and adorable were they that I would have gladly drawn a mustache just above the baby's smile.

Betty had persuaded the bracelet's owner to take a photo of the jewelry, which she was sending. Betty had decided that she would mail the picture to the American embassy in Istanbul and ask someone there to "run out" and get her a copy of it. It was all a little crazy. My mother seemed to feel that the State Department owed her some sort of favor. I guess she needed a little something; the bracelet appeared, something to hope for, something to change the way she was feeling.

She never went out of the house anymore. She was scared to leave my father. She was caged.

My job? To find the address of the embassy and help word the letter. "That's what you do," she said, "you write. I never ask you to do anything."

She didn't. I had to beg her to let me do anything for her. She was too proud.

I said I was going nuts. I told Betty about the deadline. She wanted the bracelet. I told her about the mistress. "How," she asked, "did you get mixed up with that?"

Finally, I managed to get her off the phone. I was so busy; she was not one to chat, but this time she wanted to hang on. Was it really the bracelet she wanted? Did she want me to say that this was not our family's last Christmas together, that my father was not so sick as she was finally letting herself see?

For a solid month I had been shut up in the East Side apartment of the author of the piece, Tessa Neely—a famous reporter with a reputation for destroying lives, personal assistants, and editors. For many days I had desperately begged and cajoled her to actually write, while she, ignoring my pleas, worked out with her trainer and attended Christmas gatherings.

Finally, we had a draft of what seemed hundreds of pages. Graydon, bored with it all weeks ago, had approved the piece but ordered it cut by thousands of words. Tessa was peeved, hissing.

Now as Betty was reluctantly saying good-bye, all at the magazine were scurrying, though Tessa still refused to budge. This is "fucking history," she cried again and again, jabbing my arm with the end of her pen but turning soft as a baby as she waved to Graydon on his way out. She was wearing a pink Chanel suit. It was getting later and later. The managing editor, Jan, was not pleased by all the delay.

Everyone was irate at Tessa and at me for not being able to corral her. I was so angry that when Tessa went to the bathroom, I threw her pink jacket out the window. It floated down through the air like a big, colorful bird. Tessa demanded so much. Betty demanded so little. But the bracelet thing was crazy. Betty was worked up in a way that was so unfamiliar to me. The weather had been bad at home. She had been cooped up for days.

She called back. When I had told her that the bracelet plot was going to be pretty hard to pull off, she seemed hurt. "I am here, by myself, all alone, with him," she said. "I need you to help me with just this one thing. Can't you help me just this once?"

Jan's assistant, Lulu, a whopping Texas girl, came in to say that she had to get something off her chest. She said that she had missed her therapist's appointment because she had to stay late to help with the piece. She felt angry and unsupported. I thought that this was probably the day that Lulu and her analyst had planned to discuss her feelings about cheese.

Tessa was soon looking for her jacket. When the phone rang, it was

Betty again. "I need to get out of here," she said. "We are just stuck here. I'm just stuck here, about to go nuts."

"I don't like the way you sound." Betty said again and on the phone, time after time, night after night. "I don't like the way you sound. Are you all right? Are you all right?"

"I'm fine. I'm fine," I told her a hundred times, but she didn't believe me. "I don't like the way you sound. I don't like the way you sound."

I was her focus, but as my father's face got grayer, turning a more ashy color, she became obsessed with him as well, though it was just a bit late, her waking up to take in what was happening.

My father spoke of waking to find my mother, her face right up in his, checking to see if he was breathing. "I'm dead, Betty. I'm dead," he'd say. "Well, how would I know if you were?" she'd respond. "I'd have to wake up and find you.

"I don't like the way you sound. I don't like the way you sound. Are you all right? Are you all right?"

"I am fine. I am fine."

Sucking on a Camel cigarette, hair arranged with perfect artfulness, Graydon, who had grown more and more hostile, eyed me with an expression that nearly knocked me out, a kind of contempt.

"Why," he asked me, as he surveyed a marked-up Streisand photo ("Don't tint the lips," she had demanded), "do you always have to try to be so fucking perfect? Why can't you let the writers be themselves?"

After that, nothing was really right between us. He ridiculed my outfits, my coffee brand, my story ideas. He exiled me from meetings, accused me of always looking bored. I somehow knew he would never be there anymore, I would never win his affection again. Yes, I had grown increasingly testy; yes, I was holding things up, trying to make the writing fine, missing deadlines; yes, I was marking up my galleys so endlessly that I had blinded more than a few copy editors.

Yes, I was on drugs, but only enough to kill a rock band and only at the end. Whatever it was that took me away from what I didn't want to feel or remember, I sniffed right up. I had, at some point, made a mistake. I was running fast. I think maybe I had forgotten that Graydon wasn't my father. When things are changing too quickly, things can get confused. All hands were empty now. No one was reaching out.

"Put Daddy on the phone."

"He doesn't want to talk. He hasn't left his chair all day. I don't know what to do about him. He won't do anything."

I started to go out alone. Early mornings on Sundays, I often found myself at the Sound Factory, dancing in a sweaty mob. Junior Vasquez was the DJ. The bass beat boomed. I sniffed this and that, took this and that, watched it all, sometimes joined in. Disco kites flew in the air above me. Flashes of strobe lights flashed on crazy eyes, slices of bare chest, tiny Japanese girls twirling in swirls of Gucci. Beside me one night, two large black women, dancing with gestures so perfect that I still remember them. There were street kids, ballet dancers. There were blacks and Puerto Ricans, whites, big-chested gay boys from Chelsea, fashion models, and people who looked distinctly dangerous. There were silhouettes of dancers on a screen bursting with colors. Everywhere was the current of sex, drag queens from the Houses of LaBeija or Extravaganza, doing runway turns on the sidelines. Work, all those crazy writers, my boss: They did not exist. I was alone, falling into situations I had never expected to encounter.

The disco ball spun fast; glitter fell from the ceiling and liquid smoke swirled on the dance floor. Flash forward, through faces, names I never bothered to learn, taxis with the music blaring, speeding through the late-night streets through the streams of light: It was 2 a.m., 3 a.m., 4 a.m., I was picking up a cell phone, dialing a drug dealer.

It could not last. I knew that, knew I would have to pay. And I did. I would pay and pay and pay. I am paying for it still, all those nights.

Around this time, I met a friend for coffee. He had made a sensible match, given up the party life. "I think I am out of control," I told him. "You always were," he said. "You just didn't know it."

I told none of this to Giorgianni. I told no one, admitted nothing. I kept my secrets battened down. Giorgianni and I talked about work, about how angry I got if one day passed and I was not, after all my hours, after all my work, after all my effort to get it right, singled out for special praise. If I was not told I am good, I was a wreck. If I was not perfect, I was nothing at all. If I am not successful, I am nothing at all. I tried to turn my pieces into masterpieces.

I was thirty-five years old, desperate, though I didn't know it, empty, though I didn't know it, raging in a way even I could not have managed to just ignore, though I did not know why. Often I could keep it in check, but when I needed most to be calm and confident, when I was exhausted, sleeping deeply, almost unconscious, I would spring a leak and all my anger would come out. I was a wreck. That is what happened when the phone rang on a Saturday afternoon while I was sleeping so deeply that I could barely manage to rouse myself to answer. When I picked up the receiver, I heard my aunt's voice saying that we had lost my father.

19

Every Wednesday night, on the way to our favorite restaurant for the prime rib special, Betty and I pass the empty Presbyterian church in Perry, another town with one foot in this life and another in wherever little towns go when no one lives there anymore. Many churches in this area barely survive on the donations they collect. Congregations have dwindled and worshippers are mostly old, living in dire need of church communities, but existing on fixed incomes. People without jobs have little cash for collection plates. Those who might once have shown up on Sundays watch celebrity ministers broadcasting from megachurches. They post passages from the Reverend Joel Osteen on Facebook, promises of prosperity from a man who lives in a ten-million-dollar house in a neighborhood populated by oil millionaires.

On the highways there are new temples of faith, Pentecostal congregations, tabernacles of the Holy Spirit, often housed in the kind of sheet-metal outbuildings once used for machine sheds and equipment storage. It is the old churches that are on the verge of closing their doors. The merchants who sustained them are gone. Wal-Mart, the store that wiped out the merchants, shuttered everything, has never offered a lonely widow a turkey dinner, a day of fellowship among friends, or hope.

In Perry, at this church with stained glass windows that the sun still shines through, the end came, almost unnoticed by many. Last year, in a special final ceremony, the ancient Bible with the names of all the members of the congregation through all the years was carried out to be stored. The big old building stands waiting with rows of plants for sale along the sidewalk in front, though there is talk of a mini-mall with booths for antique dealers and purveyors of home craft items.

My mother fears the day that our church will be vacant. The notion of her town without her church, her life without her church, her world without its center is enough to make her turn her head away.

Like Betty, I am scared about the days to come and am reluctant to desert the place where people who know of my mother's bad days come up to embrace me. They say they will do anything to help. A guy I went to high school with wants to know how I am doing and asks if I want to accompany him and his family to Branson to see Kenny Chesney. I thank him, but say I cannot forgive Kenny for what he did to Renée Zellweger.

"You always were real different," my friend tells me, touching my arm and smiling a little before getting into his vehicle.

Gradually I have come to feel that I fit here, at least a little. I suddenly know people again and am Dear Abby for those who are real different. A week or so ago, a woman from my high school class stopped me to say she is stuck in a trailer with a son who thinks he has a black woman living inside him.

"Tell him to let her out," I said.

Politically, I have a lot of differences with many I encounter here. When visiting the homes of reactionary friends and neighbors, I enjoy hiding their copies of books by Glenn Beck and other lunatics around the house while my hosts cook or adjourn to relieve themselves. Ducking into a garage to deposit the latest ravings of Ann Coulter into a bag of aging peat moss lifts the spirit as unfailingly as a summer tent revival. But I am trying to behave. I have a Cardinals cap, but cannot always remember what it is they play. Yesterday, when I heard that Evie Cullers is sick, I took her a dessert and listened to her talk and talk. She was recovering nicely from her respiratory difficulties, but I fear that after my sludgelike pudding, life support will be required. "Where did you come across this?" she asked when she gazed into the bowl.

I water the roses, try to keep them alive as there is still no rain. I no longer think of selling this house my father built. Maybe my attachment is temporary nostalgia, but I don't think so. I'd like to come back here in the summers at least. This is my home, my trees. Because of the drought, a lot of trees have died or are dying, and according to an article in the *Post-Dispatch,* many have been so damaged that the losses will continue for three or four years, even if the clouds finally decide to open. My father would be hurt to see this. He worked so hard to give his little trees a chance.

The last time I saw my father was over Christmas a few months before he passed away. His face was pale; it had gone from gray to pallor hard to gaze on without fear. Because of his arthritic knees, stiff after two operations, he could barely get around, though he made a cane for himself in his workshop in the basement. He kept calling my attention to that cane; he had tried to make it special, something beyond an old man's walking stick. When, unbeknownst to him, I watched him trying to go a few steps without it, I knew that the life we had shared together was coming to a close. A few days before my arrival, before our last holiday, he pulled his sciatic nerve struggling with the mattress on the antique bed where I try to sleep, trying to make it comfortable.

A few days before I left to go back to New York, he was in such pain that I took him to the emergency room. Betty stayed at home, but—still astonishingly spry then—ran out into the street as we left with the gloves my father forgot to wear, old work gloves from his lumberyard days. It was the coldest kind of winter afternoon and he hurt so badly that even breathing seemed hard labor. I watched him as he dragged himself to the admissions desk—weak, sad, and sick. He needed something fast for relief, but when the nurse said we would have to wait, probably for a couple of hours, he made no complaint, just shrugged his shoulders and made a joke. He made the old starched nurses feel like babes.

I remember my father at church, passing the communion plate

during the service to the old, blue-haired high school principal, finally retired. "Take two," he told her as he handed over the tray with the grape juice in tiny cups. "They're free, you know."

For the longest time, there in the emergency room, he got no help and we sat with me on guard, watching him, his cheek still wet from melting snow. So tightly did he clutch the handle of that cane that I thought his fingers would leave their marks in the wood. Finally someone saw the shape he was in and ushered us into an examining room. A doctor scrawled a prescription, but Big George could barely make it back to the car. When I found an open pharmacy, I think he was scared to wait alone. His heart was so vulnerable, ready to give out; something could happen and we both knew this and it was hard to leave him even for a moment.

He watched me, my every step away, from behind the frosted window of our old Lincoln as I trudged across the snow to buy the pills. On the way home, he looked straight ahead, not at me, and whispered, "Getting on time to die."

When he did leave us, he was all alone, in the basement at his workbench on a quiet Saturday afternoon in February. The night before, I had finished editing four or five articles for the Hollywood issue of *Vanity Fair* at midnight. The phone rang at 4 p.m. My aunt Alice called, my mother somewhere in the background. Betty just could not tell me, Alice said. She said Betty could not speak and had gone to her room to lie down. "Please don't leave her," I requested, but I knew she would soon be motioning Alice toward the door.

My first instinct was to call the dealer. I didn't want to feel. But it seemed disrespectful. My life felt disrespectful. For months, I had been struggling to give up drugs. Through a long, uncomfortable autumn of craving and withdrawal, I sat in a recovery group, surrounded by people who were trying to get better too. We came together in a little place with pink walls known as the Miracle Room. I took a few steps up the mountain, then would start to fall back, but someone always appeared to push me along, a little further, through another day to a place where I could feel a little better for a while.

I flew at 6 a.m. the morning after he died. At home, I felt his presence. The place was filled with him, as it had been, though he was missing and his big chair, where I had last seen him, empty. Near his workbench, I spotted two gifts, handmade, left for me to find: The first was a small cube with photographs glued on every side. To keep the pictures safe, to make them last, a coat of polish had been carefully applied. The photographs, views of our backyard at different times throughout the year, showed the way it looks in snow, in springtime when the trees are in blossom, in summer when all is green, and in the fall when the leaves are colorful. There is a picture of rain falling with the woods behind the house, just greens run together, like in some old painting. There is an image of a foggy morning when the ground is hidden and the bare trees reach out of the mist.

My father's hands were swollen when he made this memento, all the seasons of home, for me. He was dying. He could barely grip a pencil. Notes and old checks I find from this time in the drawers of his old desk are written in a hand so shaky I can barely recognize it.

In the city, in my apartment, on the bookshelf by the cube of photos, I also keep his second gift, a wooden hand created by tracing his own on a piece of wood. Like the cube, it was carefully polished. At the base where the wrist is, there are three letters carved: GAH, his initials and mine.

I was grateful for these gifts. I had wanted some good-bye and he had left it, without saying anything. My old silent man.

The night before the funeral, my mother and I talked very little. I think she was shocked by how it felt to lose him. I don't think she expected to feel so overcome. I had never seen her look so fragile and what I sensed in her strongly was regret, guilt: She should have heard him in the basement; she should have checked on him.

Finally, she began to speak. "You know," she began, "I didn't think he was really going to die. I couldn't believe it was going to happen, though I look back . . . last year . . . I had just gotten my new cornea. They wanted me to wear contact lenses, but I was too nervous to put them in. My hands shook. You remember. Every time I tried, I made a mess of it."

"Betty, quit your damn fretting."

"Your father calmed me down. I sat on the edge of the bed. He put them into my eyes in the mornings. He took them out at night. I was too nervous . . . My hands shook. Not long ago, he said I was going to have to learn to do it myself. He looked at me and put his hand on my cheek. I should have known how close it was."

"Betty, don't worry so much. Sit down. Please sit down and hold still."

One detail consoled me a little. Just before it happened, he and Betty were finishing lunch, and before he went to the basement where his heart gave out, my aunt Alice arrived with a slice of warm coconut pie. I told my mother that it was a gift to send a good man off. She just stared back until she said quietly, "I really didn't do much for him. I wish we could go back."

Before she headed into the bedroom, she said, "I don't want to go in there," so I walked back with her and laid my head on his pillow while she brushed her teeth.

On the day of the funeral, I had taken food up to my aunt and uncle's. Harry, recently sick himself, was sitting in his recliner, already in his suit, clipping his nails. When he saw me he stood, as if for some sort of salute, and put his hand on my shoulder. His face showed more pain than I had seen in him. Of all of us, he was the one who cried the most at funerals, and he and Big George had worked together almost fifty years, always arriving before the sun came up, whatever the weather.

Harry had aged since Christmas. With his eyes watering, he said, "Your father was a better man than me." I said no, but he kept on. "Your father kept us going," he said. "He could make you laugh. Sometimes it bugged the hell out of me. But the customers loved it. Everyone loved George. They came in just to see him. There was no one like him. He helped keep the business going."

At the funeral, a community choir, made up of all the choirs of all the churches, sang a hymn called "Crown Him with Many Crowns." I had not realized what a popular guy my father was, but there they all were, the people who had filled his days, his life.

My mother asked me how I could wear the suit I had chosen. "Because it was the only one I had that wasn't at the dry cleaners," I yelled at her. "I didn't plan for this."

Betty was in a mood with me. I knew I looked bad, still skinny from speed and tired from years of stress and no sleep. She treated the son of my father's sister from California as her partner in public. He was a married man with children. He had the right suit. He was appropriate for public display. All this may have been my imagination. Maybe she was just trying to show my cousin that she was grateful for his attendance. Maybe I just felt ashamed of myself.

Evelyn Fleming held my hand when they lowered the casket into the ground. After it was done, my mother looked at me, stumbled, and then caught herself, just stood there for a minute looking completely undone as if she had no idea where she should go or what came next. I went over, took her hand, and led her to the hearse, where she closed her eyes until it was certain we were far away from the grave. I never let go of her hand.

"Are you mad at me?" Betty asks today. "Have I done something wrong? I'll bet you wish I would die."

"Not until you eat this damn meat loaf," I say, shoving a casserole dish into the oven and trying not to hear her. She is an old woman, but I still hate to hear her talk about dying. "Actually, I am so grateful," I tell her, "to have you here. I cannot imagine a world without you. You know that I love you?"

Looking a bit uncomfortable, she says, "Yes, I do."

I know not to expect a response. This is not *On Golden Pond*. My mother's reticence is not something that will change. She signs birthday cards to old friends, "Sincerely yours, Betty Hodgman." She is of a generation who existed before feelings were spoken of.

We are two Americas colliding here, old and new.

When people ask Betty if she is on e-mail, she stares back and asks, "What kind of a question is that?" Every day it becomes more apparent to me, and I think to her—a woman who still calls the refrigerator an "icebox"—that her world is gone and she is standing almost by herself now, the only one who remembers how it was here, wondering half the time what it is that people are talking about.

Every magazine or paper I pick up seems to have an article on dementia, which seems to trouble almost all of those from her generation who survive. It is a plague. I have considered going from room to room with a pad of yellow squares, writing down the names of things, labeling every item.

Sometimes I think of all the people who have traveled on their own across the world, people who have gone far from home, from villages to sprawling cities where nothing and no one is familiar. My mother has also traveled—across time for more than nine decades, from one era to the next, from a world she knew to another where much she was taught does not apply. Things are changing so fast; there is no period of adjustment now for anyone. My mother tries to keep up, but it is such a complicated trip. The faces that time taught her to trust are all missing. She lives in a foreign land where it is up to me to try to make her feel at home. She has walked so far, through time.

I never wanted to hurt my parents. That has always been my excuse for not making more of an effort to force them into a reality where they could really know me, where we could have shared a little more about our lives. When the subject of my sexuality, of who I really was, finally came up, after so many silent years, I was almost forty years old. My father was gone, someplace where he could not hear my words.

Betty and I were riding through the countryside on the way home from the stockbroker's. She was talking about how my failing father, dead just days, had nearly killed them both a few months back, driving too fast near that spot, by an old one-room schoolhouse a little way past Curryville. He had been trying to get her home from an eye doctor's appointment before bad weather set in.

At some point, she asked me about my old friend David. "He never married?" I shook my head.

"Is he homosexual?" she asked.

"I am not sure," I said. "I never see him anymore. But you know I am. Surely. After all this time. You must understand this."

The passing headlights threw streaks across her face. She looked pained. It would be awhile before we would return to a safe stretch of highway. "I had thought it would pass," she said, before telling me that my father could never accept it, could not speak of it, would not speak of it. After watching the TV movie *An Early Frost,* he had commented of the father of the gay man in the film, " 'He hated it, but he loved his son.' That is all he ever said about it." That is what she told me.

"You never talked about it?" I asked. "With him? The two of you? Not at all? I just can't imagine it. Never? You said nothing about me?"

She shook her head.

There is almost no truth better not known. The harder ones are tolerated more comfortably when shared. They couldn't even talk about me to each other. I was an issue they avoided. Because of the way they had been raised to think about people like me. They did not speak of me, of who I was, even when they were alone, in the privacy of their own house.

Betty turned to me in the car and said, "Well, I guess you'll go your way and I'll go mine." After that, she stopped talking.

The radio murmured, mostly static as the miles passed, and there was nothing but the sound of strong wind. I said nothing. I wasn't sure what she meant, if we were divided now. There are words you never expect to hear. And then you hear them and it is like the news of death or disaster, they just stop you and you cannot go on for a while.

She said he loved me, my father, he loved me, but not who I turned out to be. That was the essence of it. He loved me, as so many have loved the children who turned out to be so different, "in spite of." I didn't want "in spite of." I had been afraid of "in spite of." I didn't want to hear or know that this was how it was with my dad. I just kept reminding myself that he left me his hand.

Maybe I wasn't afraid of hurting them. Maybe I just knew, always, how it would be, despite their love and best intentions. Maybe I was scared of being hurt myself and knew that finally, through no fault of their own, they could say nothing that could conceal the fact that there was part of me they could never approve of. I wasn't angry; I was just sad at this separation that would never quite be bridged, this place where, despite what we shared, we parted ways, all of us hurt. It was just a set of circumstances inflicted that we could not avoid, the legacy of our place and time—and all that they had been brought up to believe by the world and the churches that told them I was something wrong. I had grown up with the story of Jesus taking all the little children to his knee. I had thought of churches as places of kindness, but if you are on the outside looking in, if only part of you is accepted, so much is different.

No one can dispute that God or whatever force there is created the world as a changing place. I like to think that it was progress that the father or mother of us had in mind, a greater love, a growing rather than diminishing acceptance of one another, of other kinds of people, as time moves forward, but so much of what I see now does not support my notion of this design.

. . .

After my mother and I had our talk, February just went on. The days were white and empty. Night after night, I dreamed about using drugs. In the mornings, I thought of just leaving, driving to the airport and flying back to New York to hide. Just escape.

Winter is a bleak time in the country, lonely, so I stayed with Betty for several weeks after the funeral to try to help, so she would not feel alone in the house where they had lived together so long. There was low-lying fog, snow melting, lavender streaks in the fields. For days, she stared out from her window at the long blank lawn, the bare suggestions of trees. The house was quiet. Betty said almost nothing; she was papers shuffling, a voice on the phone in another room. When she opened the safe-deposit box, she took the engagement ring that her aunt Mabel, whose middle name she gave me, had left for whomever I would marry. The next time I came home I discovered she had sent it to be reset. She had made it hers. It didn't matter. It was just something I noticed.

I put dishes into the washer. I shoveled snow. I went through papers and stock certificates, dozens of extra keys to doors and cars. I sat in my father's chair, but didn't stay because, though he never had intended it, I was hurt.

My mother did not grieve outwardly, at least when I was looking, but when she sat down on the couch, it was always my dad's sweater or coat she reached for to throw over herself. When I offered to help dispose of his clothes, she put one finger to her lips to say I should not speak of this. She set the plates down for lunch, returned again and again to her window, watched the snow drop from the branches. She stirred soups, opened cans, kept all the time filled with what had to be done. She never mentioned my father, or our conversation about me, except to say one more time that they never spoke of who I was.

This is how it finally thawed with Betty: On the morning I went back to New York after my father's death, she rode with me to Lambert Field, where we were driven by the man who now took her places far from home. Her eyes were not good enough to drive outside town much anymore, and by now the highway made her nervous rather than excited. At a hotel near the airport, where we once went on hot weekends to swim, I climbed the steps onto the shuttle bus. In parting, Betty offered few words, a nod, a bunch of wrapped sandwiches, and a bundle of cookies with gumdrops, a kind difficult to bake that were once my favorite.

I thought I had seen the last of her for a while. We would, as she said, go our own ways, and I watched her every step back to the car where the driver hunched over the wheel just like my father had. But as I was waiting for the bus to pull out, there she was again, ascending the stairs of the bus, careful of every step and holding a cup of coffee, its steam rising up to her face. Walking to my seat, she offered the cup, gripping it tightly to avoid a spill, though it was very hot, and not letting go until I had wrapped my fingers around it. When she passed it to me, our hands touched lightly. She patted me on the shoulder, wavered a bit when the engine of the bus started to fire up. This is how we left it.

Gradually, we came to a truce, negotiated by distance, time apart, loyalties, and love. Silence was a condition, unnamed but ever present, or maybe just an inevitable result. There would be no intrusions, no questions, no inquiries about circumstances, details, people I might have cherished, or been hurt by, or loved. I would never miss a Christmas or summer vacation at home after my father died. I went back whenever it was possible, and there was no doubt of the love between us, but there was part of me that never went home again, at least not for a long time. I no longer felt on solid ground there. I think I am still hoping she will look up from her newspaper and ask me how my life has really been.

I don't blame my parents for any hurts. I blame myself more than anyone, my silence, but everything in the world where I was raised told me I was bad and wrong and I took it in. I didn't want to inflict it on them. I am trying to forgive myself for not getting us all through this in a better way, but lately, being here, remembering, has helped me see what I carried. Everything I heard, from every corner, when I was young told me I was bad. Nothing said the world had open arms. When I came home to help my mother and walked into the room where when I was younger I lay awake worrying about the future, I remembered all that fear and trying to put it away and sleep a night through.

What would I have done with a diamond ring? It made her think of things she thought I was missing. She made it into something that would suit the situation better.

Yesterday, on television, I heard the story of a Georgia legislator who is trying to bar gay children from attending public schools. I threw my shoe at the television and yelled out, "Fuck you, bastard."

He would take us all back to that same place. I hate that man and everyone like him. What has become of kindness?

Every week or so, a gay kid somewhere jumps off a bridge or slashes his wrists. I am told that a boy near here hanged himself because his father could not accept who he was. On television, I listen to the things they say, the right-wingers, and fundamentalists, and all the people who consolidate their power by hurting other people. I want to cover up the ears of kids and say, "Do not take it in." I took it in. I really did. I heard everything that people in the world around me said about who I was. It hurt me, but I thought I had no right to say anything because I was wrong. I didn't know what silence would cost, how it would change my life. It takes a long time to outrun the things that the world drills into you.

Our struggle for words was just a tiny battle in a small place that is disappearing. No one will remember it but me.

After my father died and I went back to work, Tessa Hadley—a woman highly attuned to issues of aging and appearance—told me I looked older. She said that the death of a parent can often bring on early menopause. Or "low T."

I didn't think I had early menopause. "Low T?" I asked.

"Testosterone."

"I don't think I ever had that much."

Tessa assured me that everything changes when parents die, when the generation ahead is gone and we are the next to go.

"The body grieves," she told me, shaking her head and raising a finger to her lips. "The body grieves."

"Be still," I told her.

I didn't look young anymore. After years of wearing contact lenses, I went back to my glasses. I just didn't care so much how I looked, if at all.

I just tried not to use drugs. I was scared to go home, to be alone, to pick up. At treatment centers, I listened to stories: the ghetto mother who gave up crack, got her children back, and rose every morning at 3 a.m. to pack lunches, iron clothes, and navigate a long bus journey to work; people who had lost people; stockbrokers who flamed out on coke, got divorced from their trophy wives, braved the wrath of their children as they kept on, trying to get clean. I heard old men and women who had weathered decades of cancer, financial hardship, loneliness, without drinking or drugging.

These stories helped me through. I wrapped these tales around me. When, unable to rise from bed or certain I would not make it through the day, I called for the help of these strangers who spoke; they came or called to talk until my crises passed. It was the stories that saved me; words rushed in to draw me back to life.

When I looked into the mirror, I did appear older; I looked more and more like my father. In the years that have followed, it has seemed to me that my dad has taken me over, seeped into me. Sometimes I think I have become my father. My body is more like his, a fact that Betty, who is already anticipating the blockage of one or more of my heart valves, is quick to point out.

In rain, my hair, a different consistency now, frizzes up like my dad's did as he strolled on the beach in Florida. I remind myself of him so often; the expressions that pass over my face feel familiar even though I can't see them.

In traffic, I lose patience, start yelling, "Damn boobs!" at drivers during rush hour. Here with Betty, I feel even more like Big George. Gradually I have slipped into his role and reactions. She seems most angry at me when I remind her of him. We relive all the old scenes.

If I have been working all night and Betty finds me taking a nap in the middle of the day, she is not amused. She hated to see my father idle. He was never allowed to relax. She hates to see me idle. I am not allowed to relax. I fall into my role. Throwing my hands into the air, I get the ladder from the garage and head out to clean what seem like decades of dry leaves out of the gutters. I get angry and manage to dislodge the drainpipe that runs from the gutter to the ground. I mutter swearwords to myself. Like he did. If Betty comes out, I say them louder. Like he did. If Betty comes out when the neighbors are around, I fling them about with abandon, as loud as I can go without actually yelling. Like he did.

But the thing is, if I am suddenly, in Betty's head, my father, what happened to the person who was me? Am I lost to her? Where did I go?

For a long time now, it has been hard to get my mother excited about anything, even going to the city. A few years back, when I took Betty into St. Louis for the periodontist, we stopped at Saks where I wanted to buy her a new outfit. It was there I noticed the depression that had settled into her, her lethargy. She looked tired and was unable to summon the energy to shop for new clothes. Later, when I went to visit another store in the mall, she waited in a chair by the Saks fitting room, the color drained from her face.

When we drove past Granny's old apartment, as she once liked to do, I told her how I always thought of Daddy when we were in St. Louis. "Well, I think this is where he would be," she said. "He probably should have stayed here. He might have been happier."

She glanced at me for a second. I couldn't put my finger on exactly what she was thinking, maybe of things she could never give him. Sometimes I think she mourns over her failings. But I think she was wrong about my father, where he would wind up if the choice was his. I still remember the picture he drew of her, our Betty, the one no one else saw, the girl on the streetcar, waiting for him to come sit down beside her, but moving away when he approached. For both of us, I think, she was always a little hard to get close to and neither one of us ever knew the reason why.

20

Sometimes I still dream I am a kid running through the rows of the fields behind our house in Madison, a little scared. Very often in the mornings, I wake up in fear of the future, of finding myself alone here on the planet. "I think," said my counselor in rehab, "that every patient I've had is scared like that."

"Don't worry, it's prescription butter," I told Betty when she eyed what I was slathering on my toast.

She said nothing; she has been irritable, mad at me, but won't explain. She just falls into it sometimes. The air-conditioning had chilled this house. Wearing my parka, I pulled the hood up over my head right there at the table. I didn't know if she was fretting over something new or returning to some festering resentment. I think she still has a little chunk of anger logged into her account book under my name, but is either reconciled to it or ashamed of its presence. It's a little island floating between us and she doesn't want to live there, doesn't want to acknowledge it exists at all, but occasionally, there she is, sitting on the sand, far off, with a look not hard to decipher.

I didn't turn out like she planned. Maybe a lot of things didn't quite, either, and almost all of the story has been revealed. We can't go back.

One morning, almost two years ago, the head of the publishing house where I worked called me in when no one else was around. Red-faced, he blurted out the news, said the department was restructuring. I was leaving. He labeled the severance "generous" and passed me a white form I was to sign. "You'll want to do that as soon as possible," he told me. "If you want to get the severance."

Back in my office, I reviewed the form calling for everything but organ harvest and the renunciation of God and country. It was lengthy. I got a little emotional. I felt like Jane Fonda in *They Shoot Horses, Don't They?* When I tried to call my authors to tell them what had happened, I froze. Within moments, the publisher was back at my door.

"Have you signed the form yet?"

I didn't respond. My head was full of voices; I went outside to try to get it together. As I passed the publisher's office, the question came again:

"Have you signed the form yet?'

I stayed in bed for days, listening to the voices fling curses. I hadn't worked hard enough. I hadn't gotten it right. Work was all. I am nothing, nothing without work. No one is. Not without work. Harry worked hard; Bill worked hard; Mammy worked hard; Betty worked hard. Shut up.

I considered possible options (migrant opportunities, Bedouin lifestyle, armed retaliation, drug mule). When I told my mother about the "restructuring," she kept using the term "firing" and it stung. "I wasn't fired," I kept saying. "I was restructured. I now have an atrium lobby."

I went to the Miracle Room and screamed at a few street people. I didn't use drugs, though I wanted to. After all the years, I still wanted to escape. Work was what I had, who I had always been. It was where I was most comfortable. It was gone.

This morning, trying to fit all the dirty dishes into the dishwasher, I listen to Betty on the phone with Betsy, a close friend whose calls perk my mother up like nothing else. Betsy is seventy or so; to Betty she is practically a teenager. She gets invited to lots of parties. My mother is flattered by the attentiveness of one so young and popular. And wealthy. Betsy has money, land.

Betty has been scared that Betsy and her husband will move to Florida, where they have a condo, but now my mother is laughing, suddenly very pleased. Betsy, diagnosed last spring with breast cancer, has completed treatment, and overhearing Betty's responses, I sense happy news.

"I love you too, Betsy," says my mother. "I love you too."

It is strange to hear her say these words out loud. It stops me for a minute because my mother is so open and sounds so cheerful.

Betsy's eldest daughter was once considered the prettiest girl around, but she got involved with a man—"from *Joplin*," Betty says, if that explained everything—interested in her parents' money. There were ugly scenes, gossip, my kind of relationship. Finally the couple divorced and Betsy's daughter has never remarried. Betty calls this is a tragedy. People forced to live by conventions are always the first to enforce them. I think this applies to my mother. A practical investor, she bought stock in the usual choices because they ordinarily pay off without risk or pain. She never imagined they could betray her or that anyone close would break them.

Never a practical investor, I have always gone for the crazy horse.

I am alone. I don't have a regular job now. Betty believes I am a bit of a tragedy, like Betsy's daughter and this makes my mother angry. She would never admit it, even to herself, and she would never hurt me, but I feel her disappointment sometimes. I've done my time with it, this sense of letting her down.

"Did you hear Betsy's news?" Betty asks. "She's going to be okay."

"I guess she and Ed can go ahead and move now."

My mother's face falls. I have lobbed a little bomb. I have to do something to change my mood—something you don't purchase by the gram or liter.

After scanning the Internet, I head to a recovery meeting in Hannibal, on the Mississippi, a hilly place where, in the minds of schoolchildren, Huck and Tom will always wander. River towns seem to always draw drunks and druggers, and this one hosts an especially large number of group homes for addicts, alcoholics, and the mentally ill. At the meeting, a woman is standing at the bottom of the steps of the church, wearing old black tennis shoes with black socks. Her hair, a tumbling tower, is strewn with little butterfly barrettes to hold it up. Her name, she says, is Mary. She is seven years off alcohol. When I tell her I am from New York, she says, "Jesus. That far."

When I say I am staying with my mom, Mary responds, "Gotcha . . . Here?"

"In Paris."

Mary says that for a while she cleaned for a woman a few streets away from us. "A well-known bitch," she claims.

Mary may clean for money, but this group is her real vocation. She has clearly made herself the leader, and if she has to swat a few drunks or some addicts' asses to keep them straight, she will.

In the church basement, there are six or eight people, including a guy who looks like a construction worker; a clean-cut middle-aged man who is perhaps a salesman; a housewife type, going at her gum; a tattooed boy slender enough to pack and fold. I fix on a tough-looking young woman with a bad complexion and short shorts who has just been released from a women's shelter. Her drug is meth. I understand the attraction. Anything that took me up was good. Back in the old days, I never wanted to be down, or sleep, or even nap.

When the woman heads off to the bathroom, Mary whispers, "Float-through. Comes and goes, gets a day or two, then meets some new asshole and it's off to the races."

Still, when the girl comes back, Mary grabs her hand and rests it in her own lap, where its sweat leaves a few fingers.

The young woman is named Brittany, as about a quarter of the women in this state seem to be. She has a pack of Camels rolled in her T-shirt sleeve and taps her foot in the air. Her face is slick, drenched with sweat; this room is hot, closed, and still, and she is detoxing. Recovery hurts. Every feeling you escaped comes to slap you in the face.

. . .

Seven years or so after my first recovery, I relapsed. I never told anyone why or how because the truth sounded like such an excuse, something to let me off the hook. But what happened was this: I had a book to edit, a book about the James family that was eight hundred pages long. My company had paid way too much for us to earn our money back unless it was . . . perfect. I had a week to do the job and it had complicated problems. I wanted it to be perfect, so I took speed and stayed up for days and the work was actually good. Never had Henry James flown through life with such exuberance. Alice? What a charmer. But I lost it. I couldn't stop using. It all accelerated very fast. I did what I had never done: I lied and lied, stopped talking to sober people, missed work, fell asleep at meetings, did things I have a hard time claiming, though the voices in my head have never forgotten.

A few months later, I found myself sitting on the steps in front of my apartment building with a suitcase and a trash bag full of unmated socks. I was on my way to rehab in Pennsylvania, waiting for a friend to pick me up. My suitcase was full of dirty clothes, the only kind I had. The socks were in the bag because I had at first forgotten to pack them and didn't want to open my suitcase again. I was tired, coming down: It seemed too much to try to open that suitcase one more time.

A few days before, I had overheard one of the executives at work, a decent woman, holding nothing back, talking about me. I have never been suicidal, don't believe in it, but I might have gone out the window if I had been able to unlatch it. At home, I got higher than ever, and as I was bare and empty, the voices hit full attack mode. I lay facedown on my pillow, almost disappeared for good. I did not want to breathe.

I think people who have always felt okay in the world will never understand those of us who haven't.

Mary asks Brittany, the newcomer, if she wants to talk, but the young woman shakes her head. "Y'all know my story," she says. "I ain't never going to get this right, and I might as well just keep going. The center made me come. I don't want to be here."

Mary reaches out, encircles Brittany with her arm, and pulls her head down onto her shoulder. I think Mary's hair is going to fall down for sure, but it does not. Sometimes a few decades of Final Net are all an honest woman can count on in this life. When tattoo boy gives Brittany a nasty sort of once-over, Mary shoots him a look that could burn the rest of the crops.

In the car to the rehab in Pennsylvania, I thought of the many great Americans who have made such a pilgrimage: Truman, Liza, Elizabeth Taylor, maybe an Allman brother. At a truck stop on the highway, we stopped for coffee, and as I paid I noticed that for some reason I was holding my trash bag full of socks.

At the rehab, they put me first into an infirmary to detox and it was freezing. A man who looked a little like Jesus said the last time he was in the infirmary, a woman had tried to eat her coins and keys.

It was October in Pennsylvania and on the first morning the ground was frosted. As I walked to breakfast, some guy yelled out, "Thirteen inches in the Poconos."

"Is that a porn film?" I asked.

On the morning of the second day, I left bed, reluctantly, for a bowl of cereal; there were hundreds of boxes in the kitchen—brands I thought had been discontinued. Trust an addict to love a Fruit Loop.

Sitting at the table was a woman who had floated by during registration: Beth. In front of her was a bowl of Rice Krispies and, next to it, a small unopened container of milk. She stared into space, looked down at the cereal, then at me, and said, "I don't want to be a fucked-up mother."

"Me neither," I said, spacey, but managing somehow to pour the milk into the Rice Krispies for her. "Snap, crackle, pop," I said to her. "Am I going to have to clean the toilets?"

"Do you want to stop taking drugs?" they asked in rehab.

"I want to stop humiliating myself," I answered. "Or just go away."

. . .

Sitting at the meeting in the heat that will not break, I watch Mary guard Brittany. A man with a toothpick in his teeth tells his story without its ever falling out. His daddy was an alcoholic; his granddaddy was too. "And it goes like that," he says. "I come to this natural and I give it up only because of no money. My kids had signed off on me. My wife signed off on me. I was living in my car. I got a house and a job now. My kids don't call, but my wife brought over a cake for my birthday and we sat and ate it."

At rehab, I talked, hour after hour, to Beth, who had a smoky voice. Her addiction began when she was in junior high. She started trying to get sober when she was nineteen, but it never clicked for long. Her kids had seen her strung out. Together, we sorted through our sloppy days.

It wasn't the first time Beth was forced to leave her family—a husband and two little boys—to stay in treatment. One Sunday, I met her kids. Watching them climb up the hill to their mother's waiting arms, the thing I noticed was their clothes. Both had on T-shirts and shorts of blazing white. They looked ready for the Laundry Olympics. Taking in those boys, Beth looked like she wanted to crawl off and die: Someone else had gotten her kids cleaner than she ever could.

"Beth is so ashamed," I told a counselor.

"You spot it, you got it."

"Did you make that up just now?" I asked.

I knew that before I left that place I was going to find myself talking to chairs.

"Why are you ashamed of yourself?" they kept on asking me. "You put yourself down every time you open your mouth. You have obfuscatory tendencies."

"Do I need a vaccination?"

"Why do you do that, the joking?"

"Because if I say what you want, I sound so damn pathetic."

I could not think at all, could not connect to what they said, stopped talking in group.

"You're withholding," said a nosy chatterbox who grew up amid the Pennsylvania Dutch. I will always picture her in wooden shoes.

"You're withholding," she kept saying. I found her intrusive.

"Bitch, do you think you work here?" I said to her. "What makes you think you've got everyone pegged so right?"

"You're withholding."

"You're withholding."

"You're withholding."

"Why do you feel ashamed?"

"Why do you feel ashamed?"

"Why do you feel ashamed?"

"Because I'm fucking bad," I screamed out one day. "Because I'm wrong."

They clapped. It was just like *Ordinary People*.

"Oh, screw you all," I said. I didn't think I had hit some sort of jackpot in terms of progress. I just gave up and said what they wanted. I just wanted to eat some Fruit Loops.

"When was it that you first felt your emotions shut down?"

"I'm not sure they were ever opened up."

"Try to connect."

"I can't do this. Everything you say makes me want to be ironic."

When I left New York to go to rehab, I told Betty that I had gone to Pennsylvania for work. She would have done her best with all this, tried to help, but I could not tell her what had happened, could not find the words. I am not sure I will ever develop the knack of letting her know just who I am, and had to put her on a shelf with all the things I could not think about then. I read recovery manuals, spiritual books, memoirs of addiction and alcoholism by rock stars and minor Kennedy wives.

I didn't think I could trust my mother not to fall apart. I never trusted them to be able to take in anything about me that seemed even slightly out of sync.

"Maybe you misjudged them," said Miss Withholding.

"Aren't they ever going to fucking send you home?"

"Why couldn't you talk to them about your sexuality?"

"Because I thought they didn't want to know."

"I think your mother would have liked for you to have opened up to her."

"Did they give you a job here?"

"Your mother sounds pretty strong."

"I thought I had to protect them."

"From what?" a counselor asked.

"From me, I guess."

"Who said you were bad?"

"Are you, like, new to this culture?"

"Do you wish your parents had said more, made you talk to them?"

"I wanted someone to help me . . . It was a long time back. It wasn't like now. We didn't know what we were doing."

After the meeting, Mary takes Brittany for a bottle of water and I walk with them. Brittany is shy, and when she finds out I am from New York, she gets quieter. I figure she maybe finished high school. Her skin is pockmarked and clearly prone to sunburn. She does not have money for water. I have a car that doesn't look about to fall apart and a shirt with a man on a horse playing some game she has never heard of. I had parents who cared, who were there or tried to be. I can't imagine she has ever had anyone.

"Honey," I say to her, "believe me, I know how it feels to screw up."

She asks, "Do ya?"

I do. It takes so long to feel better.

"What can we do for you?" asked one of the counselors at rehab.

"Keep me here forever. Give me a condo where I can see a Pocono."

One night, during the hour allotted for phone calls, I got Betty. She had been to her cornea specialist and, for once, admitted she was worried. She had lost some vision. Transplanted corneas have a shelf life. She was afraid hers were wearing out and confessed that she didn't want to go through more operations. As I tried to count on my fingers how many surgeries she had gone through, I said that if she had to have another, I would come home, but before I could get through the offer, she was saying, "No, no, no. I'll be fine."

She never mentions not seeing well, but that night was not herself. I asked what she intended to do, whether she was willing to have more surgery. "I'll do what I have to do," she said. "I am not going to be blind. I'll do what I have to do."

I decided I would too. But it was hard. Every time I tried to joke, the rehab shut me up.

"You're running from your feelings."

"I know. I hope they're fat and slow and can't keep up."

At night, I could not sleep. My mind would not click off and I thought and thought, just hung out in my head for hours and hours: I had made myself up and it had not worked. Someone else kept poking through my little act, tripping me up. One night, very late, a man from Connecticut trying to make the break from painkillers came to our room in the middle of the night to ask if anyone wanted to play golf. I said maybe later. The next night, I was awakened again—by one of the counselors who was there to search my things. Someone thought I seemed a little too energetic. "They always do that," Beth told me. "These people are all ex-addicts. They need drama."

"Babe, fuckup might as well be my middle name," Mary tells the girl from the women's shelter whose face looks even whiter in the sunlight. "I got two kids in Memphis and not even a Christmas card and they never gonna forget what a tramp I was and you just learn how to live with the shit."

I tell her, "You just close your eyes and say over and over, 'I'm okay.'"

What I don't say is that this doesn't exactly work. Shame takes forever to go away. Actually, it never does. You scrub a little every day. The thing, I think, is to know, to realize it is there, waiting to trip you up.

At rehab, there was a priest—Bruce, an alcoholic, a repeat offender, from New Jersey. One day, he was informed that his congregation had decided to take him back after his relapse. I wondered if the world would take me back. This is what Bruce said to me one night after a session where I was told, once more, that I had disconnected somehow from my feelings: "You must always, always tell the truth. If you are mad, say so. If someone asks you anything, try to find the exact words to describe what you have to say. If you try to tell the exact truth, always, you will ground yourself, become yourself. The truth connects you. It hooks you back up."

I didn't joke. I took it in. I believe the truth does hook you to yourself, but it takes so long to get in the habit of saying it out loud. I like a bit of camouflage to spruce things up a bit.

Words are my business, but I had only mastered them on paper. I will always struggle with the problem of avoiding uncomfortable words.

"Do you always tell the truth?" I asked Bruce.

"Not so much," he said.

I stayed in rehab for a month. Near the end, they gave us our evaluations. They wanted Beth to stay for another long-term treatment and she cried all night. The next morning, the tears . . . She could not stop crying. Later, she said she could not leave her boys again, that they would never forgive her.

At mine, a counselor asked me if I blamed my parents for my addiction. "Of course not," I said. "Of course not. We all got hurt in a way because we didn't talk. They just went by the rules they were taught."

"What about your mother?" asked the counselor.

"Maybe," I replied, "she was a little overdemonstrative."

The people in the interview knew I had tried hard. They laughed a little bit, let me have one.

"I am also available for weddings and bar mitzvahs."

"You do know, don't you," asked my counselor, "that you are not a joke?"

The counselor said my addiction was a trickster and that I was a secret keeper. I was told I should not go back to the city, that I would be unable to resist falling into the same patterns, but I had to keep my job. I left early on a Thursday morning. A man in a van was to take me to catch a train. On the way out, I took a last look at the line of people who were too anxious or depressed to function and who waited at this time of day for their rations of prescribed medicines. I wandered over to the place where I was to pick up the things they confiscated when I arrived. Bruce motioned me into his room and, in the dim light, blessed me, hugged me, and gave me his phone number.

"I want to stay in rehab forever," I told Beth, who looked at me and said, "Well, it looks like I'm going to."

On the first morning I was to return to the publishing house where I worked, I left my apartment at 7:30, but had to pause at three different Starbucks to collect myself before I could walk in the door. I arrived a little after nine. At the end of the day, a woman I liked came to my door, sat down with me, asked me if I was okay. She came in each day for a while. Her kindness made me feel okay.

Since then, I have not picked up again. I have attended hundreds and hundreds of all kinds of recovery meetings. I have chanted, meditated, stood up in front of people to tell my story. I have tried to reconnect. When I lost my job, I thought I was going to just fall down. "I feel ashamed and scared," I said. I told the truth. It was the strangest thing to not try to cover it up.

You can spend your whole life revealing very little to anyone. You can stay smoke and mirrors and, if you give them a laugh or two, no one will say or ask much. I never really wanted anyone to know that much about me, but I didn't even realize that. I didn't know what I was doing.

I can never be a person who has not made mistakes. But I can be someone honest who has lived through them: one of those who look you square in the eye and say, "This is how it has been, and it is okay." It has been a long, long struggle to hold my head up. I think I have survived because of Betty, more than anyone. I will never stop remembering my mother's strength, her struggle to remember words, to hang on to the world. I will always hear her at the piano, an old woman practicing, still trying to get it right, to find the right notes. I will see her walking, haltingly, in the dark, doing her best to find her way. We have sometimes struggled with words, but I am Betty's boy. There are so many things I will carry when I leave Bettyville with my old suitcase.

At home I just slip in quietly and go to my room to read. For weeks, I have been trying to start *A Gate at the Stairs* by Lorrie Moore, but I cannot get beyond the review quotes in front. There are, like, ninety. I have been fixated on them. "Reverberates with quiet lingering power that leaves the reader pondering the randomness of life and death and the wisdom and futility of love," says the *Sacramento Book Review*. This seems too much for a Tuesday afternoon.

"Where have you been?" Betty asks when she sees me.

I say I went to take some pictures.

"Of what?"

"The scenery."

My mother is still in her gown. For her birthday, I got her three new ones and a robe, but she won't wear them, says they were too expensive.

"I want to call that girl, you know," Betty says. "You know her name."

"Who?"

"The one from the dinner, the dinner at Jane's. You know her name. Her husband . . . She had to find him."

"I know." Betty has been obsessed with Jamie for weeks. She wants so much to think of some way to help her.

"I don't think a person can ever get over that," Betty says. "I want to try to help some people before I die."

There are things that everyone carries. I don't really know the things inside my mother, but I know she feels so much more than she says.

I never wanted a child for myself, but I would have liked to have seen them all, all my family, once again in someone. I would like to have kept parts of them in the world. But that was not my life. I want my mother to know that I may not be what she expected, but I am someone who tries to be good. I cannot give my mother the kids we might have liked with Mammy's eyes or Aunt Bess's crazy, gentle ways. I cannot bring her the child who sings with my father's voice. But I can wait with her through these strange days for whatever is going to happen. I can sit on a chair by her bed when she is too flustered to lay her head down on her pillow and stay with her until she can close her eyes.

21

Things My Mother Does Not Do

1. Complain.
2. Dispose of almost anything, including years-old margarine tubs possibly hoarded for the dispersal of emergency rations.
3. Ignore a coupon.
4. Put anything away.
5. Allow me to talk "long distance" for more than three minutes without yelling in the background.
6. Give up without a fight.

One night late last week, not long after 10 p.m., Betty screamed very loudly. I bounded into her room, certain that this was it. The end. When I got in there, she was perched on the side of her bed, looking sheepish.

"What on earth?" I cried out, reaching for the phone. "Are you all right? Do you need an ambulance?"

Betty just looked at me.

"Why did you scream?" I asked.

"Why do you need an explanation?"

"Because you screamed."

Some moments passed.

"I thought I felt a bedbug run across my leg," she confessed.

For several days, she'd been reading about a bedbug infestation in Columbia in the *Tribune.* On the night of the scream she had read the most recent story aloud to me. She seemed to expect me to fumigate immediately.

"The bedbugs are in Columbia," I said. "It's fifty miles away."

"They travel."

"But they don't drive," I said.

"Do you need a Xanax?" I ask a few minutes later.

"I'd rather have a gin and tonic."

The next day we were in the office of Dr. C., one of Betty's eye doctors, a cornea specialist. In Columbia. As I took her into the examining room, she said to the assistant: "I read you have a lot of bedbugs over here."

"I don't know," said the young woman, "but I got scabies from a patient once."

My side hurt. I wondered if it was gallbladder. My mother says everyone in our family gets gallbladder sooner or later. Her much repeated advice over many years, her admonition for after she is gone: "One of these days your stomach is going to feel it is about to explode. Remember I told you. Gallbladder. You are going to feel awful."

I thought the whole thing was stress. I didn't want to see Dr. C. I never do. He has hated me for twenty years—since I tripped on my untied shoelace and collided with an extremely delicate and apparently expensive piece of diagnostic equipment that was waiting in his hall to be installed.

He eyed me coolly.

"So you're still around?" he asked.

"I think I have gallbladder," I said, but Betty interrupted before I could list my symptoms.

"How many grandchildren do you have now, Dr. C.?" Betty asked.

"Forty-one."

"Good God," I cried out. I couldn't help it. I blurted.

Doctor C. eyed me as if he planned to detach my retina.

"I love children," I said.

. . .

Our weekend was okay, except for a major snafu at the farmers' market. The woman who makes the cinnamon rolls was late. If you cannot count on the Amish to be punctual, where are we? How long does it take to throw on a bonnet?

On Monday, Betty is normal and energetic. She moves around the house, semispringy, even speaking of making chicken salad. Any sign of her taking part in something is enough to almost make my day. By Tuesday, though, she is a gray ghost, hunched over, so small now, and does not seem to want to move at all. She moans; she groans; she whines; she emits tiny whimpers, chuckles without mirth, mutters to herself, bubbles up with small utterances. It is as if she is trembling verbally and repeating the same phrases again and again: "Let's go. Let's go. Let's go."

Nowhere in the house, it seems, is there a place her noises cannot penetrate.

"Well, you've got it upside down," she says to herself. "This is upside down. What? What? What?" It is as if these repetitions give her some control. Every word is like a brick in the wall guarding her against some intruder she cannot name or get a glimpse of. The phantom is frightening; sometimes it seems she is on the verge of tears. Betty. On the verge of tears. Sometimes she talks to herself, half sentences, little cries out as she shakes her hands or fists. It is like there is someone else inside her, the real Betty, anguished and panicked, and she cannot get out. She is trapped inside.

I e-mail a friend who cared for her mother, who suffered from dementia before her death. "Did she make sounds?" I ask. "No," she responds, "but demented people are like snowflakes. They are all different." I cannot see this. Snowflakes drift so peacefully, but Betty has no calm, quiet ground to stop her fall or rest on.

By Wednesday, I cannot take it. Everywhere I look in the house, there is a mess. Everything is falling apart. "Where's my lunch?" she asks. It is 2:30. I have forgotten there is such a thing as food. I take things from the refrigerator, but stop: Suddenly I do not know how to make a sandwich. I cannot remember, cannot complete the act.

I drive her to the Junction in Perry where she can have a catfish sandwich. It is our haunt. In the glass case in the adjoining gas station, there is a large selection of skull rings and a ZZ Top poster.

On the road, Betty is quiet, almost normal again, though she still shakes her hands, fingers outstretched, as if they are wet and she hopes the air will dry them. There is something about riding in the car. She seems quiet and calm, but then I hear her whisper, "Lisbon. Portugal. Scottsdale."

As we sit down at the booth at the restaurant, she says, "You look so sad today. Is there any way I can help you? Is there anything I can do? You look so sad."

Later, back at home, she goes off to my aunt's to play bridge; Anita, a woman from our church, picks her up. I have no idea which Betty will show up at the bridge table, or exactly what she will do. When she returns, I ask how it went. "A lotta old women and bad cards," she replies, before going back to her room to change into her gown, which, as she has her pants to take off and a pullover to get over her head, is tough. In an hour or so, she comes back into the family room in her jeans, not in her gown. I don't know what she is thinking.

I am lying on the couch, curved on my side with my rear to the back of it. Betty plops down in the middle, so that she is sitting right in front of me. Something new has passed through her: a wave of playfulness or perhaps happiness. She pokes my nose and stomach with her finger and smiles. She pushes my hair off my forehead affectionately. "What did you do tonight?" she asks. "Are you drunk?" Then she pokes my stomach again.

"You are," I tell her, "so going to Monroe Manor."

By 9:15 or so, I am exhausted and have to go to bed. "Where are you going?" she asks. "To bed," I say. "I just told you."

"You're not staying?" she asks.

"I cannot keep my eyes open." I have been so worried today. I just need to close my eyes and rest, but it takes me a bit to settle down. After maybe an hour, I hear her shout and then there is a big thump. She has hit the floor. "I've fallen," she cries out. "I've fallen." There are tears in her voice.

I run toward the family room where she is sprawled on the floor. She cannot get up. She is wearing her jeans and I know exactly what has happened. When my mother sits down on the couch, she will often undo her pants at the waist, making herself more comfortable. Then, pants falling down to her hips, she will get up and try to walk to the kitchen. Or wherever. Always scared she will trip on her pant legs, I have cautioned her again and again about trying not to walk with her pants falling down. But as usual, as with everything, she has ignored me.

My mother is scared now, on the floor, trying to sit up, and I am too. I am not sure if I should move her. What if she is injured? Will I make it worse? But, watching her, I see that she is moving well enough. I try to lift her up from behind, with my arms under her arms, but this is not successful. We make it to the point where she is kneeling before me. "Do you want me to get the walker?" I ask.

"No," she answers with force, with determination. "Get me a chair." I do, and, making use of it, she hauls herself up. I hold her, steady her. She seems okay. "I was just lucky," she says. "I was just lucky."

"Shouldn't we go into the hospital to make sure? What if you wake up in pain?"

"No, I want to finish my book," she says. "I'm fine. I'm fine. Be still." She must make everything all right again as fast as she can. She must return to normalcy as soon as possible. I say again that I want to call the paramedics, but she says, over and over, "I'm fine, I'm fine, I'm fine," slamming the door closed on my concern. I am worried about her tailbone, which she bruised during her last confrontation with the floor, in the middle of the night in her room before I came to stay.

"I am all right," she declares, plunking down in the recliner. "I have to finish this book," she repeats. "I don't just want to lie in there awake." She does seem to have emerged unscathed. I watch her trying to read, struggling to make out the print, trying to pretend all is normal, that nothing has happened here.

I wonder about going back to bed. When I leave the room, she says again, "You're going to leave me. Are you going to leave me?"

I go back to the bedroom, bring pillows and a blanket to spread on the couch next to where she is sitting. I carry in Mabel's quilt with the names of all the women stitched around the edges to wrap around her legs. I study the names (Mildred, Lucille, Amy, Cody, LaDonna), note one I like especially, sewed on with a flourish: Evalena. It sounds like a mountain to climb.

Time after time, I open my eyes, checking, checking again, but she reads on. "You can walk?" I ask again and again. "You can walk?"

"Be still," she says, "be still," but she says it quietly this time, as if I am a baby she is trying to get to sleep.

I want Betty to go to sleep now, just get a little rest, a little calm, a quiet hour or so, but at 1 a.m., I hear her moving. I have fallen asleep and she, apparently, has finished her book. I walk her into her bedroom and make sure she is okay. I rub moisturizer onto her face and Lubriderm onto her legs, which flake with dryness. She makes her whimpering noises, mutters to herself. It seems as though to her I am not there at all. I am touching her, but she does not notice. She is alone.

"Don't fall," she says to herself. "Don't fall. Don't fall. Don't fall." She is more upset now than before. The scrim has been torn away. She is unable to summon the part of her that covers all her fear. I stay until she is still. I sit in the corner after bringing her an extra half of Xanax, which she takes. But she still ignores me. She does not see me. No one is here but her. Suddenly she yells out, "Someone has to make the coffee. I forgot."

Heading back to the kitchen to make the coffee, I pass my old room, which my father made into an office after he retired. On the shelves above his desk there are hundreds and hundreds of seashells, polished, but a little dusty now. In the corner there is my old stereo, bought with birthday money.

There is a scene I remember that always sums up my last moments of living with my parents in the house my father built. During my last year in high school, my last months truly at home, there was a song on the radio called "Second Avenue," a ballad I liked. I wanted the album and asked Betty to find it on a day she was going into St. Louis to take Mammy to the eye doctor's. It was ten o'clock or so before my mother got home. She looked exhausted, worried about Mammy, sitting at the kitchen table in front of something cold.

I adjourned to my room to listen to the music with my headphones on. I played the record over and over, even after my parents went to bed. That night, for some reason, I found myself singing along to "Second Avenue." I did not imagine anyone listening and couldn't hear myself because of the headphones, but my parents, next door, were apparently still awake.

An hour or so after they turned in, they opened my door and stood together, looking in, smiling, looking happy, amused. "We heard the sweetest voice," said my mother, hair in some disarray, despite the use of her satinlike Beauty Sleep pillow. "You're probably going to be a rock star," my father added, his bare chest just beginning to show the contours of an older man, "but tonight you have to get to bed. Go to sleep now. Go to sleep."

That night I loved them so much.

22

It is Labor Day, late morning. The neighbors have left for the Lake of the Ozarks or Table Rock to fish and ski. They have gone to cook out and laugh with family and friends. We have nowhere special to go. My mother is standing at her window, watching the sky. Quietly she announces, after a few minutes, that it is raining. The Midwest's worst drought since the 1930s has finally broken. The weatherman has gotten it right. He has predicted rain all over the state and now it is here.

I come to stand with her by the window. She seems relieved, as if the fate of all the world depended on this rain falling from the sky, as if this was just her rain, something sent to bring her peace.

Yesterday, I found myself at our church, the First Christian Church, Disciples of Christ. I believed it would be open; there is a prayer room, a refuge for people. I thought of all those I have known in this church, in this town, who might have come here in times of trouble. All the people who have come to ask for help and gone.

The church was not open. Everything was locked up, so I sat on the step by the side door and said, out loud, to whoever was listening, "Help Betty, please help Betty. Please give her health, and happiness, and peace. Daddy, John Hickey, get your asses in gear."

As I sat on the step, so many things came rushing back to me, so many days, and words, and scenes. Through the years of watching my mother there are a few things I have come to understand.

All Betty will ever say of my infancy is this: "You cried and cried and cried. Every time I picked you up, you cried more." When she says this—and she does not admit it often—she looks ashamed, as if she should have known how to quiet me. She tells me how she would give me to my father, who would rest me on his big warm stomach and cradle me in his hands. "Your father could always calm you down. Or I'd give you to Mammy. Mammy could always calm you down. I never could. I could never make you stop crying." She doesn't believe she ever got it right.

Several years ago, my mother, my aunt Alice, and I went to Springfield, Illinois, where my parents lived when they were first married. We went by the apartment house where they started out, and I asked if she had been sorry to leave, to go back to Madison, where my father began working at the lumberyard. "Mammy needed us," she said. "My father was dead. She needed help. Harry needed help, though he wouldn't admit it. I liked Springfield. We had made some friends. I was young and kind of pretty. There were places to go there, a group of nice young couples, a pretty lake."

After our drive, we went to visit our cousin Dick, who lives in a nearby suburb and whose daughter, Kim, a midwife, was visiting from California. Kim has a child, Macao, maybe a year or so old then, young enough that he was still likely to stumble a bit when he walked. Macao had long, shiny black hair, and sweet fat legs, and chubby hands. He was, as they say, a beautiful child. When Kim, holding him, offered him to Mother—the woman who always avoids babies—she said, "He doesn't want me. I'm not so good at that."

I picked up Macao, held him up in the air, waved his hand at Betty, and danced him around. My mother looked wary. "Don't break him," my mother said. "Don't break the baby."

I said, "I don't think you can really break a baby. Here, you take him. I think he wants to come to you."

Betty said, "Watch out. You would never forgive yourself if something happened to that child."

"You cried and cried and cried. Every time I picked you up, you cried

more." She was scared, nervous, frightened she would do something wrong, and I have come to believe that I, just a baby, sensed her fear and cried out when I felt it go through me. She never quite believed she could or would get it right with a baby, with her baby. She was not the type who could care for a child correctly. She was not good enough and then he turned out broken and, after all, someone had to be blamed. Someone had to have made her boy turn out wrong. She thinks she was the one. My sense of this is so strong, though I would do anything to make it not so.

Later, Macao was walking around and kept looking at my mother. Again and again he walked over to her and gazed up at her face. Shyly, she reached out for his hand and took it, very gently, in her own, his little fat hand. In a few minutes she stood up, trying so hard not to scare him as he waited to see what she would do. She walked with the baby so carefully, reaching down to hold his hand and guide him. They went outside where she told him the names of flowers, pointed out this and that.

After lunch was over, she even picked him up, took him outside again. It was as if she wanted to be alone with him, on her own, away from anyone who might spy her making a mistake. She held him as if he were a piece of delicate china, too fine to ever take down from its cabinet. Her fingers seemed wary, so full of caution. From the window, I could see her lips moving, whispering to him, but I could not make out what she had to say.

When she came back in with the baby, she grinned a little and announced, "He likes me, I think. I think he might like *me*."

Betty thinks she is the one to blame for who I am. She was the one who got it wrong. There has never been anyone to tell her differently, because she never spoke of her fears. My father said nothing to reassure her. They didn't talk.

For years and years, Betty tried her best to do everything right, to make me okay, to be good enough. When I was a child, as far back as I can remember, my mother read to me: *The Story About Ping, Scuppers the Sailor Dog, The Happy Hollisters,* poems from *A Child's Garden of Verses.*

Night after night, year after year, after she finished the dishes or the wash and smoked a secret cigarette in the bathroom, she sat on the edge of my bed, in the light from the lamp, reading until her voice got tired or until I slept. Sometimes she added her own commentary:

"Let the crocodile have him. I'm sick of him," or *"That was kind of silly."*

She thought it important for me not to be ignorant, to read. My mother gave me words, though she has rarely been inclined to use them herself.

She made me fish, play football. She took me to endless lessons, dentists for braces, the dermatologist for antiacne pills, St. Louis for clothes. She made certain I ate the proper foods. For years and years, if I was leaving to go back to the city on an early-morning flight, she always got up at 4 or 5 a.m. to prepare steak and eggs, cinnamon toast, to stuff my suitcases with special treats, the things I liked best that only home could offer. She did everything, everything she believed she was supposed to do. Now she can do none of that. This clearly grieves her, I see. When I leave for a plane now, she says, "I feel so terrible. I cannot offer you anything to take. I should have made you something nice." She worries that after she dies, I—a man alone—will go untended.

I have tried my best to show her I am okay. I have done everything I know to show her she did all right with me. I have told her. I have reminded her of all the things she did, said time and again that whatever happens, I will never forget the things she has done for me. But it has never quite seemed to sink in.

For years I have tried to tell her that she has been just the mother I wanted, that I am the one who made my own mistakes, that I am not broken at all, that I am just human. But I don't think she has ever believed it. This is why, I think, she cannot speak of my life, because she somehow got it all wrong from the beginning. Or so she believes. This is why she has stayed, why she has waited, watching out the window, always looking out for the moment when I will turn into the driveway, always trying to look her best for when I come in the door. She has struggled to keep on, trying not to fall. To try to help me. She has not wanted to leave me alone. She has always wanted to be here for me, to do what she could.

We stand at the window. We see the rain falling on the yards, gardens, and flowers. I imagine it coming down on the beans that may bloom now on their twisted vines, on the burned corn, and highways, and back roads, and little white houses. It is raining on the trees and on the graves where, years after my father died, Betty and John struggled, summer after summer, to make the grass grow.

Last night, after I returned from my time on the church step, the evening began softly, but changed. Although her face was a battle of frustration and confusion, Betty sat, without agitation or sound, poring over her stack of bills again. I asked to help; she shook her head. When she reached the end of the stack, she started again. This happened over and over. I watched her go through this process until I began to get nervous and interrupted. "Let's see if there's a movie," I said. "Surely there is something on all those channels." My mother does not much like television, except for the news, but she agreed. On one of the HBO channels, a Richard Gere film was just starting.

"Who is that actor?" she asked.

"Richard Gere."

After an hour or so, time she spent staring, seemingly not quite comprehending, at the screen, she asked again, "Who is that actor?"

"Richard Gere."

In an hour, the same question: "Who is that actor?"

"Richard Gere."

I dozed off in front of the television as she crinkled the newspaper. Richard Gere was running down a city street, pursued by someone. When I looked up, she asked again, "Who is that actor in that movie?"

I see the rain falling on the deserted church in Perry, and on Madison's once-lively Main Street. It is coming down in Holiday, and Middle Grove, and Duncans Bridge, Clarence, Monroe City, Mexico, Moberly, Macon, Boonville, De Soto, Washington, Bonne Femme, Brunswick, Santa Fe, Granville, Huntsville, Salisbury, LaPlata, Keytesville, and Higbee. I see the old farmers with wrinkled faces, looking up at the sky.

Last night she was fitful, pacing around her bed, shaking her head, and getting after herself for something, or so it seemed. She was mad at herself for something. She was angry and so agitated that I knew she would never get to sleep, but I succeeded, finally, in getting her into bed. I fluffed her pillows, and arranged the blanket, and asked if she was too warm or not warm enough. I took her hand to feel if it was cold, then pulled the sheet up to her waist as she stared at the ceiling, shaking, half crying, half laughing, half herself, half gone, half knowing, half not.

As I turned to leave the room, she glanced at me and I saw that she was smiling at me, not the smile of recent days, the smile that seems connected to nothing, but the smile of the real Betty, the one who has not quite left forever.

When I left the room, she would not let me turn out the light. I noticed the card by the bedside table. On it, she had written:

Eggnog
Richard Greer
Anne Wallin
Lisbon
Richard Greer

Eggnog: something she served on holidays when she gathered the family together.

Richard Greer: a stranger running with purpose through her night's confusing streets.

Anne Wallin, called Nona, was the aunt she lived with in St. Louis during her days as a secretary who rode the streetcar home.

Lisbon, I think, is all the places she wanted to go.

We stand at the window for the longest time and do not move. I see the rain falling on the dry shores of the Mississippi and the Missouri. I see my mother's face in the glass with the rain coming down. We are both standing there, behind the glass that separates us from the world. The fragments of our faces are there in the glass, partly there, partly not. There have been so many Bettys. But I think I like this one best, this old lady in the flannel gown and slippers. She tries so hard.

You tell yourself that something has to happen. You tell yourself that somehow, someone is planning some sort of rescue. You say this cannot be true, that this is not happening to her. You say she is just an old woman whose time has come, who has lived a good life, who is departing, but cannot go and is so frightened of what will come if she must stay. You tell yourself that so many others have suffered more, lost more, lived less. You say that it is just her time, your time to bear sadness and farewells.

Many times in my life I have felt adrift and worried, screwed up, lost. When these moments start to shake me up, I remember coming home from St. Louis in our old green station wagon, lying in the back watching the lights on the highway signs, surrounded by bags of dresses with my fingers blackened from the hard licorice drops my father procured on every visit to Stix, Baer & Fuller, where they once had a candy counter stocked with everything. Sometimes I rode in the front seat, between my parents, and would wake up after what seemed only moments of travel to find us driving into the driveway of the house in Madison.

"Mind your own business."

"You are my business."

It is raining on our old house, on my grandmother's house, on the corner where the ladies used to gather, on the place where the lumberyard was, on the sidewalks where we walked, on Mammy's house with the many chimneys, in our backyard, on my father's thirsty trees. We watch the rain fall: her silences, my secrets; my secrets, her silences.

I watch the rain overflow the gutters and fall in cascades into the overflowing hanging baskets. Because of the holiday, I have bought her all the things she likes, special treats of the kind to please a little girl.

"The winter is coming," she says.

"I know, but we will stay warm inside our house."

As I draw closer beside her, she allows me a rare liberty: I stretch my arm across her shoulder. But she stands with her arms held stiffly at her sides. She does not touch back. We say nothing at all.

Epilogue

The night before our first visit to the oncologist, I sat in my father's office, looking over his seashells and waiting as Betty brushed her teeth and prepared to lie down. Most nights, when she falls back, she doesn't hit the middle of the mattress, only the edge. I am always terrified she will fall off in the night. Now, before she sleeps, as she protests, I put my arms around her shoulders and under her knees to lift and position her in a safer spot. She hates it, cannot stand relinquishing her body to someone else's control.

After turning out the light that night, I put my hand across her forehead, hoping to quiet her distress. Panic showed in her eyes. "You're okay," I said. "Now try to sleep. I will get you through this. You're my partner."

I thought that the doctor would say she was dying. I was prepared to let her go, to spare her pain, if that was what she chose. My father died months shy of my parents' fiftieth anniversary. "Fifty years," he said to my mother the Christmas before he died. "Fifty years! That's too damn long." And then he laughed and slapped my mother on the rear end.

"Too damn long": This is what my mother thinks about her life. She seems to believe she is taking someone else's time. This is part of what it is to be very old. Part of her is ashamed to stay here longer; she doesn't feel entitled to more.

That is what I was thinking about that night, about her deciding to leave, about having to allow her to go. By her bed I noticed her sandals, her poor old sandals, waiting for another morning in the world.

. . .

The summer of the drought was followed by an autumn where the leaves left unburned changed color quickly and were gone. All winter, the house was chilly in the mornings. We found out that Betty is not eligible for Tiger Place; they felt she needed too much special attention.

"I thought that was the point," I said.

On the first Wednesday of March, Betty awakened, complaining of pain in her side, worried about her heart. When the ache spread to her side, I took her to Columbia to the emergency room. She sat in the examining room in her pink Mizzou T-shirt, saying nothing; but when the doctor pressed her abdomen, she screamed out and I knew. She was very ill.

Betty demanded to go home so loudly that I could barely hear the doctor describe, after the CAT scan, the blockage in the tube leading from my mother's kidney, probably a tumor. There was also a mass in her spleen, but the kidney was the immediate concern. She would probably lose it and was admitted to the hospital and given painkillers and an IV.

She told the doctor, begrudgingly, that she had been experiencing pain for a while.

"What?" I asked.

"It wasn't that bad," she said.

"It's cancer," I asked the ER doctor, "isn't it?"

"It's a very odd thing," says the doctor, "family members always have a premonition. They're usually right."

"Are you her health care proxy?" asked one of the faces floating past me that afternoon.

"My mother makes her own decisions," I replied.

"Does she have a signed copy of a living will?"

"Isn't it a little soon for that?" I asked.

"It's standard procedure."

"I'll bring it tomorrow," I told her, but decided not to.

. . .

I sat by her bedside for a few hours, feeding her orange sherbet from the pantry.

"People can live without both kidneys," I told her.

"Veda Berry had just one kidney," she said. "She drank water *all* the time. I thought she was going to burst."

"Your hands are so cold," I told her.

"Cold hands, dirty feet, no sweetheart," she said, laughing a bit.

It wasn't until she finally lost consciousness that I looked out the window, noticed it was dark, and realized the day was gone. I hated to leave her, but our new puppy, Raj, was waiting in the car. He needed food, water, attention. I hadn't left him in his crate because I thought we might not get back that night.

I thought she might not get back at all.

I thought I would return to an empty house where those sandals by the bed would make me sadder than I had ever been.

When I opened the car door, Raj jumped into my arms, and I sat holding him because I did not want to return to the hospital and because he is scared of strange places. I was scared of watching her die. I hoped she would be carried off quickly without suffering after seeing something of spring, a few jonquils. I would drive her through town where the rosebud trees were blossoming.

Betty once threw a shoe at a tramp who dared intrude when she was alone in the sanctuary of the church in Madison practicing the organ. I think she went there to get away from me and my dad. Not long after this, on the way home from school on an extraordinary day, I caught her in a rare mood, relaxed and sitting on the front steps of the church with her sheet music, eating some sherbet from a plastic cup.

"Missouri in the springtime is pretty hard to beat, little boy," she told me as she reached to take my hand.

. . .

Everything revolved around Raj in the months before her illness. Maybe I wanted to make her jealous. All through fall, I cruised the humane societies of north-central Missouri, holding puppies, almost committing, but never quite committing. Then, just before Christmas, I saw Raj, pictured on the Web site with a plaintive look on his face. He had spent half of his eight months on the planet in confinement. No one wants black dogs, and he was also "extremely submissive and shy," not the type to make a Christmas present. At the shelter, he would not approach me for the longest time.

When I told Betty about him, she threw a fit that dissipated as I described his troubles and long wait to be adopted. "He's been abused," I said, revving up the story a bit. Finally, she nodded. I told her that he reminded me of John's dog, Bob. "You loved Bob," I said.

"Did not."

"You look like you have a lot of love to give," the woman at the shelter told me.

"Are you saying that because I'm fat?" I asked.

For two nights, I had pored over a booklet called *Super Puppy,* which detailed hundreds of confusing instructions for puppy parenthood. The booklet advised potential masters to establish themselves immediately as pack leader. It sounded a little like the Cub Scouts. I hated the Cub Scouts.

Driving across town after we left the shelter, I kept one hand on Raj's scrawny back as he adjusted to the car. He yelped. So did I. In the parking lot at PetSmart, where I had scheduled a bath and nail clipping before his introduction to Betty, Raj tentatively descended from the car. At the desk, the woman asked, "Do you want his anal glands expressed?" I was astonished. "I don't know," I answered. "Do they have something to say?"

On Sunday, the morning after Betty was admitted, I arrived at the hospital at 5 a.m. with Raj riding along again. He looked woebegone when I left him, but I plied him with treats. "My mother is very sick," I said. "Don't be a dick."

Betty was groggy from a pill. My cousin Lucinda was there. In an hour there would be a procedure to explore Betty's kidney blockage.

As they wheeled her out the door, Betty waved a tissue she had balled up in her palm. The nurses were too cheerful, as if she were being taken off to join a big parade.

All her fears were in that tissue. Watching as the procession headed off, I saw it fall to the floor.

On Raj's first night in Paris, Betty eyed him. "He has a long tail. Is it too late to cut it off?"

I moved his rug near my bed, stroking his head. I watched him turn around in a circle three times before committing to a sleeping position. I listened as he snored through the night, occasionally kicking a bit.

The next morning, I took him out, despite his strong resistance, but stumbled. A stick cracked under my foot as, off balance, I loosened my grip on the leash, and Raj reared up, tore the thing from my hand, and bolted.

It wasn't light yet; he was just gone. I hadn't taken in how scared he was. I just hadn't paid enough attention. I whistled and whistled, drove around, looking for his orange collar. I went down to the woods, searched as best I could, emerging with my glasses broken but nothing else.

"The thing about dogs," Betty said, "is they always break your heart."

Early the next morning, I heard a single, solitary "woof." Out back, our neighbor held Raj in his arms, the leash still dragging from his collar. All day, we celebrated. A friend from Vermont confessed that her father had been a dog trainer and that she grew up eating dog biscuits.

Carol confided that Betty had instructed her to find another dog, another Lab, to appear on Christmas. This just didn't seem like my mother. Later, coming back from the bathroom, I heard Betty, alone in the room, talking to Raj.

"You are a bad dog," she said. "You upset my boy. Now don't wet on me."

After the kidney procedure, my mother's urologist was a kind voice on the phone in the white hallway filled with light. The cancer floor, recently redone, was plush. I expected to see Jennifer Lopez outside drinking a Cuba Libre by a swimming pool.

The urologist told me that Betty had no tumor or stone. Her kidney was being cut off by some sort of growth, but they had saved the organ with a stent.

Betty came back to the room gray, the gray of the ocean in South Carolina, the gray of my father's face during his last days. "Where's the dog?" she asked groggily. "Is the dog here? Who is tending to the dog?"

"There's a big black nose sticking up here," Betty always says when Raj turns up begging at the table. "Mister, I'll skin you alive."

All morning the room was gray, like Betty, as if invaded by fog, and now and again my mother rose up out of the haze to say she was thirsty. I brought in more sherbet she liked, grateful for the color, the only bright thing in the room. Lying there, Betty reminded me of her aunt Bess, a little woman. It seemed my mother's body had dwindled overnight.

Betty was tall; Bess was small. When walking together on sunny days, they cast shadows suggesting mother and child or partners in comedy from some silent movie. Bess's waves of hair never lay quite right. As she lingered at store windows, Betty stood behind her, smoothing her hair down with the kind of care she usually had no time for.

"I will take care of Bess," Betty told Mammy and my uncles when they wanted Bess to go to a nursing home. "Just don't you worry about it."

I told myself I would take care of Betty. Over and over, I told myself I would see her through.

I would make it go just right. I would take her home, sit on the edge of the bed, and tell her funny stories about people we loathe.

I would be her soldier.

"You can do this," said a friend on the phone.

"I know."

That afternoon, on my way to purchase an extremely large cinnamon roll, I spotted a large woman from church in the hall. Betty glared at me. "Did you tell her I was in here?"

"No."

"Well, you talk to her. I'm going to shut my eyes. Tell her I died."

I hid in the men's room and ate my cinnamon roll.

The doctors began to speak of lymphoma. That night, the pain pills nauseated Betty's empty stomach. I watched the lights on I-70 from her window and worried about Raj. "You've been so good to me," Betty said to Cinda, who answered, "Well, George is the one who got you here."

Betty said nothing. I pretended not to notice.

That night at home, quite late, I made spareribs with barbecue sauce, Betty's favorites, as Raj watched, hoping for a treat. He has food addiction issues.

I had somehow convinced myself that we would have a little party after Betty's tests, when she could eat. I saw myself arriving, her savior with Tupperware, sauce still on my fingers. When I went to my mother's room to search for a fresh bottle of eyedrops to take to the hospital, I found the program from my father's funeral under her pillow along with all her lists of all the words.

At 2 a.m., I found myself in the yard, angry at Raj and screaming, "Poop, dammit, poop. Doesn't anyone have any consideration for me?" All night long I sat in my father's old recliner with an armful of warm, sleeping dog.

Each morning of my mother's hospitalization, I drove in the early morning across the lightening plains to arrive in time for the doctor's morning rounds. I traveled on roads and highways I have known all my life. From these mornings driving to see Betty, I will remember the lights going on in the little white houses; the tall display horse rising from the dark at Hobby Horse in Centralia; Raj waiting behind the steering wheel, gazing at me from the window as I came from Casey's with doughnuts. (Betty didn't always get hers.)

The faces on the elevator to the oncology floor became familiar. We nodded at one another and were so courteous. On the elevators, we were so determined to let others exit first that the doors practically closed before any of us got out.

Before Betty's biopsy, the radiologist started talking about nodes in Betty's spleen and abdomen. "No more parts," I wanted to cry out. "You cannot add any more parts."

Sitting outside the room where she had been taken for the test, I heard her scream. The anesthetic was administered through a needle in her spine. No more of this, I vowed. I would take her home and lift her into bed and wait with her for all the pain to end. But I didn't really want that. I was ready for anything, but I still didn't want her to die.

The morning after the tests, before she told us we had to leave the hospital, our doctor mentioned lymphoma again. All night long, Betty's stomach had been in an uproar. She was sicker that day than any other. But we had to leave the hospital. The tests were over. There was nothing else they could do and she had to go.

As we were getting her ready, a caseworker appeared to question us about who would care for her at home or whether she would be going to some sort of facility, as they strongly recommended.

"Wait a minute," I said. "Who cares what you recommend? You send her out of here when she is terribly sick and then you come in here and pretend you care what is going to happen to her?"

Sensing the possibility of battle, Betty perked up.

"That's not really the situation," the caseworker said.

"Well, then, what is the situation?" I asked, before the woman made her exit.

As I wheeled my mother down, she looked at me and said, "You've taken good care of me."

All the way home, Betty lay in the backseat with her head on her hand. Raj sat with me up front. "We're almost home," I said when we hit Centralia, then again when we turned on C, then on T, then finally, over and over, as we headed east on 15.

The next day we waited and waited for the doctor to call with the test results. At 5:30, the phone rang and the doctor, munching what sounded like an apple, confirmed the lymphoma diagnosis.

Betty vomited all night. I did not sleep and found myself throwing the ribs I had made for her homecoming into the trash as the sun came up. It was a shame. I had finally cooked them right.

That morning, before we left for the oncologist's, I found Raj by Betty's bed. Though he is never supposed to enter her room, he is fond of her Kleenexes, winter boots, and house slippers. Oddly enough, he will not touch the one thing I would love to see destroyed—the sandals we have warred over for so long. Labradors apparently prefer pumps.

I let Betty wear the sandals to the oncologist's, edging her tender feet into them.

"Is this dog neutered?" Betty asked me on the drive over.

I nodded. "I guess you're not going to get to be a grandmother," I told her.

"I never wanted to be a grandmother," she replied. I could think of several reasons why she might have said this. One is that it is the truth. One is that she wanted to keep me from feeling bad about not having children. I told myself it was the latter, but I think it was both. My mother hates to be called "ma'am." I don't see her loving "Grandma."

. . .

In the office of Dr. Tennan, the oncologist, I waited, in a chair that smelled like it was sick, for Betty to be called. I watched my mother, her last looks before learning she was dying.

But I was wrong. It turned out I was wrong about it all.

Dr. Tennan, a very good-looking man, flirted a little with my mother, told her she didn't look her age, said nothing about dying. He recommended treatment: two weeks of daily radiation (painless he assured us) and several more weeks of IV infusions. It wasn't chemo; a different drug is more effective with lymphoma. It wouldn't make her sick or cause her to lose her hair or suffer in any way. He said there was no reason not to go forward with it.

I thought she would say no, but she spoke up. "I want the radiation," she said. At ninety-one years old, my mother chose life, chose to fight to keep it. She wanted to live. For herself. She spoke right up. I also had to make a choice for myself. I had to think about finding my own life again. She had spoken up so quickly for hers. Maybe this was a trick I could learn.

Betty smiled at that doctor as if she were still young, ready to line up for the Miss Legs contest at the university.

All the way home, I thought of places I plan to go when my job here is finished. I want to go all across the world, just as Mammy imagined me doing. I want to learn to take photographs, to write, to maybe try to write a book of my own.

"Did you get to death's door and decide maybe it didn't look so good?" I asked Betty, still surprised that she agreed to treatment.

"Dr. Tennan is a good-looking man," she said.

I took a risk. "Dr. Tennan is a sex machine. Let's have him over for dinner." Betty was still chuckling a little when we pulled in our driveway. We had been through something and there was an opening, a crack of light that seemed, surprisingly, to delight her. If I had a photo of her that night, I would put it in a special frame, though I have wondered since if I saw more in her face than was really there.

The next day, we began radiation. They put stickers with black arrows on both sides of her chest and stomach.

I decided that the good thing about cancer is that wherever patients gather there are snacks. Unfortunately, they are often healthy. On the first day, however, I almost stole a bag of Doritos from a bald woman. I wasn't going to eat them. It was only to save her.

At the place where my mother goes to get radiation, there is a huge, unfinished jigsaw puzzle on the table in the room where people wait to go in. Every day, there is the same old farmer man, bent over the puzzle that has, like, nine hundred million pieces. He goes in for his treatment after my mom. His wife is dead. He walks on a plain, cheap cane, but he has driven himself to Columbia from High Hill every day for thirty-seven days for his treatments.

I asked him about the radiation. "It don't hurt more'n a sunburn I'd get out on the tractor," he told me. He goes to Country Kitchen for biscuits and gravy every night before he heads home. "You get a good plateful," he said.

"How much longer do you have to come?" I asked him yesterday. "Long enough to finish this damn puzzle," he told me.

He is a Missouri man. So am I.

It is something to witness, all of them trying, keeping on.

Lesbian waiting for her treatment at Missouri Cancer Institute: "Gay women do better than straight women with chemo. We already have the baseball caps."

Coming home from one treatment, Betty said she wanted to go to St. Louis to get her hair done. "I mean someone who can do it right," she said, "who can make it look halfway decent. You could use a haircut yourself. You look like a ragamuffin."

"Mother," I said, "I want you to shut up about your hair."

I feel better. I have steered my mother through this crisis, taken charge.

"I am pack leader," I tell Raj. "I am pack leader. I am fucking Arnold Schwarzenegger." I was so damn butch, I scared myself, but he paid no attention. Sometimes I think Raj believes I am merely an oddly shaped refrigerator. I smell like dog all the time now, but later, when he is lying on top of me with his head over my shoulder napping, I hear his breathing in my ear and try to forget that he has eaten half the couch.

It is interesting, gratifying even, to watch this almost human let down his guard, warm up, grow less frightened. I have watched him transform from a pup reluctant to leave his mat or crate to a daring household forager who considers it his God-given right to poop copiously in the middle of the living room. "Get some OdoBan," a neighbor advises when I share our housebreaking problems.

"How much," I ask, "do I take?"

On Betty's journey, I have learned something I had not known: I am very strong, strong enough to stay, strong enough to go when the time comes. I am staying not to cling on, but because sometime, at least once, everyone should see someone through. All the way home.

When Betty got an infection, we went back to the hospital and I returned to my early drives across the dark countryside and my mind turned often to High Hill and the old farmer making his way to his truck on his cane in the cold wind. I have kept going too. Through all the years. Maybe it is time to give myself a little credit.

Sometimes it is okay to be broken open, even if it is sadness that finally connects you to everything you are feeling.

If I scream at Raj after he has an accident in the house, Betty glares at me harshly. "Now is that any way to talk to him?" she asks.

"Be still," I say. I am tempted to greet him in the mornings as my father once did Toto: "Hello, you old tail-wagging sonuvabitch."

I tell Raj I love him, dozens of times a day. I want him to feel okay—safe, at home in the world. Betty doesn't hear me when I bend to whisper to him. She seems to have become a little more deaf since her cancer and her memory has declined along with her ability to walk unassisted. Something in Betty's head is surrendering. It is harder and harder for her to keep her balance when walking. After the ten o'clock news, on the way to her bedroom, she stops every two or three steps and looks around, uncertain and shaky, as if on a long trek. She no longer pauses to check the hymns.

Night after night, I follow behind her with my hands on her hips to keep her steady until we reach the bedroom where she puts on her gown, a nightly challenge as it is hard for her to raise her arms. She is always relieved when the gown, soft on her shoulders and my cheek when I hug her, is finally on.

I have ice cream when she is sleeping. I keep an old-fashioned long-handled teaspoon hidden in a cabinet and use it to ferret out pieces of chocolate and caramel from the bottom of the carton before anyone else can get to them. I call it my digging spoon. Betty is outraged when she discovers that the chocolate nuggets or bits of candy bar are missing. "This is supposed to have Heath Bar in it," she cries out.

"Toffee causes tumors," I tell her.

In another life, the gods may send me someone powerful or glamorous to share my existence on this earthly plane. But in this one, for now, Betty and Raj are fine enough. Already they are conspiring against me; I expect to be out of the will in about fifteen minutes. I ponder the question of whether there is an organization designed to rescue humans from rescue animals.

"Do you not understand that he doesn't know what you are saying?" my cousin asks when she hears my endless conversations with my dog.

"He's not human!" I say, "I know he's not human, but I think I may be a Labrador."

I will move on. This won't last forever. For now, the sound of Raj's paws clicking on the floor as he prances makes me almost as happy as Betty's occasional smiles. If I go to the store, she insists on looking out for Raj; she hates to see him have to go into his crate. When I return, I find them on the couch together. He is our loving friend, our little black dog.

Since he arrived and she became more engrossed in his activities, she makes her sounds much less. He is the noisy one now. I know this home is just for now, but I treasure our days. I feel different than when I arrived. Nothing magical or radical, just a little more comfortable with myself. A few more pieces have shifted into place. In my head there is a kind of early-morning quiet. Because I have come through for her. It has taken me so long to feel okay in my own skin, but I feel better, more at home in the world. Most days.

"What," Betty asked suddenly one afternoon, "will you do in the future, after I'm gone?"

"Marry Dr. Tennan," I said. It just flew out of my mouth.

"You could do worse," she said.

Sometimes I think of how it will be when I am old. I am lying in my bed in the Liza Minnelli ward at Villa Fabulosa. I can hear the old queens singing songs from *Evita* in the Madonna Conference Room. Madonna is gone, but her cone bras and bones are on display at the Smithsonian Institution.

Someone comes into the room, tucks the sheet under your legs, asks if you are feeling like you can sleep tonight. He may or may not really be there at all; maybe you just need someone to listen, to answer. But you think he is there, a real person to break the night.

He is a kind man, and in the end, kindness is everything. The night is suddenly lonely. You cannot get your bearings. You have no idea where you are, so you ask questions, to try to keep from forgetting everything, who you are, where you have come, the people you loved the most:

"Where am I from?"

"Missouri," says the man. "You have told me about it, the rivers and flowers and trees."

"That town I remember with the foreign name?"

"Paris. It is gone now, I am sorry to say. There were floods, but the people you knew were gone before."

"The roses are gone?"

The roses were beauty, faith, sharing, work, perseverance, memory, consolation. The roses were care.

You picture pink petals floating on still water.

"What is the capital of Portugal?" you find yourself asking.

"Lisbon."

"Who am I from? Who were my people?"

"Betty and George?"

"She almost married the governor. My father would not have liked it. He loved her."

"What is that stuff you drink at Christmas?"

"Eggnog."

"Where is the place I said was pretty?"

"The green yard behind your old house."

"Who am I from?"

"Betty and George . . ."

"Where will I go when this is over?"

"To see them."

The young man leaves the room and you begin to say your prayers. You remember the days she said them with you, her hand on your shoulder, gentle and almost frightened, as if she was scared to break you, as if she was scared the world would. She knew you would have to be strong.

Acknowledgments

I always wanted to try to write a book and it has taken a lot of people to get me to the final page. I must thank my agent, Betsy Lerner, my buddy who possesses many rare attributes, including the gift of real friendship and that rare thing, the kind of generosity that actually desires great things for her friends. My editor, Carole DeSanti, has taught me—I wish I had learned this years back—that the best editing is done with a whisper. She has offered a rock-solid foundation of advice, edits, and encouragement, along with the time to do one more draft.

The writing of this book has been a relay, and every time I fell and lost hope there was someone to pick me up and carry me to the next day's work. The bane of writing is self-doubt; the gift is friends, real friends, who save you. Kathryn Shevelow and Sara Switzer, both fabulous and wise critics, have been there for me every second since page one. So has Ann Patty. I have felt them strongly in my corner; what a gift, lasting and true. Lauren Lowenthal, a brilliant woman, demanding in the best and most helpful ways, showed up just in time to get me to the end, kicking and screaming. Jennifer Barth, well . . . thank you, Jennifer, for so many things, including your readings and endless aid to the cause, my cause. I am grateful to you and for you. Nancy Collins: Thank you for your considered comments, your love and humor, and, most of all, for the title, which I recognized immediately when you uttered it.

There are so many more to thank: Adrienne Brodeur, Betsy Cornwall, Walter Owen, Beth Kseniak, Johnathan Wilber, Rux Martin (who edited the first draft), Deanne Urmy, Edward Shain and Laura Popper,

William Middleton, Debbie Engel, Rob McQuilken, Casey Schwartz, Marie Brenner, and Steve Weinberg. Amanda Urban has been a great booster for years. Vanessa Mobley, Terri Karten, Jonathan Burnham, and Helen Atsma also helped provide the confidence to get to Bettyville and back.

Anthony Shadid continues to inspire me every day; I so wish I could thank him in person. Lucinda Baker has been my partner in tough times and a wonderful cousin. Carol Crigler has given endless support to my mother and to me. For decades now, Paul Giorgianni has put up with my complete looniness and tendency to forget appointments. Lastly, Raj Hodgman has been a great partner in the labor, despite a weak bladder and the tendency to howl.

Thank you, Viking, all of you, for buying this little book and rising to support it. I appreciate the work of Chris Russell, Roland Ottewell, Paul Buckley, Hal Fessenden, Nancy Sheppard, Gina Anderson, Carolyn Coleburn, Paul Slovak, Clare Ferraro, and everyone who helped me bring these pages home.

Author's Note

Memoir and memoirists labor under suspicion and I wanted to fess up about cosmetics used and make some reassurances. All conversations quoted here occurred though sometimes—intentionally or because of the tricks of memory—have been combined or moved in time. Digressive discussions have been shortened. There has been editing, but not at the cost of essential accuracy.

For reasons of privacy and respect, the names and details surrounding some of the characters have been altered. A few very minor characters are composites.

The imposition of structure to any story, I have discovered, alters realities. Scenes plucked from the fabric of life are changed, inevitably, when removed from a larger context. Nuances of character are sometimes lost to the considerations of narrative. I regret that, but have done my best to remain fair, generous, and faithful to truth. Still, this is only my Bettyville, created from memories filtered through time, arguable perceptions, and my own consciousness. Other travelers may have their own stories, thoughts, interpretations. My greatest wish is to hurt no one, though I believe we are often the most triumphant when revealed at our most human.